# APPLYING SOCIAL

## The role of social resea
politics, policy and practice

David Byrne

First published in Great Britain in 2011 by

The Policy Press
University of Bristol
Fourth Floor
Beacon House
Queen's Road
Bristol BS8 1QU
UK

Tel +44 (0)117 331 4054
Fax +44 (0)117 331 4093
e-mail tpp-info@bristol.ac.uk
www.policypress.co.uk

North American office:
The Policy Press
c/o International Specialized Books Services (ISBS)
920 NE 58th Avenue, Suite 300
Portland, OR 97213-3786, USA
Tel +1  503 287 3093
Fax +1 503 280 8832
e-mail info@isbs.com

British Library Cataloguing in Publication Data
A catalogue record for this book is available from the British Library.

Library of Congress Cataloging-in-Publication Data
A catalog record for this book has been requested.

ISBN 978 1 84742 450 1 paperback
ISBN 978 1 84742 451 8 hardcover

The right of David Byrne to be identified as author of this work has been asserted by him in accordance with the 1988 Copyright, Designs and Patents Act.

The statements and opinions contained within this publication are solely those of the author and not of The University of Bristol or The Policy Press. The University of Bristol and The Policy Press disclaim responsibility for any injury to persons or property resulting from any material published in this publication.

The Policy Press works to counter discrimination on grounds of gender, race, disability, age and sexuality.

Cover design by Qube Design Associates, Bristol
Front cover: image kindly supplied by www.alamy.com
Printed and bound in Great Britain by Hobbs, Southampton
The Policy Press uses environmentally responsible print partners

# Contents

# Abbreviations and acronyms

| | |
|---|---|
| ABI | area-based initiative |
| ABM | agent-based modelling |
| AcSS | Academy of Social Sciences |
| ANC | African National Congress |
| ASAS | Advancement Support Advisor |
| CDP | Community Development Project |
| CG | cultural governance |
| CHC | Community Health Council |
| EPA | Educational Priority Area |
| ESRC | Economic and Social Research Council |
| GIS | Geographical Information System |
| IPPR | Institute for Public Policy Research |
| ITSC | Independent Sector Treatment Centre |
| KONP | Keep our NHS Public |
| LINk | Local Involvement Network |
| LSP | Local Strategic Partnership |
| MEANS | Means for Evaluating Actions of a Structural Nature |
| NEETs | Not in Employment, Education or Training |
| NHS | National Health Service |
| NIHR | National Institute for Health Research |
| NPM | New Public Sector Management |
| ONS | Office for National Statistics |
| PCT | Primary Care Trust |
| PFI | Private Finance Initiative |
| PPIF | Patient and Public Involvement Forum |
| QCA | Qualitative Comparative Analysis |
| RAE | Research Assessment Exercise |
| RCT | randomised control trials |
| REF | Research Excellence Framework |
| SSRC | Social Science Research Council |
| UNDP | United Nations Development Programme |
| URBAN | Urban Community Initiative Programme |
| WEA | Workers' Educational Association |

# Introduction

This book is entitled *Applying Social Science* and that is exactly what it is about. But what does this expression actually mean? A good approach to disentangling the meaning of a phrase is to look carefully at the meaning of the particular words that make it up and then see how they actually work when brought together. Two sources for establishing meaning are the *Oxford English Dictionary Online* (OED) and *Wikipedia*. I make no apology for using the latter, despite its own wise warnings to students about the dangers of using 'tertiary' sources in the presentation of work. If what it says makes sense, then use it; this is particularly the case when we have, if not quite triangulated with three points of reference, then at least established another validating cross reference. This works well for the meaning of words and expressions since meaning is established in use – the exact principle which informs the definitional practice of the OED and the underlying mode of construction of Wiki definitions through community specification. So below are definitions of the individual words and some of the component elements of the expression 'applying social science' from these two exemplary sources:

- **Science** (from the Latin *scientia*, meaning 'knowledge') refers in its broadest sense to any systematic knowledge-base or prescriptive practice that is capable of resulting in a prediction or predictable type of outcome. In this sense, *science* may refer to a highly skilled technique or practice.

  In its more restricted contemporary sense, science refers to a system of acquiring knowledge based on scientific method, and to the organized body of knowledge gained through such research. This article focuses on the more restricted use of the word. Science as discussed in this article is sometimes called experimental science to differentiate it from applied science – the application of scientific research to specific human needs – although the two are interconnected.[1] (http://en.wikipedia.org/wiki/Science)

- **Science,** in a more restricted sense: a branch of study which is concerned either with a connected body of demonstrated truths or with observed facts systematically classified and more or less colligated by being brought under general laws, and which includes trustworthy methods for the discovery of new truth within its own domain. ... In modern use, often treated as synonymous with 'Natural and Physical Science', and thus restricted to those branches of study that relate to the phenomena of the material universe and their laws, sometimes with implied exclusion of pure mathematics. This is now the dominant sense in ordinary use. (OED Online)

- **Applied:** designating a discipline, or that part of a subject, concerned with the use of specialist or theoretical knowledge in practical or functional contexts, as *applied biology*, *applied chemistry*, *applied economics*, *applied kinesiology*, etc. Also: designating an expert in or practitioner of such a subject. See also Special uses. Freq. opposed to *abstract*, *pure*, or *theoretical*. (OED Online)

- **Applied science** is the application of knowledge from one or more <u>natural scientific</u> fields to solve practical problems (http://en.wikipedia.org/wiki/Applied_science)

- The **social sciences** are the fields of <u>scientific knowledge</u> and <u>academic scholarship</u> that study social groups and, more generally, <u>human society</u> (http://en.wikipedia.org/wiki/Social_sciences)

- **Social science:** the study of human society and social relationships; a subject within this field, as economics, politics, sociology, etc. (OED Online)

There is broad agreement between the OED and Wikipedia. Science is about the systematic construction of knowledge about the world in all its aspects. Application is about the employment of that knowledge in practice for the achievement of human objectives. The first – science or quite often 'pure science' – comes before the second, the application of science. Both sources also identify a tension. First there is 'science' defined very much in the terms which were specified by the Gulbenkian Commission on the Future of the Social Sciences, and which is the sense in which the word 'science' will be understood throughout this present book. Science is: '… systematic secular knowledge about reality that is somehow validated empirically' (1996, p 2). That definition is plainly influenced by the way the words in German – *wissenschaft* – and the Slavonic languages – *nauk* – the usual translations of the English term 'science', have never quite acquired the restrictive character of the English word, that is restrictive to science based on the deployment of *the* (and the definite article necessarily implies singular) scientific method. The OED definition above recognises the tension here, whereas the Wikepedia definition merely notes it and then takes the route we might call 'scientistic' – that is, endorsing <u>the</u> scientific method. In this book the word 'science' will always refer to 'systematic secular knowledge about reality that is *somehow* – in other words perhaps in different and multiple fashions – validated empirically. The term 'scientistic' will be deployed pejoratively, for the restricted usage.

Wikipedia recognises this issue when it comes to defining:

- **Human science** (also, **moral science** and **human sciences** as typical in the UK) ... a term applied to the investigation of human life and human activities via a <u>rational</u>, <u>systematic</u>, and <u>verifiable</u> <u>methodology</u> that acknowledges the validity of both <u>data</u> derived by impartial observation of sensory experience (objective phenomena) and data derived by means of impartial observation of psychological experience (subjective phenomena). Its use of an <u>empirical</u> methodology that encompasses psychological experience contrasts to the purely <u>positivistic</u> approach typical of the <u>natural</u> <u>sciences</u> (which exclude all methods not based solely on external sensory observations). Thus the term is often used to distinguish not only the content of a field of study from those of the natural sciences, but also its methodology. (http://en.wikipedia.org/wiki/ Human_sciences)

While the emphasis on the distinctiveness of methodology is correct here, the emphasis on 'psychological experience' as the distinguishing character of the methodology of 'the human sciences' is inadequate. Chapter One of this book will deal exactly with the methodological issues which arise in relation to the social scientific empirical investigation of reality and will do so in a fashion which insists not on a distinctive methodology for the social alone, but on a radical distinction between the artificial and abstract – the domain such as it is of 'scientism' – and the much more interesting domain of the real, which includes much of the traditional territory of 'scientistic' science and in particular any intersection of the natural world and human action, that is the whole of ecology. In other words it will argue for complex realism as a methodological foundation for many methods in the investigation of reality in all its aspects.

So far – for many if not all social scientists – so conventional. Arguments with <u>the</u> scientific method are the stuff of methodological debate even if we will find them ignored and/or dismissed in some surprising intellectual locales. Now let me be truly radical. The necessary point has been made, and made beautifully, by one of the anonymous referees in their report to The Policy Press when commenting on the proposal I made to them for this book. Here is 'Anon':

In essence David Byrne proposes to redefine social science, or least give it the definition it has always deserved. It is an expansive definition that emphasises the interwoven nature of applied social science, policy, and democratic governance. His definition elevates it from step-child to first born, showing in different ways that it is not derivative of conventional social science, stuffed into disciplinary packages, but instead transcends those different 'disciplined' ways of dong social research through its engagement with the larger society. (Anon, and very grateful to her/him I am too!)

There is a lot in this observation. Let us begin with the first element. This book will challenge the ordering of 'pure' or discipline-based science and applied science. That is to say in contrast with both the OED and Wikipedia who entirely accurately represent the normal understanding of applied science as the application of knowledge generated in the pure disciplinary sciences to human purposes, it will argue that much and perhaps most of the useful knowledge about the social world is actually constructed in the very process of active intervention in that world, and this is also true of interventions in relation to the interaction of the social world with nature itself. Pure/disciplinary science does not come first. Indeed in relation to the essentially social, there is a serious question to be asked as to whether there is any value at all in a conception of pure/disciplinary sciences separate from application.

However, my anonymous reviewer also identified another crucial characteristic of applied social science, that it is interwoven into the very fabric of policy formation and governance in contemporary 'post-democratic' (a term which we will define in a moment but is due to Crouch, 2000) states.[2] To illustrate what is meant here let me say that one stimulus for undertaking this task was provided by a comment made by May in response to a methods article in a journal (*Sociology*) when I was one of its joint editors:

The state in contemporary Britain is increasingly characterized by new kinds of reflexivity, mediated through systems and institutions of technical expertise – in which policy rooted in *evidence* is central to its strategic practices, and thus to political discourse. These are expressed in many ways, but involve a central shift towards the primacy of (largely quantitative) knowledge as the foundation for an increasingly active and managerial model of state intervention across a range of policy fields. The emergence of this imperative towards *evidence-based* policy in the final decades of the 20th century is one important ideological feature of the apparently post-ideological character of contemporary British politics. In the British case this has involved the rapid development of policy mechanisms and agencies through which this work can be effectively delegated to the Academy. ... One outcome of this is that sociologists might now find themselves among the outsourced civil servants of the evidence-based state. This is why political contests about methods are important. (May, 2005, pp 526–7)

That rings true but it is only part, although a vital part, of the story. Social research is certainly engaged in the construction – a word used here very deliberately – of evidence but it also plays a crucial role in a range of other governance processes apart from the 'simple' demonstration of 'facts'. So we find a great deal of social research conducted to evaluate – to generate a special kind of evidence about 'what has worked or not' and 'how' that has happened. Not only do all institutions of governance seek to evaluate, to find out 'what works' in relation to interventions in the social world, they also seek to use the findings of research to justify. In other words we are often dealing not with evidence-based policy – the rational development of policies on the basis of evidence, although this approach itself assumes a common and general interest which seldom exists in practice. Instead we find continued examples of policy-based evidence, of the selective use of research findings to assert that policies have worked, continue to work, and will work in the future. When ideology seems not to matter, then demonstration of technical competence replaces it and research becomes politicised as a process of bolstering justification. Despite valiant efforts by statisticians to protect the independence of official statistics there has been pressure even on this fundamental source material but the selective interpretation and publicising of research findings is even more common. So research serves as part of the process of social legitimation in terms of its products.

We find also that social research has a 'process legitimation function' in that research is now a crucial component of consultation procedures, which certainly generate 'evidence' but which also form part of the participatory process in 'post-democratic' governance. We find research co-mingled with action at every level of professional and related practice and at many levels of policy formation and implementation, particularly if we recognise processes of policy development and implementation as so often being processes of action research themselves. Often, particularly but not exclusively in domains of policy and practice where ecological and social issues intersect, we find research being used to describe the sort of futures (the plural is deliberate) which might emerge from the implementation of particular policies. This always involves modelling although it is only sometimes done in relation to the construction of models which are actually called by that name.

All of these processes – the construction of evidence; evaluation; consultation; modelling; research as social action – will be dealt with here through a combination of account of their essential nature, a careful methodological discussion of their social scientific character, the presentation of real examples of them in practice, a critique of those examples, and a consideration of how we might develop good applied social research in the future. That word 'good' here has two inter-related components. One relates to the scientific status of research practices, with that status not understood in some narrow scientistic way but rather in terms of how we might, to reiterate the Gulbenkian Commission's definition, construct useful empirical knowledge about social reality and do so in a fashion such that we can maintain the however localised and scoped validity of the accounts of the past, present and potential futures which we generate in doing this. The other aspect of 'good' is of course normative. The norms being asserted here are those of democracy – of the right of the governed to be able to have an informed say in the processes of governance and the principle that information in all its aspects should be based on truthful accounts of the reality of things that matter for those processes. The democratic norm in the contemporary world is, however hypocritically asserted, generally universal. In putting my cards on the table I will also say that to raise a much more contentious ideal, I am committed to a radical and solidaristic egalitarianism – *fraternité* and *égalité* as well as *liberté*. That commitment will colour the arguments presented here.

For some 30 years I have been engaged in teaching undergraduate and MA students research methods *and* the methodological foundations of those methods in what is now named as what it always was: a school of applied social sciences. Those students have included some whose primary focus has been on an academic discipline – sociology, anthropology, history, politics, even economics – but many have been working on projects in the fields of social policy, social work, community work, health policy, urban regeneration, and so on. The students have included not only full-timers but also lots of part-time students actually working in practice, some of them explicitly as social researchers but all dealing with applied social research. Many of those who pursued a disciplinary route at Master's and even PhD level have subsequently become applied social researchers both outside the academy and in it. At the same time I have worked on a range of applied social research projects as a typical contemporary social science academic forming part of May's outsourced workforce. My contribution has invariably been as the 'methods person', and I have worked on research projects and scholarship in a more traditional academic mode, which have been concerned with the critique of social policies and social practices in the same fields where I have been working as a master technician. May's argument pushed me towards trying to make sense of this in a formal way, to develop an academic argument about issues which had frequently been the basis of rants; informed rants, but rants nonetheless. The key organising principle which has made that move possible has been the recognition that we can think of all social research including applied social research as a set of processes – of things which are done, done in particular ways, and which have particular consequences. That has provided me with a framework for this book.

The remainder of this introduction will consist of an explanation of the organisation of the text. However, before turning to that it is necessary to present the promised definition of 'post-democracy'. This matters because a central argument here is that the socio-political context of applied social research – particularly in the UK, which provides an extreme example of these developments, but rather generally across most societies globally which appear to be democracies in the old sense of that word – is now post-democratic. Crouch defines this situation as one in the following:

> while elections certainly exist and can change governments, public electoral debate is a tightly controlled spectacle, managed by rival teams of professionals expert in the techniques of persuasion, and considering a small range of issues selected by those teams. The mass of citizens plays a passive, quiescent, even apathetic part, responding only to the signals given to them. Behind this spectacle of the electoral game politics is really shaped in private by inter-action between elected governments and elites which overwhelmingly represent business interests. (2000, p 2)

One aspect of post-democracy – given that a major element in it is essential ideological consensus about the relationship between state and market coupled with a subordination of politics to business interests – is that a key claim made by political parties in seeking office is relative technical and managerial efficiency in the achievement of public goals. The roles of social research here, as May indicates, include the development of practices to achieve those goals *and* the demonstration that they have been achieved through evaluation. Evidence is a key product in both processes. To this I would add participation. Evidence is, to use the language of cybernetics, about the processes and products of learning feedback. Participation plays a role in this but it also has a crucial function of apparent legitimation. In summary, applied social research in post-democratic societies is not just engaged in description and evaluation; it is also deeply implicated in the ongoing making of those social orders themselves.

## The organisation of this book

This book is primarily organised around the processes which constitute applied social research. So of the ten subsequent chapters, the middle seven have titles which begin with a gerund – with the active noun form of an English verb: constructing, surveying, evaluating, legitimating, consulting, modelling and acting. However, actions happen in contexts and two sorts of establishment of context will bracket that set. The first will deal with the methodological foundations of applied social science. The second, Chapter Nine, will address the role of applied social sciences in the contemporary academy – in the formal organisation of intellectual practices in the social sciences today. The final chapter – Concluding – will revert to the gerund specification and do just that. Let me outline these chapters in turn as a guide for readers.

Chapter One will address 'the methodological foundations of applied social science'. It will be a clearing of ground and a precise and assertive specification of methodological position. The argument will be very much pluralist in relation to deployment of the methods and techniques of social research and at the same time prescriptively authoritarian in terms of the actual methodological framework which should inform all aspects of research practice – that is design, execution, interpretation of research products,[3] and action during the research process and subsequent to it. The chapter will begin with a critique of existing meta-theoretical positions through a consideration of the implications of understanding social research practice as necessarily post-positivist, focusing in particular on the implications of realism for applied social research. So the focus will be on constructing a viable meta-theory with a demonstration of the value of a scientific/critical

–

realism as a methodological foundation for applied social research. The chapter will develop an account of 'complex realism' based on the implications of understanding the social world as composed of complex open systems. In part this will be done by showing how the framing of issues of policy and practice as 'wicked issues' is essentially a way of saying that they are set in a complex social world. 'Complex realism' provides us with a methodological approach which enables us to construct proper understanding of these issues and which offers the potential for the development of practice in relation to their resolution.

Having established the meta theory/methodological frame of reference which will inform subsequent discussion, the chapter will deal in summary with two opposing methodological positions which have had considerable influence in relation to formal discussions of the methodological foundations of social research. It will demonstrate the weaknesses of traditional crude positivism in terms of the inadequacies of the causal account that that approach and its primary method, the controlled experiment, can generate in relation to the social world. Equally, it will deal severely with the extreme relativism of most post-structuralist/post-modernist discussions of social theory. Some attention will be paid to actor-network theory, precisely because that approach is sophisticated, intelligent, and has some interesting things to say, while at the same time having an ontological foundation which in effect denies the possibility of the production of useful knowledge.

Next the chapter will review arguments about quantity versus quality: this section will assert that the methodological disputes between quantitative and qualitative modes of social inquiry were always fatuous and are now wholly redundant. It will develop the argument about the interpretative character of all research processes presented in Byrne, *Interpreting quantitative data* (2002) and show how good social research, but especially good applied social research, draws on both the quantitative and the qualitative modes preferably, but not invariably, together.

The last part of Chapter One will turn to issues surrounding knowing and acting – the content of the Greek term 'praxis' which is the foundation of all conceptions of critical social science, particularly but by no means exclusively as informed by the thinking of Marx. This section will consider the implications of praxis – the obligation to act appropriately in relation to the process of knowing and that which is known – for the ethical foundations of applied social research. It will draw in considerable part on the arguments of Paolo Freire and the phenomenological, Marxist, and liberation theological traditions which informed his work.

Chapter Two is about constructing evidence. That is to say it deals with the development of knowledge which is to be applied in order both to understand what works and to show what has worked – with the improvement of practice and policy and with claims for competence in the development of solutions to the problems of contemporary life – the policy domain, and in the implementation and execution of those policies, the practice domain. The use of the words 'constructing' and 'construction' in relation to the production of evidence does not here mean that such evidence is necessarily merely reification, that is, bears no relationship to reality. Instead it conveys the meaning that our evidence is made out of something which is reality itself, but also made in particular ways and for particular purposes. So the purpose of this chapter is to consider the general issues which arise in relation to the making of evidence. In other words we will begin with a discussion precisely of the issue of just what evidence, the product of applied social research, actually is. The chapter will continue with a critique of any classification of evidence which ranks it according to the means which have been used to make it. This section will refute the arguments presented in particular by the Cochrane Collaboration for health, but also with some qualifications endorsed by the Campbell Collaboration in relation to general policy, that it is meaningful to construct a hierarchy of modes of production of evidence with the meta-analyses of randomised controlled trials occupying the highest position in that hierarchy. It will show that for complex open systems this is absolutely not the case and that instead we have to understand methods as different ways in which we construct narratives and see them as complementary and equal modes of knowledge production.

Despite this critique of the Cochrane and Campbell Collaborations' ranking exercise in relation to evidence, we must endorse their more general project which is synthesising knowledge. The projects of assembling existing knowledge developed by the Campbell and Cochrane Collaborations demonstrate the significance of existing knowledge and the importance of systematic process in addressing that knowledge in applied social science. There is more to this than meta analyses and systematic reviews, although these are important tools in synthesis. Synthetic narratives provide an overarching way of understanding how knowledge can be brought together as a whole. The chapter will then consider the issue of variables versus cases by taking forward the complex realist methodological arguments developed in Chapter One and showing how variable-based approaches which understand variables as real social agents are essentially useless in applied social research. It will argue that we should regard social measurements as variate traces of open complex systems. Set theoretic approaches to the systematic comparison of cases, exemplified by Qualitative Comparative Analysis, do represent an approach to causality which enables us to address complex and contingent causation and generate useful understanding for application in practice.

Chapter Three is about surveying the social world. It will develop the arguments presented thus far in relation to the main areas of policy and practice in which applied social science has been deployed by picking up examples of existing issues, good and bad practices, and interesting methods. The word 'surveying' will be deployed in terms of Patrick Geddes' description of the logical order of planning: survey – establish what is known; plan – develop a set of policies for the future; implement – proceed to apply them; and evaluate – assess their impact. So here the focus will be both on the ways in which the social sciences have established knowledge *and* on the nature of that knowledge.

Social surveys usually generate quantitative data and we will consider examples primarily drawn from health contexts which are quantitative, although these will include surveys which are much more dialogical and iterative than was possible before the web made interactive surveying and mapping possible. However, there are qualitative modes of research which we should think of as surveying. In particular work in the tradition of Mass Observation has this character and part of Chapter Three will be devoted to an examination of this mode and of its considerable potential for applied social research. Again we should not draw a rigid distinction between quantitative and qualitative modes of work. Qualitative surveys can generate quantitative data, particularly if we regard data not as measures of disembodied variables but as measures of the traces or attributes of complex systems at particular time points. This potential will be demonstrated with reference to how qualitative inspection reports can be used to generate quantitative attributes in the form of classifications, which can then be used to explore causality through systematic case comparison.

Chapter Four is concerned with the process of evaluating – with the role of social science in the establishment of outcomes and effectiveness in the achievement of those outcomes. That is to say it will deal with understanding what has happened and to what extent policies and practices have been successful in doing what they were intended to do. In brutal summary it is about 'what works and why it works'. The 'why' means that it will be concerned in substantial part with issues of causality. The chapter will review the role of evaluation in the relation to policies in all areas. It will deal with the actual politics of evaluation, that is to say the way in which political pressures intrude into the evaluation process with examples. We will develop a realist/complexity-founded approach to evaluation – drawing here on a synthesis of the arguments of Pawson and Tilley (1997) with the complexity frame of reference.

Understanding what works and why is not only a task for social scientists. It is also a task for policy makers, practitioners and general publics. By this is meant rather more than that the products of evaluative social science should be accessible to those audiences but that policy makers, practitioners and general publics all have an active, if you like an agentic, role in the process of evaluation itself. This means that evaluation is a process in which multiple voices must be heard – it must always contain an element of dialogue. Considerable attention will be devoted here to this dialogical aspect of the evaluative process.

The argument will be developed by drawing on examples of evaluation in practice looking at education, health and anti-poverty programmes. Illustrations will come from a range of agencies and locales including evaluation in development contexts where dialogical practice is best established, and in particular the issues surrounding evaluation in complex social interventions. The last has been a problem for social science at least since the work of the Ford Foundation Grey Area Projects in the US in the 1960s and is very well illustrated by contemporary work in relation to AIDS prevention projects worldwide.

The next process, examined in Chapter Five, will be 'legitimating': that is to say the *selective* use of social science in justifying policy and practice. The chapter will focus on the politics of evidence. Are we dealing with evidence-based policy or with policy-based evidence? That is to say, is evidence used to inform policy in a rational fashion, which in and of itself is by no means as simple a process as that statement implies, or is it deployed to justify policies in a way which is selective and partial? We will examine the political factors in the construction, publication and use of evidence generated by applied social science. It will show how political factors always enter into these processes and review the implications of this for applied social research in general. Particular attention will be given to the way in which governments selectively and often inaccurately present the results of applied social science investigations in order to justify policies and defend their record in relation to the technical efficiency of their administrations. These issues have arisen in relation to the use and abuse of official statistics but also relate to the ways in which academic studies have been seized on to 'demonstrate' effectiveness in relation to the achievement of policy outcomes. Examples include UK assessments of changes in income inequality and social mobility, the use of 'crime statistics' in relation to assertions around 'public safety', and a range of discussions relating to the relative efficiency of private versus public provision in health, welfare and education. The chapter will note that many, but not all, academics have 'willingly' entered into this process, sometimes in terms of ideological assertion (this is particularly true of economists), sometimes in relation to funding opportunities. It will also note that some civil servants, and in particular statisticians, have an honourable record in resisting the pressure for 'good news and only good news' and discuss how the examples of statistics commissions provide a basis for 'honest' applied social research.

Chapter Six will examine the process of 'consulting'. Consultation has become an essential component of the repertoire of political administration in post-democracy. The reasons for this were well expressed by the Skeffington Committee's Report on People and Planning:

> Life ... is becoming more and more complex, and one cannot leave all the problems to one's representatives. They need some help in reaching the right decision and opportunity should be provided for discussions with all those involved. ... Planning is a prime example of the need for this participation for it affects everyone. ... This becomes all the more vital when the demands of a complex society occasion massive changes; changes which in some areas may completely alter the character of a town, a neighbourhood or a rural area. The pace, intensity and scale of change will inevitable bring bewilderment and frustration if people affected think it is to be imposed without respect for their views. (Skeffington Report, 1969, p 3)

In principle consultation serves the three functions of providing necessary information to decision makers which has been elicited from the relevant 'publics'; engaging the relevant 'publics' in the actual decision-making process; and legitimising decisions made because they are based on complete information and real public engagement. In practice the actual degree of engagement in decision making is limited and almost never extends to strategic issues but is confined to details of implementation. Experience demonstrates that, far from legitimating decisions, processes of consultation very frequently anger those who have been consulted. This chapter will examine the role of social science in consultation with reference to:

---

- the delivery of existing evidence to those who are being consulted;
- the use of quantitative survey methods in consultation;
- the use of qualitative modes including such participatory mechanisms as citizens' juries;
- the reality or otherwise of dialogical engagement in participatory processes.

The discussion will be informed by examples drawn from health service re-organisation at the local level, and the development of Academy provision in the English secondary school system. The chapter will be informed throughout by the sceptical perspective inherent in Ambrose Bierce's definition of the word 'consult' in his *Devil's Dictionary* written in the early years of the 20th century: '**Consult:** get people to disagree with a decision which has already been made'.

Chapter Seven will address the process of modelling – the creation of versions of reality by whatever means – physical, mathematical, as computer simulations – in order to work out what might happen in the future if various actions and/or contextual developments are applied to reality in the same way as they are applied to the model. The easiest illustration of what this means is by reference to physical models, a technique not much employed in the social sciences! Naval architects in the past built models of the hull forms of ships and subjected them to various scale wave conditions, mostly in the UK in a large tank in Wallsend on Tyne near where the present author lives, in order to see how the hulls would stand up to turbulence – a chaotic process not easily subject to formal mathematical analysis – in reality. In other words the model was considered to be a simpler representation of the thing but one which contained its essential characteristics, and therefore could be used to predict future outcomes. Note the emphasis on simplification, which is always going to be an issue in relation to complex systems.

The development of formal models has been part of the application of social science, particularly since the availability of real computing power in electronic form. This has been primarily a matter of the application of econometric techniques, particularly but not exclusively in health contexts, although traffic flow models developed by civil engineers always had a considerable social content and the first working economic model was one based on water flowing in pipes to represent the UK macro economy – an analogue physical simulation actually rather like the ship models in the tank. Now we find considerable use being made of electronic simulations dependent on binary computing, particularly in domains where the ecological and the social intersect. This chapter will:

- identify the limitations of linear and equilibric models in relation to social processes; this will necessitate a severe rejection of the utility of much of traditional economic modelling in social policy;
- review the implications of modelling non-linear developments in open complex systems;
- discuss the potential *and* limitations of simulations as predictive models in relation to the impact of social interventions;
- argue for the development of general multi-method narratives of the future as the basis of modelling in applied social science.

The last of the 'gerund' chapters, Chapter Eight, will deal with acting – the role of social science in action research. Action research as an explicit mode of applied social research is widely deployed across a range of policy areas. I have had a particular interest in this mode since I wrote my MSc dissertation on it in 1970 and developed this in practice as Research Director of the North Tyneside Community Development Project (CDP) in the late 1970s. It can be argued, and this chapter will argue, that in addition to research projects which are explicitly identified as 'action research' much of the process of policy formation and implementation has a strong action research component. That is to say, research not merely informs the beginning of the process but there is a constant iterative feedback of research findings into the process as it develops. This chapter will:

- establish a methodological basis for action research in contrast with notions of 'pure social science';
- explore the relationship between action research and the notion of praxis in social research;
- illustrate with examples drawn from community development, development projects in the global south, health projects and education projects;
- consider the role of action research in participatory governance.

Again the chapter will draw on examples of action research in practice including the UK CDPs of the 1970s, perhaps the most explicitly politically informed example of action research in an 'advanced industrial society' in which I was a very active participant.

Chapter Nine will consider the existing and proper relationship between social science as practised in the academy (that is, in institutions of higher education and related bodies) and in organisations such as think tanks which stand between the academy and the processes of political administration. It will challenge the notion of the 'superiority' of the pure disciplinary perspective with special reference to the necessary development of a post-disciplinary mode of thinking in 21st-century social science. So it will both review the meaning of the terms 'multi-', 'inter-', and 'post-disciplinary' in practice and challenge the notion of any meaningful distinction between a pure and applied social science. It will critically review the claims of the core disciplinary social sciences – sociology/social anthropology, history, economics, psychology and geography (political science being inherently interdisciplinary) in relation to application, and review how the fields of education, the urban, health and general social policy, have deployed those knowledge claims. Particular attention will be paid to the role of statistical reasoning across the academy in relation to the application of knowledge. The argument will again draw on the Gramscian distinction between traditional and organic intellectual roles and work.

In this context 'think tanks' can be considered as a crucially important example of organic intellectual practice and the relationship of think tanks to funders provides an interesting example of the relationship between corporate interests and the production of knowledge. Of course not all think tanks are on the effective payroll of corporate capitalism and all will reflect to some degree the interests of their funders, but in applied social research done by think tanks we always have to consider the degree to which he who pays the piper calls the tune. This is even more the case of commercial applied social research done by private consultants outwith the academy. The relationship of commercial applied research and the academy is not simply a matter of the pure incorruptible academy versus the crass commercial but has become substantially more complex given that academics themselves, particularly in relation to evaluation research, work on a commercial contract basis.

The concluding chapter will draw on the arguments presented in preceding chapters in developing a proposal for the proper forms and role of applied social science in the 21st century with a particular emphasis on the role of knowledge in relation to present interwoven ecological and financial crises. It will argue for a responsibility in terms of praxis – in effect reversing the arguments Max Weber made at the beginning of the 21st century for a distinction between the academic and political modes of practice. These themes are by no means new in academic debate. In relation to a core discipline they were raised by Alvin Gouldner in *The coming crisis of Western sociology* (1971) but Gouldner saw this entirely in terms of the role of the traditional intellectual. We have to consider carefully how this works out when applied social researchers are 'in the state' and in a range of other contexts where the independence of traditional tenure is not part of the contractual package. This is not to say that 'employed professionals' are in any way mere hacks of those who pay them but they are clearly in a different position from distinguished professors in the university, as it used to be. The actual social location of social researchers is a frame for their work but it is not an absolute constraint. Praxis is perhaps the fundamental ethical issue in application, in marked contrast to 'ethical codes' which can often be back-covering and concealment exercises by elites in both the public and corporate sectors, and particularly in relation to the increasing intersection between those sectors. All these issues will be examined here.

To conclude let me indicate the style of this text. The introduction and the conclusion are written primarily in the first person singular to emphasise that these are chapters which derive from my own world view as it influenced the decision to write this book and as it developed in engagement with the material and arguments reviewed here. Other chapters will be written in the first person plural as they are about collective and general arguments in the social sciences as a whole.

**Notes**

[1] Underlining here and in other Wikipedia quotations indicates a cross-referencing link to another definition.

[2] I originally wrote 'the post-democratic state' and then realised that to use the definite article implied a degree of abstraction of, if you like, ideal typification, which is wholly alien to the methodological spirit of this text.

[3] Because research makes products rather than finds them, but makes them from something rather than nothing.

# ONE

# The methodological foundations of applied social science

> Methodology: the strategy, plan of action, processes or design lying behind the choice and use of particular methods and linking the choice and use of methods to desired outcomes … Theoretical perspective: the philosophical stance informing the methodology and thus providing a context for the process and grounding its logic and criteria. (Crotty, 1998, p 3)

When we do research we do it in relation to the world and we have to engage with the nature of the world and how we can know it. In other words we work with what Crotty calls a theoretical perspective, although others use the term 'meta-theory' to mean the same thing. That theoretical perspective must include an ontology, that is a worked out understanding of what the world is. Crotty rejects the use of ontology in this way (1998, p 10) but here we are following Blaikie, who asserts that ontological assumptions constitute: 'ways of answering the question':

> What is the nature of social reality? These assumptions are concerned with what exists, what it looks like, what units make it up, and how these units interact with each other. (2007, p 3)

Ontology comes first because the epistemological position, that is the approach to how the world may be known, depends on that fundamental understanding of what the world actually is. And here we have to emphasise by using 'is', a form of the present tense, we are dealing not only with what is but what has been and what might be; with the past, the present and the future.

If we were cosmologists what has been said so far would delineate the issues to be addressed in this chapter. In other words if we were 'pure' scientists dealing with phenomena over which human beings can have no influence whatsoever given our present state of technology, then we would need to say no more. However, we are applied social scientists and both those adjectives – 'applied' and 'social' – require us to go further. Let us start with the implications of dealing with science which is social science, in other words science which is concerned with social reality. These implications are ontological, epistemological and have a third mode of constructive ontological engagement in which both what is known and how it is known have a constitutive effect on social reality itself. In brutal summary we have to address the issues that arise from the social being socially constructed, from knowledge about the social being itself socially constructed (although from something, not from nothing – this is extremely important), and with the ways in which knowledge of social reality itself plays an important part in the ongoing reconstruction of social reality. The word 'applied' absolutely reinforces the importance of this 'reconstructive' element of science. Of course all applied science has implications for the ongoing constitution of the social world. When chemical engineers apply chemistry and chemical physics to the manufacture of new polymers all sorts of social consequences flow from this, right through to the level of cultural consumption and the forms of possible mass media. Think mobile phones. Applied social science is not merely, as say Giddens would have it, doubly reflexive. It is reflexive almost in a series to infinity in its interaction with what the world will become. There is an ongoing iterative relationship between the knowledge of the social world which we apply to shape the social world, the reshaped social world – which might very well *not* be reshaped in the ways we intended from our interventions – and knowledge of that social world as it has become. In reality – a very telling phrase here – given that the social world comprises a whole set of nested and intersecting complex systems, most of the time the social world as a whole and the systems within it are remarkably robust BUT when they do change, the changes that matter are large scale and fundamental. They are changes of kind, not of degree.

The term 'complex system' has been introduced explicitly into our discussion. Likewise, if somewhat implicitly, there has been mention of realism. The arguments presented here about the nature and purposes of applied social science are explicitly set within a meta-theoretical framework in which these two terms are brought together, that of complex realism. That is to say, they are based on the synthesis of the critical realist programme most generally associated with the work of Bhaskar (1979) and the programme of what Morin has called 'general complexity' (2006). Reed and Harvey define the nature of complex realism thus as:

a scientific ontology which fits Bhaskar's philosophical framework: one which treats nature and society as if they were ontologically open and historically constituted; hierarchically structured, yet interactively complex; non-reductive and indeterminate, yet amenable to rational explanation; capable of seeing nature as a 'self-organizing' enterprise without succumbing to anthropomorphism or mystifying animism. (1992, p 359)

There are numerous texts which elaborate either the content of complexity theory or the general perspective of critical realism. Particularly useful for the former is Cilliers (1998) and for the latter Danermark et al (2002), Carter and New (2004) and Sayer (2000). A warning note is required in relation to the character of complexity theory. While critical realism is by no means an intellectual domain without arguments and differences, there is a more or less general agreement about the foundations of the intellectual current. This is not the case for complexity science where what Morin (2006) has described as 'restricted complexity' asserts that complex systems can always be understood in terms of emergence from the interaction of simple, or at least simpler, elements, usually on the basis of rules of action. For an elegant exposition of the reductionist argument see Holland (1998). Here our colours will be nailed firmly to the mast of the opposing vessel of general complexity, which while not denying either simplicity or restricted complexity, considers these to be limited sets within a world where most systems are complex in a way which goes beyond emergence from simple interactions. Readers who want to take things further are referred to the above texts and to Byrne (1998, 2005b) but here we need to lay out in brutal summary the essentials of critical realism, of general complexity and of their synthesis as complex realism.

Let us begin with critical realism and in particular with the ontological scheme proposed by Bhaskar and the understanding of causality which flows from that scheme. For Bhaskar there are three levels to his deep ontology. The first is 'the real' – the domain of generative mechanisms which underlie the world as it is and are expressed in it, contingently – a word which matters a great deal, at the second level, that of the actual – what is. So for example the deep causal processes underlying the Earth's core are expressed in interaction – another word which matters a great deal – with context and with, as we now recognise after Lovelock, particularly the biosphere, in expressing the nature of the Earth's surface in terms of atmosphere, continents and seas. The third level is the level of the knowledge we construct about the actual and the real, the level of the empirical. In epistemological terms critical realism is constructionist but it is a constructionism which, while admitting the social, also allows a strong voice for reality itself, a position wholly in accord with the phenomenology for example of Merleau-Ponty. The words 'contingent' and 'interaction', which have overlapping, if not quite synonymic, meanings, are important. They matter in relation to critical realism's understanding of causality. Pawson and Tilley (1997) express this in a formula which is presented here in slightly modified form after Byrne (2002):

Mechanism & Context => Outcome

Here the ampersand '&' stands for 'in interaction with'. Note also that we do not have an equals sign = but a directional sign => implying an irreversible arrow of causality. What this means is that how the causal mechanism works out is determined – which word here means both limited in range of possible outcomes *and* influenced in relation to specific outcome – by the context in which it operates, with context very widely defined in cybernetic terms as the whole of its surrounding environment. So, to deploy an often used example, the necessary cause of clinical tuberculosis (TB) is the exposure of an individual human being to the TB bacillus, which has causal potential but can only express that in an actual organism. However, whether or not that individual develops the clinical disease will be a function of their own resistance to infection which in turn will be a function both of their genetic makeup and of their general health. General health in turn will be a function of the whole set of social circumstances they have experienced throughout their life up to the point of exposure. The TB bacillus is the ultimate cause of tuberculosis but while necessary, it is not sufficient.

What this means is that any effect, and we will define what we mean by an effect in complexity terms in a moment, usually has more than one cause and that moreover the same effect can have different sets of multiple causes. Likewise, ultimate generative causes may not result in expressed effects since the effects depend not only on the ultimate cause but on a whole complex set of intervening factors. So, for example, if we take secondary schools in contemporary England and look at the success profile of cohorts of pupils passing through them, we find that almost all schools which select pupils by ability for admission do well. Selection by ability is a sufficient cause of high average achievement of cohorts. However, other schools which do not select by ability also do well and when we explore the pattern of causation here, for example by systematic comparison using Qualitative Comparative

Analysis (QCA), we find multiple causal sets – to use Ragin's (1987) term, 'configurations' – which produce high average achievement. We find other sets which do not and we find sets where some schools do well and some do not – contradictory configurations which drive us to look further (see Byrne, 2009b for a development of this example). We will find that systematic comparison is a key tool in any effective applied social science.

Let us turn to the essential of general complexity theory. Essentially this is a systems theory which deals with complex systems. Complex systems are characterised above all else by emergence, by the possession of properties which are not amenable to description in terms of the elements which describe the system. In other words the analytical programme of reductionist scientism is not capable of describing such systems and is especially useless in understanding causality in relation to them. We can describe complex systems in a variety of ways, for example as 'far from equilibric', but the essential characteristic is the significance of emergence. Complexity must not be confused with 'holism', that is to say with the view that we can only describe and understand things in terms of their properties taken as a whole. On the contrary complexity is interested in systems as a whole, in the components of systems, in the interaction of components with each other, in the interaction of the components with the system as a whole, *and* in the interaction of systems and their components, sub-systems, with things external to and intersecting with the systems, which are generally other systems. Social geography provides a pertinent example. If we are interested in what a neighbourhood (however operationalised) is like (what kind of place it is) then we have to think about the effects on the character and trajectory – an important word – of the neighbourhood, of the individuals and households which make it up, of the locality, that is the wider local geographic context, of the region, of the nation state, of the world block, for example, the North American Free Trade Association (NAFTA), and of the world system as a whole. Note that influence is not hierarchical. It is both up, from households, and down, from the world system. Moreover, what happens at the neighbourhood level can have significance for city region, and hence for the world system. Think of the role of the *faubourgs* of Paris and the islands of Petrograd in the revolutions of 1789 and 1917.

What is interesting about systems is their trajectory. That is to say, what matters is the state of the system through time. For complex systems, which are generally pretty robust, most of the time they stay much although not exactly the same. In complexity terminology their trajectory lies within a torus attractor. However, they can and do change and the change is not gradual but radical. We can describe it exactly as metamorphosis. Morphosis is change; metamorphosis is radical change as with the transformation of a caterpillar into a butterfly. Systems can cease to exist but they can also change in kind while continuing to exist.[1] In this frame of understanding we can now regard an effect as being a description of the overall state of a system or of some key aspect of the system which is of significance for us. Do they stay much the same or do they undergo radical transformation – in complexity language, a phase shift? If we are interested in cause we have to have an understanding of effect, and effects are to be understood in terms of descriptions of system states in relation to stability or radical change.

Note the unapologetic emphasis on the pursuit of causality outlined here. As Danermark et al have asserted: 'The explanation of social phenomena by revealing the causal mechanisms the produce them is the fundamental task of social research' (2002, p 1). Of course description – the presentation of coherent accounts of what is – is an absolutely necessary precursor of the elaboration of causality, but without some sort of understanding of causality we have no licence for intervention in order to engender change. In other words we need a causal story in order to act. So we can now dismiss as utterly irrelevant to applied social science those versions of post-modernism/post-structuralism falling into the category labelled by Pawson and Tilley as 'hermeneutics II' which 'starts from the point of view that all beliefs are "constructions" *but* adds the twist that we cannot, therefore, get beyond constructions. It insists, in other words, that there are no neutral/factual definitive accounts to be made of the social world' (1997, p 21, original emphasis).

This is absolutely not a dismissal of interpretation or of qualitative modes of social research, as Pawson and Tilley make clear in their endorsement of the legitimacy of 'hermeneutics I' described in terms reminiscent of participatory action research. On the contrary interpretation and engagement are essential for research which seeks first to understand and second to change.

We can develop this point in relation to the arguments of 'actor network theory' in relation to method, for which see Law (2004). In many respects actor network theory is essentially a constructionist approach which takes an entirely epistemological and relativist position on scientific knowledge of any kind, and at the same time is underpinned by a serious and coherent programme of real social research, in marked contrast to the literary theoretical foundations of most 'hermeneutics II'. The key issue is the nature of the real. For critical realism reality exists and has depth. Actor network theory has a very shallow ontology which is essentially subsumed into epistemological construction. In contrast with post-structuralism actor network theory is both coherently expressed and has an empirical foundation in ethnographies of scientific and technical practice but its fundamental position is that scientific knowledge is a construct of a reality which is in deep flux and does not take form until science fixes it for us.

> Contrary to Euro-American common sense, they (Latour and Woolgar) are telling us that it is not possible to separate out (a) the making of particular *realities*, (b) the making of particular *statements* about those realities, and (c) the creation of *instrumental, technical and human configurations and practices*, the inscription devices that produce these realities and statements. Scientific realities only come along with inscription devices. Without the inscription devices, and the inscriptions and statements that these produce, there are no realities. …particular realities are brought into being with and through the array of inscription devices and disciplinary practices of natural and social science. Reality, then, *is not independent of the apparatuses that produce reports of reality.* (Law, 2004, p 31, original emphasis)

In another very interesting passage Law asserts that:

> The world as a 'generative flux' that *produces* realities? What does this mean? … in this way of thinking the world is not a structure, something that we can map with our social science charts. We might think of it instead, as a maelstrom or a tide rip. Imagine that it is filled with currents, eddies, flows, vortices, unpredictable changes, storms, and with moments of lull and calm. Sometimes and in some locations we can indeed make a chart of what is happening round about us. Sometimes our charting helps to produce momentary stability. Certainly there are moments when a chart is useful, when it works, when it helps us to make something worthwhile: statistics on health inequalities. But a great deal of the time this is close to impossible, at least if we stick to the conventions of social science mapping. (Law, 2004, pp 6–7, original emphasis)

A lot of the present author's male ancestors on his mother's side were Master Mariners and the family actually ran a navigation school during the 19th century. Now navigation on the oceans in a calm is a nomothetic process by which position and hence course – direction in which the vessel should travel – can be established by reference to fixed elements, in the old days by use of sextant and chronometer to fix longitude and latitude and now by calling up a GPS reference. However, when it comes to inshore waters the vessel needs to be piloted, to be managed through a location where dealing with what happens depends on deep local knowledge of the particular form of local currents and obstacles. Things vary but not in a way which is wholly unpredictable. A pilot's knowledge is based on a deep understanding of the way seabed and land features interact in context with tide states and weather. Any current condition is contingent but it can be understood and managed. In other words Law's example fits very well with critical realism but not with a notion that the useful is the exception. The chart is a basis but what has happened since it was made and what is happening now is the content of pilotage knowledge – contingent but not separate from the generative mechanisms of seashore and bed and tide in interaction with weather. Law's example of health inequality statistics is a good one to consider here. These are exactly empirical products of the actual form of expressed health in human bodies which are the product of the inequalities expressed contingently in different capitalist social orders and even in different localities with different housing and health systems. That said, the capitalist mode of production is precisely the mechanism – the real, which produces what is – the actual, and what we measure – the empirical. Measurement is crucial here.

We need a little more consideration of the modes of inquiry which are appropriate in relation to the simple, the restricted complex, and the general complex. The simple can be understood by analysis – by the abstraction from the world as it is and the creation of an artificial domain of the experiment within which single causal relationships are 'established'.[2] Hayles (1999, p 12) calls this 'the Platonic Backhand', in which the world is understood as simple and complexity is regarded merely as fuzzying noise. Plainly if we do have complex causation, then we cannot establish it by experiment. For restricted complexity the technique of choice is some variant of simulation to deliver what Hayles calls 'the Platonic Forehand'. Here we start with the simple in terms of rules for discrete micro-agents and see meso and macro complexity emerging from interactions based on those rules. However, the approach ignores all context. It does not allow for any kind of causality pre-existing micro-interactions and having causal potential. John Westergaard, in criticising the post-structuralist turn, could in many respects equally well be speaking of restricted complexity:

I think sociology has gone through twists and turns from the 1970s onwards, some of which were counter-productive and then produced a counter-reaction on the part of sociologists themselves. I'm thinking of the neo-marxist movement of the late 1960s and early 70s. Although I'm a marxist, I didn't agree with its abstract theorization which was very far removed from the business of trying to apply theory to contemporary realities. It was more concerned with exegesis of original marxist thought. It then picked up a strand of anti-positivism which was also present in ethnomethodology and symbolic interactionism which otherwise were its polar opposites. But this shared anti-positivism became virtually an epistemological relativism which I found particularly troubling in the case of marxism. I understand marxism to be inherently empirical but this was anti-empirical. It helped to give sociology a bad name which it didn't otherwise deserve, and sociologists, unconsciously I think, retreated from that into a more cautious stance altogether. Curiously enough, postmodernism is a further development, an extrapolation of some features of the ethnomethodological turn of the 1970s, and with later 'cultural turns' it curiously survived right into the 90s. I'm not sure that it's still surviving but there again there were counter-productive features in its anti-structuralism. O.K., 'structure' is only a metaphor, but useful to denote persistence and causal force. I think the strand of postmodernism which I found most unfortunate was, again, an epistemological relativism which, if taken to its logical conclusion, makes you think 'well, what the hell are we doing?' If we can only look at perceptions, and at other people's perceptions only as they are coloured by our own perceptions, what are we in this business for at all? (2003, p 2)

To be fair to those practising restricted complexity, they certainly do not deny reality or assert that it cannot be known. Indeed they are most assertive in arguing that simulations, Hayles's Platonic Forehands, are isomorphic with the world not just as pragmatic engineering descriptions (see Crutchfield, 1992) but as isomorphic with reality itself. The point is that they have no structure, no social before the micro interactions. This is wrong. 'Persistence and causal force' matter enormously.

Let us remember that word 'critical', so far simply deployed as an adjectival qualification of 'realism'. In the last part of this chapter we will elaborate on the notion of 'critical' but let us here and now recognise that critical social research is about change and is necessarily about change which is partisan. In the terminology of liberation theology it is to 'take an option for the poor' with poor here understood to stand as a generic term for all exploited and dominated social groups.

Before leaving complex realism we have to engage with a necessary limitation of any scientific description given that we are engaged with complex systems. When we are dealing with the simple we can through reductionist techniques produce adequate models of systems and of causation which are simplifications of the things we are seeking to understand. We cannot do that with complex systems. An adequate description would have to be as complex as the system itself, which as we shall see is a major problem for the simulation of complex systems. However, to recognise this is not to abandon the prospect of a useful social applied social science. We can know:

> The most obvious conclusion drawn from this perspective is that there is no over-arching theory of complexity that allows us to ignore the contingent aspects of complex systems. If something is really complex, it cannot be adequately described by means of a simple theory. Engaging with complexity entails engagement with specific complex systems. Despite this we can, at least at a very basic level, make general remarks concerning the conditions for complex behaviour and the dynamics of complex systems. Furthermore, I suggest that complex systems can be modelled. (Cilliers, 1998, p ix)

So we always simplify, but we must also remember that we do so in engagement. It matters enormously that we are not in any real sense external observers. We are actually part of the systems themselves. Whether this makes the task of science easier or harder, or indeed both things at once, is something we will explore as we develop the argument of this book. In any event we consider that complex realism provides a meta-theoretical framework for methodological practice which resolves the problem identified by Unger: 'a practice of social and historical explanation, sensitive to structure but aware of contingency, is not yet at hand. We must build it as we go along, by reconstructing the available tools of social science and social theory. Its absence denies us a credible account of how transformation happens' (Unger, 1998, p 24).

Complex realism and a set of practices derived from it provide us with just such a form of practice, hence with a way of understanding the causes of transformation, and consequently with a means to intervene to some effect in the social world. Let us clear some more ground before proceeding to a detailed examination of the processes of such intervention.

## Beyond quantity versus quality

> I have many objections to the way quantitative social research is conducted today, but I nevertheless believe that quantitative research is essential for sociology. Although qualitative research can be important for the development of explanatory theory, it lacks the reliability and generalizability of quantitative social research and this is critical if sociology is to be a rigorous science of the social. (Hedstrom, 2009, p 101)

The first sentence of this quotation is absolutely correct and the second is, if not absolutely because qualitative research is certainly important for the development of explanatory theory, mostly wrong. The words 'reliability' and 'generalisability' are the key here. What Hedstrom is looking for is a set of explanations couched in terms of 'social mechanisms' which are: 'constellation[s] of entities and activities that are organized in such a way that they regularly bring about a particular outcome' (2005, p 33). In the original this is in the singular and as we have noted in our discussion of a realist version of causality we should consider that there are multiple mechanisms which can generate the same outcome, but that aside there is nothing to quarrel with in this project. What we have to question is the notion that these kinds of explanations can only be achieved through quantitative work. Reliability is about reproducibility. It is a concept which derives from the way in which psychological measurement wanted to have the status which we can attach to experiments in the realm of the simple where we can intervene in an abstracted artificial version of reality and get the same results every time we do the same thing. Note that this works very well in the realm of the simple. When you measure the relationship between resistance and current in an electrical circuit with a constant electrical potential, there will always be the same inverse relationship expressed in Ohm's Law. It works somewhat in the kind of statistical experiment typified by a randomised controlled trial of a new drug if the drug is actually effective. Note 'somewhat' because only for really fantastic drugs is the actual effective drug better for all cases in the treatment group than the placebo administered to the control group. Probabilistic relationships have an element not of randomness but rather of contingent complexity. It does not work at all for complex systems and in relation to interventions within them.

In the domains to which we apply social science we are never working with the sort of simplicity which can be addressed by the bench-controlled experiment. Sometimes, for example in pedagogical innovation, there is enough simplicity for us to use statistical experimentation but mostly we are dealing with complex systems and complex interventions. Teisman et al point out the implications of this very clearly:

> Our starting point is the empirical observation that governance systems and networks are often in states of change which make them difficult to analyze, let alone manage. Stability of governance systems seems to be the exception rather than the rule. Further more, any changes that do take place are often capricious. Processes seem to unfold in unique and non-replicable ways, making it difficult to learn from successes and failures and to develop general theories. ... This then begs the question of how to develop knowledge about such an elusive subject of research. An attempt is made here by starting from a complexity theory perspective, with the assumption that the interactions in governance networks are complex: the outcomes of interactions between parties do not only result from the intentions and actions of these two parties, but also from interferences from the context in which the interaction takes place and the emerging results of such interactions. This means that the output and outcomes of the same interaction can differ in different places and at different times. A governance approach or organizational arrangement applied in two different contexts can result in very different outcomes. (2009, p 2)

The clear implication of this is that we need narratives, certainly as we will see as the basis of systematic comparative investigation of causality in relation to complex interventions but also in relation to the construction of any social scientific account relevant to application. So, for example, we need narratives of lives to explore the trajectories of young people into adult life in order to identify the multiple and complex causal mechanisms which produce different outcomes at the completion of this transition. Of course narratives can, and where possible should, have a quantitative component. That after all is exactly what survey-based cohort studies construct – multiple narratives in a quantitative form. Qualitative Comparative Analysis is precisely a method which enables us to transform deep qualitative information into a quantitative form in order to explore multiple and complex causation but we should not regard the qualitative as merely a stage on the way to the quantitative. On the contrary we often need detailed and careful qualitative narrative as the basis often for quantitative exposition of causality and that quantitative exposition often leads to further qualitative investigation. One way of describing this style of work is to call it 'process tracing', a term employed by George and Bennett, who quote Hall quoting George himself: 'process-tracing is a methodology well-suited to testing theories in a world marked by multiple interaction effects, where it is difficult to explain outcomes in terms or two or three independent variables – precisely the world that more and more social scientists believe we confront' (George and Bennett, 2005, p 206).

In a complex world stories matter. The arguments presented here are important both in general methodological terms but especially in relation to the processes of constructing evidence and evaluating effectiveness in relation to outcomes. In particular we have to challenge the notion of any hierarchy of evidence which privileges the quantitative over the qualitative. We will do this somewhat forcefully in Chapter Two.

An interesting and important comment on the actual role of numbers, in effect on why it seems to be true that 'some numbers beat no numbers every time' was made by a participant in the research workshop series 'Focusing on the case' during a focus group discussion: 'And what you said about policy makers not being able to add up three and four, I think this is part of the explanation of why they give so much more value to numbers because they don't understand them ...' (quoted in Byrne et al, 2009, p 517). Certainly the quantitative seems to have a semi-magical quality which it has possessed in some degree since Plato, as expressed in Kepler's Renaissance ontological belief that everything in the universe is arranged according to measure and number. The 19th century turned this into an epistemological principle with Maxwell stating: 'To measure is to know', and Kelvin even more firmly asserting: 'When you can measure what you are speaking about, and express it in numbers, you know something about it.' But what is measurement? That question matters because if we reject a simplistic positivism in which the things in the world are brute facts and speak to us directly, and no science since the development of instrumentation has been able to work on that basis, then we have to think very carefully about what we are doing when we measure. Let us make it plain – measurement is a process of interpretation, no less than the processes of interpretation which underpin qualitative research practice. Kritzer put this very well:

> That interpretation is important in quantitative social science should not be surprising because interpretation is central to analysis of human [we might say all actually] phenomena. In literary analysis, one is typically presented with a text for interpretation. In qualitative social science the analyst must construct the interpretation. In quantitative social science, the analyst constructs both a first order text (in assembling the data) and a second order text (in the form of statistical results). With each additional step in the process, the role of interpretation increases, as do the technical elements that must be considered as part of the interpretative process. Thus, rather than being divorced from the human process of interpretation, quantitative social science probably involves more levels of interpretation than does qualitative social science. (1996, pp 2–3)

If we allow that the data, the elements of the first order text, are themselves constructed rather than assembled and raise an eyebrow at the use of the word 'analysis' with its inevitable reductionist referent, then this passage really hits the nail on the head. Kritzer throws the quantitative programme right into the set of Pawson and Tilley's hermeneutics I, which is exactly where it belongs. In other words the distinction between quantitative and qualitative in terms of objective versus subjective breaks down, because both forms of data/findings are made into knowledge through the interpretive process.

There are extensive arguments about the theoretical basis of measurement which are summarised in Byrne (2005b). A complex realist take regards measurements as generally being not accounts of things real in themselves which can be abstracted from the complex systems they describe, the cases – the traditional understanding of variables – but rather as variate traces of the trajectory of those cases. In this way of thinking measurement is a way of describing the position of a system in its possible state space at any time point and repeated measurement is an account of the trajectory of the system. Note that this necessarily requires multi-dimensional measurement. The only real variables are elements introduced to affect the trajectories of systems, interventions originally external to those systems, and it is only in experimental contexts that we can introduce variables without the problem of real interaction and hence contextual determination. Note that experiment here means bench experiment with physical control. Statistical experiments based on random allocation can never eliminate this issue, which is different from, although overlapping with, the Hawthorn effect problem where human subjects act on their own interpretation of experimental contexts. It was precisely for this reason that Znaniecki (1934) argued for a qualitatively based strategy of analytical induction as the only method by which the social/human sciences could hope to replicate the explanatory power of the physically controlled abstracted experiment.

The point of the foregoing is simple. There is no meta-theoretical difference between the products of quantitative and qualitative social research. As we shall see, good research practice often requires both modes but that is what they are – modes, with the crucial process of interpretation being common to both. What is important is the recognition that the dominant tradition in quantitative causal work, regression analysis and its derivatives, is not compatible with a proper understanding of causality in relation to complex systems but systematic comparison integrating qualitative and quantitative reasoning is.

## Praxis – the critical part of the methodological programme

> The philosophers have merely described the world in various ways. The point, however, is to change it. (Karl Marx, Thesis XI on Feuerbach)

The above is carved on Marx's tomb in Highgate Cemetery in North London. It is the essence of the idea of praxis – one of four Attic Greek terms relating to the character of knowledge which we need consider here. Another is 'episteme', the root of epistemology, but which has a different meaning in and of itself. It refers to abstract knowledge, to knowledge which is the product of some form of reasoning separated from immediate context, whether derived from deductive or inductive process. Traditionally its contrast is '*techne*', the root term for technology. *Techne* is knowledge which is specific, is in context, and is applied without abstract reasoning. The class, ethnic and gender hierarchies of slavery-based ancient Athens of course appear clearly in this distinction.

We are contrasting the gentleman with the artisan, even if Socrates was himself a stonemason. It is worth noting that technology, our contemporary word, is more than *techne*. Technology is the application of abstract knowledge in context but it is based on abstract knowledge. The masons who built Durham Cathedral and Saint Magnus's Cathedral in Orkney (the same men for both) could be described in terms of *techne*, possessors of profound contextual knowledge about materials and structures but not basing their work on abstract calculation and experimental knowledge about the properties of materials. Contrast this with Gaudi, the architect of Sagrada Familia in Barcelona, who had a profound engineering knowledge of structures and based his use of materials on careful bench experimentation. This distinction will be of some importance.

The fourth term which has recently been revived in arguments about social knowledge is '*phronesis*'. This is deployed particularly by Flyvbjerg in a book directed towards *Making social science matter* (2001) written with an explicit intention of getting past the issues raised by understanding science only in terms of episteme. Flyvbjerg defines and argues for *phronesis* thus:

> *phronesis*, variously translated as prudence or practical wisdom. In Aristotle's words *phronesis* is a 'true state reasoned and capable of action with regard to things that are good or bad for man' ... *Phronesis* goes beyond both analytical, scientific knowledge (*episteme*) and technical knowledge or know how (*techne*) and involves judgements and decisions made in the manner of a virtuoso social and political actor. I will argue that *phronesis* is commonly involved in social practice, and that therefore attempts to reduce social science and theory either to *episteme* or *techne* or to comprehend them in those terms are misguided. (2001, p 2)

The confounding of technical knowledge as possessed by Gaudi with know-how as possessed by medieval masons is a rather serious error which mars Flyvbjerg's general argument but more serious, albeit closely related, is his tendency to equate praxis with general social practices in the public sphere despite a perfectly accurate discussion of Foucault's use of that word 'praxis', and whatever Foucault's other faults[3] he does get this right. We could fit Foucault's definitions easily into the usages of 'praxis' identified in the *Oxford English Dictionary*:

A term used by A. von Cieszkowski in *Prolegomena zur Historiosophie* (Berlin, 1838), then adopted by Karl Marx 'Zur Kritik der Hegelschen Rechtsphilosophie, Einleitung' in the *Deutsch-Französische Jahrbücher* (1844), to denote the willed action by which a theory or philosophy (esp. a Marxist one) becomes a social actuality. Action that is entailed by theory or a function that results from a particular structure.

1953 E.L. Allen *Existentialism from Within*, ii. 27 The Greeks did not speak of 'things' but of pragmata, implying that I have to do something (praxis) about them.

Freire, who will be very important to the general arguments of this book, defined praxis as: 'reflection and action upon the world in order to transform it' (1972, p 28). For him the rationale for action is a given but it is embedded in that idea of pragmata – knowledge is not just for the knowing. When something is known then having that knowledge imposes a moral requirement that we act upon it. The way in which Freire understood the production of knowledge in relation to the processes of dialogue and conscientisation derive in considerable part from his grasp of the moral obligations which underpin praxis. Note that we have simply taken it for granted that applied social science has implications for social life. In the terms identified by Hammersley (1999) we have specified it as having a function, essentially the set of functions we discussed in the introduction to this book. Applied social science generates knowledge for what May (2005) calls the 'evidence based state'. The techniques and procedures of applied social science in cybernetic terminology provide the learning feedback systems of governance in all its forms. However, in post-democracy applied social science does more than that. It serves as legitimation and through consultation and participation as a crucial strand of the governance process itself. It is intrinsically embedded in the ways in which the state and its allies, the essence of the term 'governance' in social theory and partnership in social practice, operate to form the social world. Of course 'the state' is not a person but the personnel of the state and of other agencies and entities are the actors and these personnel include applied social scientists. Hammersley was arguing with Gouldner's (1971) argument that sociology, although we might as well say social science, had a mission in maintaining the values of the enlightenment defined as universal. He instead endorses what is generally understood to be the position asserted by Weber[4] to the effect that sociology – again we might say social science – is no more than a source of factual knowledge about the social world and has important but limited practical utility. However, given the functions which we have assigned to applied social science, this approach is simply not good enough. Applied social science does things. Those who do it do things. It is inherently and necessarily political.

Note that this is a different argument from that advanced by Gouldner which is in important respects repeated by Burawoy (2004) in his calls for a public sociology. Burawoy distinguishes between 'public sociology' which: 'engages publics beyond the academy in dialogue about matters of public and moral concern' (2004, p 1607) and 'policy sociology':

> which focuses on solutions to specific problems defined by clients. The relation between sociologist and client is often of a contractual character in which expertise is sold for a fee. The sociologist, thereby, cedes independence to the client. ... What makes the relation instrumental is that the research terrain is not defined by the sociologist. It is defined narrowly in the case of a 'client' or broadly in the case of a 'patron'. (2004, p 1607)

This distinction is fundamentally misconceived. It privileges a form of academic work which stands outside the reality of the day-to-day life of practising social scientists and has essentially a self-referring audience among academic and related elites. Burawoy at least wants to speak beyond the academy but what is his audience? We need to start from the reality of engagement for the great majority of 'practitioners' of social science in contemporary society, which is neither as legislator nor interpreter (to use Bauman's terminology) – two modes which describe only the activity of that tiny and largely self-regarding minority who occupy anything resembling the role of what Gramsci described as the traditional intellectual – but rather as employed worker in organic mode in the apparatuses of governance or as trainers of those employed workers. If we are going to be serious about praxis we need to focus on the potential for organic engagement as a form of struggle with particular reference to the significance of evidence construction and consultation participation processes in relation to legitimation and political engagement in 'post-democratic' political governance.

Essentially the frame of argument here is derived from Gramsci but not, in accord with Gramsci's own style of working, in the form of scholastic and ahistorical repetition out of historical context. Gramsci had some good and useful ideas which can be employed in trying to understand contemporary post-industrial and post-democratic societies but we have to think for ourselves in our world, just as he did in his. The elements in the conceptual tool box employed here which derive from Gramsci are his distinction between traditional and organic intellectual roles and his understanding of the relationship between civil society and the state. Although he does not reference Gramsci as the source, Burawoy does employ the distinction between traditional and organic but only in relation to 'public sociology':

> I would also propose a distinction between elite and grassroots public sociology. The former reaches a wide but thin audience and would include books that stimulate reflexive debate ... or columns in national newspapers ... I call this form of public sociology *traditional* (original emphasis) because for the most part, it formulates a common public 'interest' and it does so at arm's length, in contrast to an *organic* or grassroots public sociology that engages the particularistic interests of more circumscribed publics – neighborhood groups, communities of faith, labor organizations and so on. Traditional public sociology assumes the limelight so we need to make the extra effort to validate the often invisible organic public sociologies. (2004, p 1608, original emphasis)

However, this distinction is couched primarily in terms of the audience and general interest conception of the 'traditional' intellectual. Gramsci himself did not consider that traditional intellectuals functioned to serve any general interest. Rather they functioned within the domain of civil society, which domain is an arena in which the dominant class acts to exert general societal hegemony, and supported that process in its general application. Certainly traditional intellectuals have characteristically asserted their independent position but Gramsci regarded this as misconceived. 'Organic intellectuals' in contrast are precisely those whose intellectual activity specifically serves a particular class, and most importantly serve to legitimate the interests of that class in terms of a claim for the general management of the state and its interface with civil society, to be conducted in accordance with the values and interests of that class. Several authorities have commented on the way in which neo-liberalism in relation both to its moral and utilitarian claims can be understood as the product of organic intellectual activity. We could certainly extend that position to cover the role of Giddens in relation to his assertion of the 'third way' – 'neo-liberalism with a smiley face'. Indeed a harsh critic could extend that critique to cover the general 'post-modernist' coloured set of projects in sociology and cognate disciplines, typified most elegantly by Bauman's writings, which in effect eliminate any scientific basis for praxis and generally dismiss praxis as something to be done. And that requirement for action is of course precisely the etymological content of the word in the first place. Praxis is in considerable part action which must be undertaken on the basis of knowledge, because when you know, you have a moral imperative to do.

Let us consider the validity, even in its own terms, of Burawoy's distinction between public and policy sociology and even more his dismissal of the policy relevance of sociology in contrast with economics. Brady (2004) has challenged both the distinction and the dismissal of the policy relevance of sociology, arguing cogently that Burawoy demonises the state and asserts that successful sociological interventions will operate only in the domain of civil society. That is a reasonable criticism but both Burawoy and Brady are making a false and far too precise distinction between civil society and the state as rigidly demarcated and separate spheres. There is certainly heuristic value in identifying economy, state and civil society as somehow distinctive but that process of distinguishing must always recognise that in messy reality they are profoundly inter-penetrating. It is precisely in the liminal contexts of the inter-penetration of civil society and state that 'applied social science' functions as a set of organic praxes and has a radical as well as hegemonic potential.

This chapter has been about making serious claims for the value of an applied social science which is founded on a coherent methodological framework – complex realism operates as constitutive in immensely important ways in the contemporary world, and has the potential for informing critical practice in order to make the world a better place. It has dismissed the claims of positivist social science, which to put it bluntly are arrogant, pig ignorant, self-serving and downright stupid. (The argument to which this is the summary will be developed in Chapter Nine.) Nomothetic claims for social science are simply rubbish. However, the chapter has likewise rejected the claims of 'hermeneutics II' – the extreme relativism which in effect dismisses the potential for any kind of knowledge as the basis of intervention in the social world – a meta-theory for the bone idle just as crude positivism is a meta-theory for the pig ignorant. Finally, in an effort to annoy as many people as possible, it has also dismissed the form of a demand for an engaged social science which separates that engagement from the actual mucky business of applying social science, and presents it merely as not so much detached critique, since its proponents are not detached at all, but outside the processes of making the social. There is not much more to this than simply informing people what is wrong with their world. Now of course this last activity is a vital part of any critical social science but the point is that it is not enough. So what is? Well, let us now work our way through the processes of applying social science in an effort to answer exactly that question.

**Notes**
[1] And of course come into existence. Think about the development of cities in North America or even in 19th-century industrial UK. In the latter case Middlesbrough literally did not exist before the 1830s and was a town of a quarter of a million just 70 years earlier, and this in a country with an urban population for more than 2,000 years. New York or Sidney are other examples of new urban systems in recent history.

[2] Popper's discussion of falsification is of course intended to demonstrate that we can never establish the truth of a hypothesis, only fail to disprove it. We are always faced with the prospect of the 'fallacy of affirming the consequent'.

[3] For example, despite Flyvberg's unctuous praise for the care of Foucault's historical research in relation to his establishment of genealogies, Foucault managed to move the era of the mass incarceration of the mad back into the 18th century from its real location in the 19th!

[4] Although others including Gouldner (1971) consider that this view is in important respects wrong and that Weber was not arguing for value freedom as political neutrality in scientific practice.

# TWO

# Constructing evidence: the development of knowledge which is to be applied

Why are social scientists interested in evidence? Because:

> we believe that the ways in which research is combined with other forms of evidence and knowledge could have important impacts on the nature, distribution, effectiveness, efficiency and quality of public services. Indeed we would go further to assert that it is reasonable to suppose that more deliberative and judicious engagement with high quality research may be sufficiently advantageous to be an important goal of public service reform. (Nutley et al, 2007, p 2)

In other words most of us subscribe to the old progressive liberal world view that we are here to do some good, what we know may help in the doing of that good, and systematic and coherent knowledge is one of the key foundations of doing good. However, at the same time many of us also recognise that a duty of those who know is to criticise. Nutley and her colleagues go on:

> it should be noted from the outset that research can be, and indeed often is used in ways that transcend the evidence-based policy and practice agenda. For example, while social research can play an important and positive role in informing and even supporting policy and practice decisions, this not always the case. Research can also seek to critique and challenge established policy and practice frameworks. (2007, p 11)

If we take the praxis position outlined in Chapter One, knowledge implies an obligation to critique and challenge in academic terms but also in all possible and acceptable action forms and especially through political action. However, knowledge is the starting point even if bitter 20th-century experience has demonstrated that while knowledge taken alone is *not* power, it is an important basis of power in interaction with organisation and mobilisation.

The particular form of knowledge which concerns us here is evidence so it is useful to consider the meaning of that word. The *Oxford English Dictionary* defines 'evidence' as: 'The quality or condition of being evident; clearness, evidentness'.[1] If we go further into usage we find that the term has a legal meaning – evidence offered in a court of law as to the facts of the matter and a meaning in science. Wikipedia – again used here as *evidence* itself – develops all these usages and does so in relation to science in general and 'evidence-based medicine' in particular in relation to, yet again, *the* scientific method. Thus we have:

- **Evidence-based medicine** (EBM) aims to apply the best available <u>evidence</u> gained from the <u>scientific method</u> to medical decision making. It seeks to assess the quality of evidence of the risks and benefits of <u>treatments</u> (including lack of treatment).

  EBM recognizes that many aspects of medical care depend on individual factors such as <u>quality</u>- and <u>value-of-life</u> judgments, which are only partially subject to scientific methods. EBM, however, seeks to clarify those parts of medical practice that are in principle subject to scientific methods and to apply these methods to ensure the best *<u>prediction</u>* of outcomes in medical treatment, even as debate continues about which outcomes are desirable. (http://en.wikipedia.org/wiki/Evidence-based_medicine)

and to follow the link to method:

- **Scientific method** refers to a body of <u>techniques</u> for investigating <u>phenomena</u>, acquiring new <u>knowledge</u>, or correcting and integrating previous knowledge. To be termed scientific, a method of <u>inquiry</u> must be based on gathering <u>observable</u>, <u>empirical</u> and <u>measurable</u> <u>evidence</u> subject to specific principles of <u>reasoning</u>. A scientific method consists of the collection of <u>data</u> through <u>observation</u> and <u>experimentation</u>, and the formulation and testing of <u>hypotheses</u>. (http://en.wikipedia.org/wiki/Scientific_method)

So the usage here refers to the development of evidence as the foundation of rational disinterested accounts of how things are, of what causes them to be as they are, and of what works in intervention in relation to changing them. This requires a developed account of how they come to be as they are, unless we proceed with what 18th-century physicians were inclined to describe as 'mere empiricism', based on observations that things worked in practice.[2] Moreover, although 'evidence-based medicine', the parent of the evidence-based movement, makes concessions towards practice-based experience and other forms of knowledge, knowledge produced by experiments is privileged above all other forms of evidence as descriptions of 'how the world works and what might work in changing it'.

Two issues emerge from this sort of understanding of evidence. The first is meta-theoretical: in a complex social world should we accord any sort of privilege to knowledge generated by procedures which require that world to be intrinsically simple? The second is socio-political: is knowledge ever disinterested and separate both from the social context and understandings of those who produce it and the social contexts and interests of those who would use – or ignore – it? We are dealing with discourses here which are sources of power both in the academy – the body of personnel whose trade it is to generate knowledge – and in the sphere of intersection among the state, civil society and the economy – the domain of politics in the widest sense.

Attention to discourse is not a move towards relativism, to what Pawson and Tilley called 'hermeneutics II'. Taylor and Balloch have asserted that: 'A fierce controversy rages within academic evaluation theory between *scientific realists* who argue for the possibility of an independent reality capable of objective description, and *social constructionists* who argue that all knowledge is contextual, relative and subjective' (2005, p 1, original emphasis).

The distinction presented in this way is misconceived. The realist position, which is the foundation of the complex realism argued for here, certainly allows for knowledge to be contextual – limited in the scope of its application – and relative, in the sense that it is related to that context and the way in which researchers work in that context. However, the subjective element, while present in realism, is confined to the requirement that those producing knowledge should be aware of their own subjectivity and explain how this relates to the character of the knowledge generated. It is perfectly possible to have a social constructionist understanding in a realist frame. Indeed it is essential. What realism does not accept is that social construction in the sense of the construction in the research process is the only element in the construction of knowledge. Reality itself has a voice. We make but make from something. And a crucial principle is always to speak as we find. As Carter and New have noted: 'Of all the philosophies of social science, social realism is probably the most optimistic about the possibility – and the necessity of reaching significant knowledge of the social world as a result of systematic principled investigation' (2004, p 1).

Let us turn to the issue of the kind of evidence which has value in relation to the description of a complex world.

## Invert the hierarchy – the stupidity of conventional rankings of evidence

> [A]n experienced social researcher with quantitative and qualitative research skills to promote the most up-to-date methods of social research and policy evaluation. The job involves advising government departments on social research and policy evaluation, delivering training to government social researchers and keeping them up-to-date on current methods and designs. ... A high level of skill in social research and evaluation (and quantitative methods in particular) is essential. ... Knowledge of experimental, quasi-experimental, systematic review and meta-analysis would be an advantage. (Advert for the post of Principal Research Officer – Government Chief Social Researcher's Office – Prime Minister's Strategy Unit)

The rationale for defining a researcher's role in this fashion was expressed by the Chief Economist and Director of Analytical – interesting word – Services at the Department for Education and Skills thus: 'Both government and social science fail too often in the only rare use of experimental evaluation and randomized control trials. From these comes the knowledge most valuable to policy makers' (Johnson, 2004, p 26). It would be easy to describe the above statement as rubbish, and at the first level of understanding it is exactly that. If policy makers want to know how a complex social world works then one thing is as sure as the fact that the sun rises in the morning – experimental approaches in general and randomised control trials (RCTs) in particular are about as much practical use in providing that information as is a chocolate teapot for holding tea. A second, and cynical, level of understanding might reflect on the fact that in many circumstances the last thing policy makers want is a truthful and accurate account of how a complex social world works so methods which utterly fail to provide that account may have considerable value after all. However, cynicism in relation to the politics of politics is not the only form of cynicism required in understanding the privileged position attached to RCTs and their derivatives. We also have to consider the politics of the academy, of the professional producers of knowledge, and in particular the role of the

Cochrane and to a less extent the Campbell Collaborations in asserting a hierarchy of the value of evidence in which:

> The pinnacle of the hierarchy is occupied by the RCT ... Other research methods are ranked lower in the hierarchy, with other types of *controlled* study second to the RCT and uncontrolled methods a poor third. In practice advocates of RCTs tend to regard uncontrolled methods as suitable only for hypothesis building with a view to an eventual controlled study. (Harrison, 1998, p 20, original emphasis)

The Cochrane Collaboration is:

> an international not-for-profit and independent organization, dedicated to making up-to-date, accurate information about the effects of healthcare readily available worldwide. It produces and disseminates systematic reviews of healthcare interventions and promotes the search for evidence in the form of clinical trials and other studies of interventions. (UK Cochrane Centre website, ukcc.cochrane.org)

It is named for the distinguished British epidemiologist Archie Cochrane who pioneered the development of systematic review of evidence in relation to clinical interventions. The Campbell Collaboration is named for the distinguished US social scientist Donald Campbell who likewise deployed experimental techniques in policy evaluation. While there seems little doubt that Cochrane would heartily approve of the direction taken by the organisation named for him, Campbell might raise some interesting questions about the extent to which the Campbell Collaboration has followed in the same direction. As he noted in a most interesting foreword to a book on case-based methods:

> More and more I have come to the conclusion that the core of the scientific method is not experimentation per se but rather the strategy connoted by the phrase 'plausible rival hypotheses'. This strategy may start its puzzle solving with evidence, or it may start with hypotheses. Rather than presenting this hypothesis or evidence in the context independent manner of positivist confirmation (or even of post-positivist corroboration), it is presented instead in extended networks of implications that (although never complete) are nonetheless crucial to its scientific evaluation.

> … in addition to the quantitative and quasi-experimental
> case study approach that Yin teaches, our social science
> methodological armamentarium also needs a humanistic
> validity-seeking case study methodology that, although
> making no use of quantification or test of significance,
> would still work on the same questions and share the same
> goals of knowledge. (Campbell, 2003, pp ix–x)

Amen to that! Let us be clear here. The objection is not at all to
the objectives of the Cochrane and Campbell Collaborations but
rather we need: 'to redirect critical attention towards Evidence Based
Medicine's (EBM) fixed hierarchy of evidence as the guilty source
of its questionable epistemic practices' (Goldenberg, 2009, p 171).
Goldenberg argues for a general pragmatism, noting pertinently that
despite the pragmatic – that is to say attention to what is adequate as
explanation in terms of effectiveness (even in a postmodernist version
as with Rorty's take, there is no necessary correspondence to causal
reality) – character of EBM, the idea of a fixed hierarchy of evidence
is profoundly unpragmatic.[3]

What is the fundamental problem with the experiment in
relation to the complex social and the social's intersections with the
complex ecological and biological? Let us first be clear as to what
sort of experiment we are dealing with. We are not dealing with
bench experiments in which material reality is both controlled and
manipulated directly in order to test a specific hypothesis in relation
to the nomothetic establishment of a general law. Those readers who
have studied even elementary physics will recall how we can test Ohm's
Law, which describes the inverse relationship between the resistance
of an electrical circuit and the current flowing in that circuit under
a constant electrical potential, by varying resistance with potential
held constant, measuring current flow with an ammeter, and plotting
measured resistance against measured current. That is a clear example
of direct control over relevant factors. Rather in almost all social and
clinical experiments we 'at best' control by randomisation or, and by the
canons of the hierarchy of evidence, much less satisfactorily, create or
observe a quasi-natural variation in relation to measured outcomes. Why
are RCTs and quasi-experiments not appropriate for the investigation
of causation in a complex social world? First we have to consider
the actual form of explanation they actually generate. It is important
to recall that RCTs do not produce constant outcomes. In fact we
examine the outcome in no single case but rather compare outcomes
for pooled aggregates between intervention and control groups. Our

description is purely probabilistic leading to the bizarre situation for the Cochrane Collaboration which Borgerson describes thus: 'While mechanistic (bench established) and probabilistic causes might intuitively be thought of as complementary ways of understanding the empirical world, the evidence hierarchy identifies probabilistic causes as epistemically superior' (2009, p 222).

There is a reason for this but the privileging of the RCT is the wrong solution to a real problem. Bench-based physiological and related experiments are very useful in relation to specific bio-medical problems but they do not generate universally generalisable results in the way that the bench-based testing of Ohm's Law generates universally generalisable results. Just as animals are only approximate models for human organisms, so any human organism is only an approximate model for any other human organism since each organism is itself a complex system with differences from other organisms which are of considerable significance. In relation to a range of basic physiological and even pharmacological interventions[4] we should, as Borgerson says, see RCTs and bench-based experiments as useful and complementary since they are addressing simple causation in relation to clearly defined outcomes.

When we move into the realm of the social we move into a complex world with multiple and contingent processes of causation, even in relation to clearly defined outcomes. In the language of conventional frequentist statistics we move into a world which is full of interactions at multiple levels. Despite assertions to the contrary, conventional linear statistical techniques are very poor at illustrating the character and significance of interaction, which in any event should be understood not in terms of reified variables but rather as representing real complex causation in complex systems. At best, and very seldom in published work, we have some relatively low order interaction terms entered into a regression equation with little in the way of substantive discussion of what this actually means in terms of causal process. From a complex realist perspective RCTs, which insist of necessity on simple causation, are not isomorphic with social reality. Greenhalgh and Russell note that '… a narrowly 'evidence based' framing of policy making is inherently unable to explore the complex, context-dependent, and value-laden way in which competing options are negotiated by individuals and interest groups' (2009, p 304).

In other words even in the context of the use of evidence, social action creates social reality. From a complex realist perspective of course the evidence has itself been created in a context of social action. Related to this fundamental ontological issue is something which is often appreciated in real efforts at RCTs applied to the socially complex, which may be found at any level from long-term interventions in health or criminal justice systems targeted on individual people up to interventions designed to deal with socio-environmental-political issues at a global level. That is the set of issues surrounding duration and the role of researchers in relation to feedback to managers of interventions during experimental processes when there is any ongoing social activity. The idealised RCT tests the null hypothesis that the intervention will have no effect. In order to do so it requires that the initial research design is maintained exactly at all stages of the intervention. A very clear exposition of this rationale can be found in the approach of Freeman, an experimentally committed evaluator, to the work of Action for Boston Community Development (ABCD), as described in Marris and Rein's (1967) account of the experience of the Ford Foundation Grey Area Projects in the 1960s. Freeman argued, and from the point of view of positivist experimental design he was perfectly correct, that the only engagement between a research evaluator and those actually managing an intervention in an experimental project should consist of the research evaluator constantly snarling to maintain the integrity of the initial strict experimental protocol. It is worth returning to Freeman and Sherwood's 40-year-old discussion of *Social Research and Social Policy* (1970) because it represents a more serious and well-constructed attempt by social scientists committed to the experimental approach to specify what is involved in experimental social interventions than recent assertions of the value of experiment. These comprise either ignorant positivist imperialism by non-social scientists and especially epidemiologists or a kind of uninformed acceptance by social scientists who have not thought seriously about what experiments really are in relation to the social world. That latter accusation could not at all be levelled at Freeman and Sherwood. Their insistence that:

> An impact model is an attempt to translate theoretical notions regarding the regulation, modification, and control of social behavior [sic] or community conditions on which action can be based ... The impact model must include a statement concerning the stimulus or impact, a hypothesis about what changes the impact will produce, and a theory or proposition about how that change will affect the behavior or condition the policy maker is seeking to modify (1970, pp 7–8)

is centered around the notion that theory matters. In other words experiments have to be informed by explicit theories of social process – in realist terms we can say that there must be a specification of generative mechanism. It is really surprising that most RCT social interventions are not founded around the specification of theory/ generative mechanism. Instead there is generally little more than a notion that an intervention will make a difference without an explicit theory as to why, with no more in the way of hypothesis than that a difference will be made tested against a null hypothesis of no difference.

Action research never works in the way Freeman wanted in any complex social situation for reasons which reflect the fundamental ontological status of the social. What is surprising is that more than 40 years on we still find what is really a simplistic and reduced version of his logic of inquiry asserted not only as a possible mode, which frankly speaking it isn't, but even as the best of all possible modes. In complex interventions things never stay the same. Even if we were to accept the simplistic version of social causation, which would be necessary for us to think that experimental modes can tell us anything in long-term projects, we could never maintain them in practice because the contexts change as things go on. However, this all too real practical issue does not actually matter because the mode of inquiry is wholly useless to start with and we should not be wasting our time with it in the first place. Social reality works differently. The wise words of McIver delivered nearly 70 years ago and annotated by Cicourel tell us how: 'the social structure if for the most part created ... Unlike the physical nexus [the social type of causal nexus] does not exist apart from the motives of social beings [and requires a methodological strategy that fits the distinctiveness of social events]' (Cicourel, 1964, p 1, quoting MacIver, 1942).

All this would not matter much if at all but for the way in which the ontological fallacy underpinning the privileging of randomised controlled trials has penetrated into the mindset of those who control the funding and resource base for the evaluation of complex social interventions. The general tone is set by the UK Medical Research Council's Social and Public Health Science's Unit in relation to complex social interventions in health:

> The International Collaboration on Complex Inter-
> ventions provides infrastructure support for investigators
> who share an interest in the design and conduct of complex,
> community-level interventions in population health. ...
> Our interest is in theory and methods appropriate for

interventions in social and physical environments. The main focus is experiments involving the allocation of some communities to an intervention while other communities act as comparisons but we are also interested in improving how much we can learn from repeatedly studying communities over time (using natural experiments, such as new housing, road building and school programmes). (Medical Research Council's Social and Public Health Sciences Unit website, 2009, www.sphsu.mrc.ac.uk/ research_project.php?prjid=EICCI&bcrumbs=EV. METHOP)

We find this reproduced in relation to research on health inequalities in the 2009 report of the UK House of Commons Select Committee on Health, where it is asserted that: 'Having a "control" group or project to which an intervention or treatment can be compared is a fundamental tenet of good research; so is randomization of the intervention so that people (or places) have an equal chance of being selected as subjects or controls in the research' (2009, p 32, para 63).

In the United States the decision in 2003 by the US Department of Education's Institute of Education Sciences to privilege experimental and some quasi-experimental designs for funding (see Donaldson, 2009, p 7) led to a serious split in the American Evaluation Association (AEA). The AEA leadership issued a rejection of this approach noting (entirely accurately if perhaps in too conciliatory a form) that:

> RCTs are not always best for determining causality and can be misleading. RCTs examine a limited number of isolated factors that are neither limited nor isolated in natural settings. The complex nature of causality and the multitude of actual influences on outcomes render RCTs less capable of discovering causality than designs sensitive to local culture and conditions and open to unanticipated causal factors. (quoted in Donaldson, 2009, p 8)

What Donaldson describes as 'an influential group of senior members' of the AEA then issued a rebuttal asserting that: 'The generalized opposition to use of experimental and quasi-experimental methods evinced in the AEA statement is unjustified, speciously argued, and represents neither the methodological norms in the evaluation field nor the view of a large segment of the AEA membership' (quoted in Donaldson, 2009, p 9).

These statements represent a rather clear specification of the issues, although it is necessary to develop the implications of the reference in the AEA statement to 'the complex nature of causality' in order to finalise the argument. The collection of essays edited by Donaldson et al, *What counts as credible evidence in applied research and evaluation practice?* (2009), is essentially a framed debate between the two positions.

In her contribution to this by developing 'An argument for social and educational inquiry that meaningfully honors complexity', Greene quotes from Simons: 'Simplicity and certainty are what governments seek. Complexity and uncertainty are what we [qualitative evaluators] habitually deliver ... The government wants to know what works and what we have to tell them is nothing works everywhere and that their best bet is to fully understand why this is so' (Simons, 2000, pp 410–11, quoted in Greene, 2009, pp 158–9). Exactly. But is there a way past this which allows us to have a systematic social science? Head (2008) suggests that in addressing complex policy problems we have to recognise that we are dealing with multiple evidence bases. He identifies three 'lenses' for understanding the 'evidence base(s) of policy debate' (2008, p 5). These are *political knowledge*, which is the sum of the knowledge held in all its forms by political actors; *scientific research based knowledge*, which: 'is the product of systematic analysis of current and past conditions and trends, and analysis of the causal inter-relationships that explain conditions and trends'; and *practical implementation knowledge*, which is the combination of day-to-day experiential knowledge of practitioners and the management/organisational knowledge of those who deal in policy and programme implementation (2008, pp 5–6). For Head, who recognises the disputes which persist over the character of scientific evidence itself:

> rigorous and systematic research has great value, but needs to be placed in wider context. Hence, it is argued that effective policy – its design, implementation, and evaluation – depends on several evidentiary bases. These are all involved directly or indirectly, in the development and assessment of 'good programs' and help us to understand 'effectiveness' in a more holistic and networked policy environment. (2008, p 4)

There is a good deal of heuristic value in Head's distinction but while recognising this we should also remember that in practice these forms of knowledge are all inter-linked given the role of scientific knowledge in relation to the educational and practice formation of both practitioners and politicians *and* the role of political orientation and interests in the construction of scientific knowledge itself. The best way to develop these issues is in relation to a specific example and we can do that by taking one which has very considerable salience in the English-speaking world outside the US – that of health inequalities.

## Understanding causality in relation to 'wicked issues' – the general problem for evidence in a complex social world

> The task of collecting evidence on [health] inequalities is especially difficult and has been described as a 'wicked issue'– a problem that is complex, difficult to define, with no immediate solution, and one where every wicked problem can be considered to be a symptom of another problem ... Assembling evidence to reduce health inequalities through social determinants certainly seems to fit this definition. The causes and symptoms are highly interrelated, and the causal pathways complex, passing through many sectors, including housing, transport, crime, health, welfare and education, all of which fall within the purview of the Campbell and Cochrane Collaborations. Better evidence to address this wicked issue therefore will involve synthesizing complex sets of evidence across disciplines and methodological divides, and understanding the process and context of interventions, while using these syntheses to inform real-world decisions. (Petticrew et al, 2009, p 454)

This comes from a Cochrane review and the lead author has been a proponent, albeit with some qualifications, of the general utility of RCTs as evidence generators in relation to complex social interventions. There is nothing to quarrel with here. What is being said accords with the line taken by Head but we need to develop the implications of thinking in this way for our understanding of the reality of applying social research in relation to evidence.

The term 'wicked issues' is very widely employed in contemporary discussions of health policy and practices. It is usually considered as having originated with Rittel and Webber (1973) and has been defined thus:

> Wicked issues are those that seem to defy solution, or where seemingly sound interventions turn out to have unexpected

consequences and results. Solutions that worked in one place fail when imposed on others. Ideas that remedy one problem can create a new set of circumstances, often with unintended consequences that then need resolution. (Hargadon and Plsek, 2004, p 2)

Note the congruence between this specification of 'wicked issues' and the discussion of the problems posed for public intervention in complex systems quoted from Teismann et al in Chapter One. Let us develop this by deploying a slide from a presentation by Blackman (2006; see table) which summarises the contrast between wicked and tame problems. It is apparent from the description, and Blackman specifically endorses this view, that wicked issues arise in complex systems with complex processes of causation in operation. This means that conventional approaches to resolution which depend upon the development of universally applicable rules and procedures *will not work*.

| 'Wicked' problems | 'Tame' problems |
| --- | --- |
| No definite formulation | Well-defined and stable |
| Continually evolve and mutate | Know when a solution is reached |
| Solutions are better or worse | Solutions are right or wrong |
| No principles of solution that fit all members of a class of problems | Belong to a class of similar problems which can be solved in a similar way |
| Many causal levels, with problems symptoms of other problems | Causes are evident with solutions that can be tried and abandoned |

Note that the political wickedness of these issues is not just a technical matter or rather by not just a matter of the problems of administering complex socio-political systems in a technical mode. In 'social democracies' and in particular in the UK, in marked contrast with the US, these issues have enormous political salience. We will return to this with reference to another health issue – the reconfiguration of local health provision – in our discussions of consultation and participation. Here let us focus on the nature of evidence which might be useful.

This was precisely the focus of the Select Committee on Health Inequalities in relation to evidence about what might lead to reduced health inequality in the UK. The committee made explicit reference to Health Action Zones (HAZs), an important initiative launched in 1997 with the explicit brief of coordinating multiple agencies, principally those of the NHS and local government, 'to explore mechanisms for breaking through current organisational boundaries to tackle inequalities and deliver better services'. This initiative has been judged as failing to do much if anything in terms of reducing health inequalities. Benzeval, who carried out a major evaluation of the initiative, in her evidence to the Health Select Committee stated:

> The evaluation started after the initiative so there was little chance to influence the design to improve the evaluabilty of either the overall initiative or specific interventions within it. Even within a process evaluation of a complex systems change initiative like HAZ, it could have been possible to employ outcome evaluation, including experimental designs, of specific interventions, but as well as issues of time and resources there was limited commitment on the ground to the idea of evaluation, they just wanted to get things going to achieve change. (House of Commons Select Committee on Health, 2009, p 31, para 56)

HAZ was a place-based set of projects requiring social action by local agents in specific places. Blackman (2006) has examined precisely both the issues which arise in the conceptualisation of *Placing health* and what methods of evaluation might be appropriate in relation to 'complex systems change initiatives'. Benzeval seems to have used this term simply to say that there was an effort to change systems and that the effort was complex. Blackman starts from the position that the systems themselves are complex, complex in the way that has been described in Chapter One, and that therefore any attempt to understand what has generated change in them must be founded on a clear understanding of the implications of that ontological specification for the construction of meaningful knowledge. He proposes the use of Qualitative Comparative Analysis (QCA) as a means by which we can understand trajectory change in complex systems. The potential for the use of QCA in combination with careful process tracing as a method for evaluating complex system interventions is considerable and we will return to it. Reading the discussion of evaluation in relation to health inequalities developed by the House of Commons Select Committee and the evidence of academics on which it is based, it is plain that 'complexity' thinking did not inform the understanding of either the committee or their witnesses. The issues were clearly identified in the debate around evaluation of complex social interventions in the 1960s and 1970s (see Marris and Rein, 1967), indeed more clearly identified than by contemporaries who are committed to the discourse of hierarchies of evidence and the general utility of RCTs. What is important is that we now have an intellectual framework, complex realism, and a set of intellectual tools based around systematic comparison, which enable us to resolve the issues which were identified a generation ago.

The conceptual discussion of health inequalities developed by Higgs et al (2004) is particularly helpful to us here. In a volume edited by Carter and New and dedicated to the objective of *Making realism work* they draw on the critical realist framework in two important ways. The first is by taking up Lawson's concept of demi-regs. Let us quote them quoting him:

> Although constant event patterns or invariant regularities may not occur in open [here synonymous with complex systems], partial regularities do. Lawson calls these *demi-regularities* or *demi-regs* and defines them as:
>> 'A partial event regularity which *prima facie* indicates the occasional, but less than universal, actualization of a mechanism or tendency, over a definite region of time-space. The patterning observed will not be strict if countervailing factors sometimes dominate or frequently co-determine the outcomes in a variable manner. But, where demi-regs are observed there is evidence of relatively enduring and identifiable tendencies at play.'

(Lawson, 1997, p 204, embedded in Higgs et al, 2004, p 93)

Let us think about what happens in relation to outcomes in any RCT, even in those RCTs which do have for example a clear theoretical conception of the mechanism relating intervention to outcome and in which the trial is carried out over very large numbers of cases.[5] In most cases there is considerable variation in the outcome across cases within both treatment and control groups. For example, let us take the case of a hypothetical RCT of penicillin when this was first developed as an intervention and was at the height of its effectiveness in relation to clinical outcomes. Some of the people in the control group would recover from any given infection although more in the treatment group would recover – in the case of penicillin at that point, most of them. However, in the treatment group some would become very ill or even die because they were allergic to penicillin. Now an RCT for penicillin would encounter much greater variability in outcomes because many infectious agents have in different strains evolved a resistance to it. Even when it really was a wonder drug and a magic bullet, there was not a universal better outcome. What we have is a demi-reg, which we can express using a modification of Pawson and Tilley's (1997) formula:

Mechanism & Context => Outcome

Antibiotic with a well-understood biological action & (in interaction with) the distinctive biological status of the patient being treated including strain of infectious agent in relation to resistance to the drug => Outcome

Outcomes vary but all the RCT generates is an average outcome across cases. This is the fundamental problem of probabilistic reasoning as the foundation of evidence from RCTs. Identifying this issue is not a basis for dismissing the utility of evidence of causation based on probabilistic reasoning BUT it is a reason for describing such evidence as simply exploratory in relation to the proper establishment of cause. All RCTs can ever generate is demi-regs. When we bring in human agency as well as context they are not even much if any use at doing that.

The other way in which Higgs et al draw on the realist framework is through a careful consideration of the idea of class, or more accurately a class society, in relation to the generative mechanism of health inequalities as a whole. In Chapter One we noted that actor network theory rejects the reality of deep generative mechanisms. Law (2004) explicitly refers to health inequality statistics in relation to his discussion of this issue. If we do accept that health inequalities are a product of a deep generative mechanism – the class inequalities which are generated by a capitalist mode of production – then the implications for the role of social science are very different from those which arise if we do not have that sort of understanding. In the latter case the task of social science is simply to assist in the development of forms of governance and practice which reduce inequalities (if such reduction is identified as a politically approved project). If we think that it is 'capitalism wot does it', then we have important things to say about the nature of capitalism as a social order. This is not to say, in the manner of various inane Marxists of the 1970s (many of whom turned coat to be cheerleaders for neo-liberalism in the 1990s) that the only role of critical social science is to call for revolutionary transformation. It is perfectly appropriate for social democratic social scientists (like the present author) to attempt to assist in the development of better practices within the present system, while at the same time generating critical information about its character and calling for reforms which in accumulation over time will transform its character. So it is worthwhile to develop evidence about what works locally in relation to health while supporting taxation, public spending, and workers' organisational projects which would change the distribution of material resources across the society as a whole towards that of a more egalitarian social order. It is possible to be a reformer of social administration and a leveller in relation to social policy.

To say this is to raise fundamental questions about the politics of evidence production, questions which will inform all of the issues addressed in this book. By way of concluding this chapter let us consider the following:

> the interests of action and experimental research ... are not at all the same. Research requires a clear and constant purpose, which both defines and precedes the choice of means; that the means be exactly and consistently followed; and that no revision takes place until the sequence of steps is completed. Action is tentative, non-committal and adaptive. It concentrates upon the next step, breaking the sequence into discrete, manageable decisions. It casts events in a fundamentally different perspective, evolving the future out of present opportunities, where research perceives the present in the context of final outcome. Research cannot interpret the present until it knows the answers to ultimate questions. Action cannot foresee what questions to ask until it has interpreted the present. .... Because it is pragmatic and flexible, an exploration also needs to be retrospectively interpreted, in a different manner from an experiment. The final outcome cannot simply be related to the initial aim and method, since these have undergone continual revision. The whole process – the false starts, frustrations, adaptations, the successive recasting of intentions, the detours and conflicts – needs to be comprehended. Only then can we understand what has been achieved, and learn from the experience. Research in this sense is contemporary history. Even though no one ever again will make the same journey, to follow the adventures of the projects offers a general guide to the dangers and discoveries in their field of action. From such a guide, anyone may evaluate the experience according to his purposes. (Marris and Rein, 1972, pp 205 and 207)

The chapter from which that long double quotation is taken has played an important part in the author's career. He first read it when he was an undergraduate student of sociology and social administration in the late 1960s, drew on it extensively when writing his Master's dissertation in social policy and planning in 1970,[6] and used it to inform his role as Research Director of the North Tyneside Community Development Programme in the mid-1970s. Although Marris and Rein do assert that experimental approaches have a role in understanding social action, they go on to specify that experiments are necessarily an abstraction from reality and that given 'the unique complexity of an historical event' it is difficult if not impossible to derive outcomes from any universal laws of human behaviour (1972, p 206). Hayles has labelled the experimental method as 'the Platonic Backhand', noting that:

> The Platonic Backhand works by inferring from the world's noisy multiplicity, a simplified abstraction. So far so good: this is what theorizing should do. The problem comes when the move circles around to constitute the abstraction as originary form from which the world's multiplicity derives. Then complexity appears as a 'fuzzing up' of essential reality, rather than a manifestation of the world's holistic nature. (1999, p 12)

She argues, convincingly, that experiment – the Platonic Backhand – shares with the new method of simulation – the Platonic Forehand – a common world view in which the abstract in the form of disembodied information is regarded in true Platonic tradition as the Real Real. In this frame of reference messy reality itself is regarded as merely the shadows on the cave wall to refer to one of the foundational myths of the simplistic model of western knowledge.

Marris and Rein pit action and research against each other as ultimately incommensurable if any notion of abstraction is preserved as the essence of scientific description. What they admit as a possible mode of understanding is essentially unique ideographic description of real historical process. That was the position the North Tyneside CDP team took in preparing our final report on the experiences we derived from our own specific interventions in community development in that locality.[7] The synthesis of complexity science and critical realism which constitutes complex realism provides us with a way of getting beyond that limitation of the unique to be interpreted but not generalised. We can address the possibility of the 'Aristotelian smash', a term coined by Byrne (2002) from badminton, to supplement Hayles' tennis-based metaphors. This involves working with an account of what is and how what is has changed – the essential character of the survey which will be the subject of the next chapter. If we are to understand what has caused how things are in a way which allows us to generate knowledge which in any way can be generalised beyond the specific instance, then we have to engage in systematic case-based comparison. To that theme we will return in Chapters Four and Seven.

## Notes

[1] Interestingly, and surprisingly, the usage examples given do not include reference to either scientific or policy evidence, which is a rare example of the OED not being bang up to date in relation to how a word is deployed.

[2] Any randomised controlled trial not based on a full causal account of the supposed basis for effectiveness of the intervention is of course 'merely empirical'.

[3] As we shall see when we discuss modelling, although it is possible to have considerable sympathy with pragmatism's objectives, realists really do want to know not only what works but how it works.

[4] Although the failure to pursue variation in outcomes in RCTs – in other words to pay attention to the outliers and deviant cases – is a real issue which in all probability derives from the interests of pharmaceutical companies (major funders of RCTs) in not allowing for any real qualification and specification in relation to the efficacy of their products. This matters profoundly when we are dealing not with an average effect measured in some scalar sense but rather with categorical condition. RCTs sometimes measure true scalars, for example, cognitive performance on a test in relation to anti-dementia drug treatments. Sometimes they use scalars as proxies for categorical condition – five-year survival post-cancer treatment is considered to represent effective elimination of the underlying pathology. However, they average out effects across multiple cases, which means that there is never any deterministic account underlying their findings.

[5] RCTs carried out over small numbers of cases, which is typical in any attempt at an RCT in relation to social intervention, are on very shaky statistical ground in drawing any inferences from differences observed in relation to outcomes. If the cases in the study are considered as components of a sample drawn from a large population, and statistical procedures which treat them in this way are routinely deployed, then numbers and variation are not really adequate for any proper random allocation to intervention and control or

inference based on difference in outcome. There are enough issues in relation to the application of frequentist statistical approaches to inference in relation to large samples drawn randomly from large populations but these are much magnified if the real populations are in reality small and limited.

[6] The quotations are referenced to the pagination in the second edition of the book but it was first published in 1967.

[7] However, we, along with some but not all of the other UK CDPs, also recognised what in realist terminology we can now identify as the generative mechanism of massive deindustrialisation as fundamental to the social experience and organisation, or perhaps disorganisation is the better word, of North Shields and places like it. In other words yet again it was 'capitalism wot done it', both in the sense that it created the industrial potential of North Shields in the first place and then, in what for capitalism as a whole may have been creative destruction but for working-class people in North Shields was destruction full stop, took the place apart at the joints.

# THREE

# Surveying the social world: assembling knowledge as a basis for action

The word 'survey' considered both as a noun and as a verb has its origins in the interrelationships between the natural and social uses of the natural. Its earliest usages are related to the laying out of land for agricultural purposes but it has been extended into the description of character of both the built environment as a whole and elements of that built environment.[1] One component here is the making of maps – of descriptions of the world as it is. Here let us consider that branch of the making not only of maps but also of charts of bodies of water – hydrography. The marine hydrographer makes not only charts in the sense of maps of the physical layout of the seabed but also notes the relatively constant but subject-to-dramatic-change phenomena which are ocean currents and the regularly changing character of tides. The seabed of the continental shelf changes regularly and has to be constantly resurveyed. In other words hydrographers have to survey complex systems and describe not only how they are but how they have changed, while noting important aspects of them, which are constantly subject to change in themselves and are the sources of change in other aspects of the systems.

The task of the social survey is essentially similar with the added proviso that the sources of change in social systems can be the willed and intentional acts of human beings expressed at all of the micro, meso and macro levels.[2] Patrick Geddes, the polymathic founder of much of modern urban planning while also being an innovatory systems biologist and significant figure in the development of British sociology, described the survey as the foundation of any kind of social intervention. He recognised that it had to be not just a static description or snapshot of what is but also had to take account of how what is had come to be. In other words all social surveys must deal in terms of change towards what is now – with the processes of becoming. We will return subsequently to Geddes' subsequent phases of planning and implementation and add to them the phase of evaluation, that is the processes of deciding what to do in order to change what is, of doing it, and of assessing what has been done. For now let us consider the elements of the survey and then see how they have been and might be deployed in relation to specific sets of social interventions.

The significance of accurate description of what it and how it has become what it is cannot be overemphasised. Far too much of both 'academic' or 'pure' social science and policy/practice intervention ignores this reality.[3] One of the essential tasks of the applied social scientist is to be able to tell it not only like it is but how it has become like it is. A key tool in this process is the measurement of the social world. The cultural theorist Raymond Williams put this point very well:

> It is very striking that the classic technique developed in response to the impossibility of understanding contemporary society from experience, the statistical mode of analysis, had its precise origins with the period [early 19th century] of which you are speaking. For without the combination of statistical theory, which in a sense was already mathematically present, and arranged for the collection of statistical data, symbolized by the founding of the Manchester Statistical Society, the society that was emerging out of the industrial revolution was literally unknowable. (1979, p 170)

This passage deserves careful deconstruction. From any complexity perspective the word 'analysis' has to be treated with extreme caution – handled with tongs, we might say in the vernacular. We should replace it here with 'description'. Likewise, although the mathematics of probability theory were in the process of development by the early 19th century, driven originally by the practical requirements of the ancient human activity of gambling, statistical theory largely developed later in order to handle the measurements produced by the collection of social data. That said, the key point remains absolutely valid. In a society which is itself enormously complex *and* is undergoing a radical phase shift, it is impossible to know either the character of the society or how it is changing without careful quantitative enumeration.[4] It is precisely for this reason that the original charter of the Royal Statistical Society[5] noted that it had been established in 1834

> to collect, arrange, digest and publish facts, illustrating the condition and prospects of society in its material, social, and moral relations; these facts being for the most part arranged in tabular forms and in accordance with the principles of the numerical method, and the same Society is now called or known by the name of 'The Statistical Society'.[6]

So a key component of any survey is quantitative. Statisticians, seduced by the search for platonic versions of reality established by abstraction, have a regrettable tendency to forget that their first task is enumerative description, a process appositely identified by Tukey as exploration:

> Once upon a time, statisticians only explored. Then they learned to confirm exactly – to confirm a few things exactly, each under very specific circumstances. As they emphasized exact confirmation, their techniques inevitably became less flexible. The connection of the most used techniques with past insights was weakened. Anything to which a confirmatory procedure was not explicitly attached was decried as 'mere descriptive statistics', no matter how much we learned from it. (1977, p vii)

The emphasis on hypothetico-deductive method, the foundation of the privileging of the RCT, as a way if not really to establishing cause pace Karl Popper, then at least to saying this might be how things work, has meant that the real task of charting change has been regarded as secondary by many contemporary statisticians. An important exception to this is provided by the contents of the UK Government's publication *Social Trends* established under the auspices of Claus Moser and editorship of Muriel Nissel with this brief: 'Social Trends draws together social and economic data from a wide range of government departments and other organisations to provide a comprehensive guide to UK society today, and how it has been changing'.[7] That is as good a definition of the task of the quantitative element of the social survey as any you could find.

*Social Trends* deals primarily with 'social facts', that is with what Bateson (1984) considered to be measurements which would be agreed on by different individuals and have the same value if considered by the same individual at different time points. Interestingly if we look at dictionary definitions of the social survey then we often find that they emphasise its role in the elicitation of opinions – things which in Bateson's terms would result in differing responses from different individuals and perhaps from the same individual at different points in time.[8] Surveys oriented towards value elements such as the British Social Attitudes Survey also offer us traces of important aspects of reality and allow us to see how values, meanings in effect in relation to key issues, change over time. This is an important part of the quantitative account of social reality.

Numbers matter but numbers are contestable, since they are not found – the literal meaning of 'data' as something which is (or more properly somethings which are, since 'data' is the Latin plural of 'datum') given – but rather are constructed by processes of measurement. In other words whenever we look at numbers we have to consider the operational definitions – the measurement rules – which have been used to make them. The example of UK unemployment statistics illustrates this exactly. UK politicians throughout the 1990s ranted on as to the comparative success of the UK economy driven by neo-liberal policies directed towards 'flexibility' in comparison with the stagnancy of Germany which remained essentially corporatist in governance processes. A key indicator of this relative success was asserted to be the lower unemployment rate in the UK as compared with Germany. Even ignoring the impact on Germany of the massive costs of reunification and the reconstruction of the former East, a major reason for this was that UK social security systems had assigned very large numbers of individuals to the category of 'incapacitated', that is, permanently too sick to work, while many of the same people in Germany would have been classified and counted as unemployed. The fracturing of the UK economy and the relative success of Germany in coping with the global financial crisis demonstrate the fatuousness of the British political elite's conception of the state of the nation reinforced as it was by data misinterpretation. Actual worklessness rates for adults of working age were always at least as high in the UK as in Germany (other than in some Eastern Länder) and often higher. It is crucial to pay attention to how things are counted.

That point should be obvious but there is a more subtle and equally important point to be made about the actual status of our measurements. We should always think of them not as 'variables' but as 'variable attributes'. Variables vary – that is they change, they have different values for different cases and/or at different time points. So far, so good but the term 'variable' has acquired a much stronger meaning in modern science than simply being about things changing. The OED identifies 'variable' as both an adjective – variable things can change – and as a noun. In the latter form the word describes not just things that change but forces which can change. The notion of the 'variable force', of a thing which both exists in and of itself and has causal potential in relation to other things, is foundational to Newtonian physics and has had a profound influence on the understanding of causality across science as a whole. It has actually had a particular impact in relation to quantitative social science especially for quantitative modelling as a basis for the exploration of causality. Measurements about cases are abstracted from the cases as if they were physical forces and understood as having causal powers separate from and prior to the cases – the real social entities here – themselves. The cases become just the simple undifferentiated objects of ideal Newtonian physics like the billiard and cannon balls which were the subject of my calculations in applied mechanics nearly 50 years ago.

This is a fundamental error. Cases, the entities in the social word constructed by our 'casing' – the term devised by Ragin (1992) to remind us that defining 'What is a case' is just as important as any operationalisation of a quantity – are real complex systems. Of course we make them by casing but they have a reality from which we make them. Cilliers puts this exactly:

> Boundaries [of complex systems and cases for us] are simultaneously a function of the activity of the system itself, and a product of the strategy of description involved. In other words, we frame the system by describing it in a certain way (for a certain purpose) but we are constrained in where the frame can be drawn. The boundary of the system is therefore neither a function of our description, nor is it a purely natural thing. (2001, p 141)

The implication of this understanding is that we should not think of variables which can vary independently but rather of variate attributes. An attribute is attributed – it is determined by us in the process of measurement in interaction, other than for complete reifications which can happen but are not general – with reality itself and it assigned to a case.[9] Attributes have to be attributes of something. They cannot exist in and of themselves. We must understand our descriptive social measurements over time as measurements of the variate traces of real social systems in relation to their actual system state. That raises an interesting question in relation to the word 'trend'. Trend implies gradual and incremental change. What really interests us are changes of kind, phase shifts in complexity terminology. Of course changes of kind can be the result of accumulation of gradual change to a critical point of transformation or tipping point – what Marx called the transformation of quantity into quality. Trend data with enough time points can enable us to see when this happens, for example in the radical transformation of the UK economy between the late 1970s and the early 1980s from one with both an employment and value-added base in industrial production to one in which industrial employment and production have become residual elements – the transition from an industrial to post-industrial society. Here we can see what has happened best if we look at a whole set of measures over time including the location of employment by sector, the value of product of different economic sectors, the gender composition of the workforce and the spatial location of production and employment. The UK still had an industrially focused economy and was an industrial society in the early 1970s. By the early 1990s this was no longer the case. There had been a phase shift which took some 20 years to complete. Tipping points are not necessarily instantaneous in the social world.

We generally tend to think of survey data as constructed by processes which are immediately recognisable as social surveys. In other words they are the product of specific data collection exercises like the decennial censuses in the UK or the British Household Panel longitudinal panel survey. However, survey data can also be the product of routine administrative processes providing those processes include a recording element which constructs the data in a standard format at specific time points. So for example almost all of our data about those in receipt of various cash benefits in the UK is the by-product of routine administrative data recording with the survey element forming part of that routine. Likewise much of our information about individual incomes (although not now household incomes) is the by-product of tax collection. Administrative data is a very important part of our survey base.

It is useful to consider the range of cases which can be and are the subject of survey. We tend to think of case in terms of individuals or households and often deal with cases constructed from these through computation of statistics for geographical areas – super output areas, wards, local authorities, and so on – by aggregation of micro data for the units from which the data was originally collected. Geographical aggregate data at different geographical levels forms an important part of our data resource and informs both description, for example in the construction of indices of deprivation, and resource allocation. However, we also have case descriptive survey data which describes cases that are not individuals or households but institutions.

Survey data describing private sector institutions is, for perfectly good reasons of confidentiality, usually only available when aggregated, typically on a geographical basis. However, data about institutions in the public sector has a different status and is generally publicly available. There are two reasons for this. One is simply that public institutions are publicly accountable and part of that accountability must take the form of statistical descriptions prepared in a standardised fashion so that comparisons can be made. Originally that was as far as things went but data is now used to generate rankings. Rankings and the data on which they are based serve two purposes. The first is to inform consumers of publicly available goods. In other words the data becomes a basis for choice by us as consumers rather than the basis of informing us as citizens. In practice in England (given different practices in devolved parts of the UK) this is largely a matter of informing parents in relation to the performance of state schools as a basis for supposed parental choice as to which school to send their children to. This certainly serves a consumer purpose and is now even published on websites which are primarily concerned with describing house prices at the level of postcode. The second is to form part of the basis of external management of the performance of public institutions in relation by gradings which can trigger external interventions, for example in relation to failing schools or underperforming hospital trusts or local authorities. Targets are set and indicator data is collected in relation to the achievement of those targets. Much of the data describing institutions is a by-product of routine administration but one of the tasks of any administration is of course surveying that which is administered in order to get useful descriptions of how things are and how they are changing. Such data is enormously useful in applied social science.

Although the visible institutions of the welfare and social state are rather well documented it is important to note that ad hoc quangos are much less well documented and are in fact rather secretive in their operation. For example it has proved necessary to deploy legal processes under freedom of information legislation in order to extract information from 'Pathfinder' projects in England.[10] However, generally data is available and while its normal form of publication is on an institution-by-institution basis it is usually quite easy to obtain spreadsheets which describe the whole institutional set.

One important set of quantitative descriptions which can be ordered through time are the sets of indices represented in England by the Index of Multiple Deprivation and globally by the United Nations Development Programme's Human Development Index. The latter was developed in an explicit effort to provide a measurement which moved beyond the traditional economic activity-centred measures which prioritised market-oriented growth such as GDP per capita. Instead the focus was to be on 'people-centred measures' framed in accordance with Sen's conception of capabilities and functionings. It has a set of components including life expectancy, educational measures and a function of GDP per capital expressed in purchasing power terms (see UNDP, 2009). The English Index of Multiple Deprivation (there are separate indices in the areas of the UK's devolved governments) is described in Department for Communities and Local Government (2007). These kinds of composite indices are examples of social indicators. *Social Trends* was established precisely as a way of delivering a set of social indicators describing social change in the UK. Social indicators have been defined thus: 'the operational definition or part of the operational definition of any one of the concepts central to the generation of an information system descriptive of the social system' (Carlisle, 1972, p 25).

The early greatest ambitions of the social indicators movement of the 1960s and 1970s, which were in effect to develop a set of social indicators which could underpin predictive models in the way economic indicators were considered to underpin macro-economic models used in governance, have not been realised. We will return to that issue in Chapter Seven when examining social modelling in some detail. However, descriptive social indicators, operating sometimes as targets despite the problems which arise when they are so deployed,[11] are a crucial element in the survey products of contemporary social science. They form a background account which is part and parcel of our understanding of what is and how that is changing.

## Constructing survey data

Any measurement of anything is made according to operationalisation rules. Normally we think of operationalisation in relation to surveys as a process undertaken solely by researchers, whether academic, governmental or commercial. We can think of stages of question selection – which in relation to questions on standard topics often draws on the resources of the Survey Question Bank which is part of the UK ESRC's data archive[12] – since this enables comparison across studies, and processes of testing and validation have already been undertaken. Otherwise, given the time and resources, survey researchers have traditionally piloted questions using techniques of varying degrees of sophistication. Sometimes pilots have simply involved the use of open-ended questions and the collection of all answers in textual form as a basis for reduction and constructing a coding frame. More sophisticated approaches have included the use of repertory grid techniques to establish the range of personal constructs. These are standard and appropriate methods for developing survey instruments.

A 2010 study undertaken by Blackman, Wistow and Byrne at Durham University developed an explicitly dialogical approach to the construction of a data collection instrument. This study deployed a QCA method in an effort to identify successful combinations of management practices and field interventions in relation to narrowing the health inequalities gap for a set of Spearhead local authorities, the 70 English local authorities that were in the bottom fifth on three or more of a set of five deprivation and health outcome indicators.

> The principal method for collecting primary data about conditions in the Spearhead areas was the completion of questionnaires by local practitioners (available at the web site noted above). These were initially based on questionnaires that had been designed for the earlier exercise commissioned by Government Office for the North West (Blackman and Dunstan, 2010). They were updated based on a literature search and a number of questions were added, including about commissioning services, the public health workforce and whether health inequalities were prioritised within the local authority area or between the area as a whole and the national average. Practitioners were then consulted at a series of regional workshops about the structure, content and phrasing of the questionnaires, with feedback from these workshops informing further redrafting. Following this, the Department of Health's National Support Teams for health inequalities and teenage pregnancy provided detailed comments, and then final versions of the questionnaires were completed. (Blackman et al, 2010, p 10)

Here the very respondents to the survey played a crucial part in its design, and as we shall see, subsequently in the interpretation of its results. Neither of these engagements is of course wholly innovative but in this study they were explicitly central to the whole research process. This kind of engagement seems essential in applied social research dealing with complex social interventions. In this case the respondent partners were senior managers and practitioners but the principle can be applied generally to members of any target group for survey research, for example to members of a local community or patient group.

Another innovative approach to the construction of survey data is that which underpins the work of the Children's Services Mapping Unit, again at Durham University. This is described in Barnes et al (2006). Here there is a voluntary live and ongoing data collection exercise in which designated 'Mapping Leads' in each of the participating organisations – NHS trusts including Primary Care Trusts (PCTs) and local authorities – make returns to a web-based data collection tool. Multiple respondents were engaged in gathering the material.

In constructing the returns made an average of 16 individuals were involved in the process in relation to each return. The data is complex and those making returns are supported through ongoing dialogue with a help desk which advises on the detail of returns and is therefore a participant in the data construction process. This is a highly developed and refined example of surveying in relation to complex and multi-agency service delivery. This kind of process might, following Savage and Burrows' (2007) specification of a 'knowing capitalism', be described as part of the process of the 'knowing state'.

The notion of a 'knowing capitalism' is an important one. Savage and Burrows recently discussed the 'coming crisis of empirical sociology' noting that:

> Fifty years ago, academic social scientists might be seen as occupying the apex of the – generally limited – social science research 'apparatus'. Now they occupy an increasingly marginal position in the huge research infrastructure that forms an integral feature of what Thrift (2005) characterizes as *knowing capitalism*; where circuits of information proliferate and are embedded in numerous kinds of information technologies. In an era where capitalism has begun to 'consider its own practices on a continuous basis … to use its fear of uncertainty as a resource … to circulate new ideas of the world as if they were its own … to … make business out of, thinking the everyday' (Thrift, 2005: 1) what is the role of the empirical sociologist? (Savage and Burrows, 2007, p 886, original emphasis)

The source of this soul searching is a recognition that whereas quantitative data about the social world was traditionally generated to a considerable degree by explicit sample survey investigations of that world by social scientists, now the enormous amount of electronic data generated by commercial transactions, linked to the data produced by the state both in censuses and through its administrative practices, is a major resource for social exploration. What do commercial organisations do with this data? Most often they sort things into kinds. Cluster analysis and other forms of numerical taxonomy, including data mining tools based on neural net approaches, are used to generate typologies which then identify market segments of consumers which can be targeted in specific ways. The growth in Geographical Information Systems (GIS) owes a lot to the way in which marketing has seized on locale of residence as a key base for typing. Actually what is happening here is that neighbourhood is being used as an organising level of description because it is possible to 'mash' (Burrows' term) census level aggregate data and private sector generated data at this spatial level and in commercial use tie it to postal marketing campaigns. Likewise increasingly we will find mashing of institutional data in a way which to some degree is being pioneered by the Durham mapping team, although this still requires specific data collection as opposed to riding to a degree on the back of routine electronically recorded transactions. However, things are bound to move on.

So measurements matter. But are measurements the only way in which we can have both descriptions of what is and accounts of how it came to be? Can qualitative research provide us with some equivalent? The answer is yes.

## Depiction and narrative – qualitative approaches to saying what is and how it has come to be

How, we must ask, is it possible to survey in a qualitative fashion, that is to say in such a way that the end products of the exercise are not data, numbers generated by operationalisation through a coding scheme, but rather what Bateson (1984) called information, knowledge about reality held by people in the natural language of everyday life? Sure, we can engage in detailed qualitative studies using the methods of observation and interviewing alongside documentary research and hybrid approaches such as focus groups.[13] But surely the products of detailed qualitative studies always encounter the problem that they describe particular contexts in rich terms, of course, but with issues when we try to consider how we might generalise beyond that specific context. We also have to confront the problem posed by the necessarily selective presentation and subjective interpretation of description in any qualitative study, although we can equally see that all surveys generating numbers select in relation to topics addressed and operationalisation of measurement in relation to those topics and agree that anything generated from quantitative data is itself the product of interpretation. We will return to issues of understanding causality in relation to qualitative work in subsequent chapters. The key issue for now is range of coverage. It is a convention to say that qualitative work, and particularly ethnography, is deep but narrow whereas quantitative work is shallow but broad. Can we have broad qualitative work?

Well, we have had it, in the form of 'Mass Observation' – note the conjunction of the words 'mass' and 'observation' in the title of this enormously important exercise. The founders of the project put it like this:

> The real observers in this case [the two coincidental events of the abdication of Edward VIII and the Crystal Palace fire when a symbol of Victorian Britain was destroyed] were the millions of people who were, for once, irretrievably involved in the public events. Only mass observation can create mass science. (Madge's letter to the *New Statesman*, 2 January 1937)

The emphasis was on the everyday and there was a twofold challenge to the traditions of ethnography as embodied in anthropology. The first was that the Mass Observation project was primarily concerned to collect rather than interpret. In effect the Mass Observers were to be their own interpreters subject to no academic authority. The second was scale – the intention was to recruit if possible 5,000 observers. The project was also explicitly emancipatory: 'It does not set out in quest of truth or facts for their own sake, or for the sake of an intellectual minority, but aims at exposing them in simple terms to all observers, so that their environment may be understood, and thus constantly transformed' (Harrisson, Jennings and Madge's letter to the *New Statesman*, 30 January 1937).

A full account of Mass Observation is given in Hubble (2006), who notes that it in some ways prefigures the development of focus group approaches in the 1990s (2006, p 3) but there was much more to this complex, indeed in some ways weird, project than that as he demonstrates very well. The key issue for us is the nature of the documentation which emerged from the actual observation. Some of this took the form of sets of simultaneous snapshots of particular issues (beards, armpits and eyebrows; the Aspidistra cult; and the private lives of midwives were among the set suggested in the second *New Statesman* letter). Better known through subsequent publications are the diaries which observers kept recording not only their own experiences but also deeply personal feelings and responses to those experiences. The diaries are of course narratives – stories ordered through time – and the role of Mass Observation before and during the Second World War means that they recorded enormous social changes. Mass Observation contributed to policy development – particularly in bringing the working class into a graduated taxation system and supporting Keynes' moves in this direction with evidence of an essentially qualitative but large-scale form. Plummer, in his discussion of the use of life histories, identifies what we get from this kind of narrative:

> concerned with depicting and discussing a particular and peculiar style of investigating and understanding human experiences, a style which simply advocates getting close to concrete individual men and women, accurately picking up the way they express their understandings of the world around them, and, perhaps, providing an analysis of such expressions. (Plummer, 1983, p 1)

There has been a rather low-key effort to revive Mass Observation with currently about 500 observers addressing topics which in Spring 2008 were: 'You and the NHS' and 'Your life line'.[14] The actual approaches and method of Mass Observation would seem to have considerable potential in relation to all sorts of social issues. Certainly the keeping of diaries is done as a research procedure. For example. we can imagine it being deployed to record the experiences of being a looked after child in the care of the state. Two interesting examples which deploy the diary method in a fashion similar to Mass Observation are Milligan et al (2005) and Hawkes et al (2009) exploring respectively health and well-being among older people, and risk and worry in everyday life. Actually diaries would seem to form a really useful part of any documentation of the experience of complex social interventions of any kind and the diaries would include diaries both of practitioners and those who were the target of the practice.

The contemporary equivalent of Mass Observation is probably the focus group. Focus groups have none of the radical potential – radical in both methodological and political terms – of Mass Observation, but they do represent a qualitative method of generating descriptions of aspects of the social world. Although observation and reporting of group discussions has formed part of the ethnographic method since that was developed, it is usually considered that the deliberate creation of groups for discussion was an invention of Robert Merton's in his role at the Bureau of Applied Social Research. There is an extensive literature on the practical use of focus groups (see Krueger and Casey, 2008) and the reader is referred to it for guidance on practical application. Often focus groups are used in marketing and political opinion research to give information – exactly 'information' in Bateson's (1984) meaning of that word, knowledge expressed in the natural language of everyday life – about attitudes in relation to products and issues of the day. Indeed the political usage (and somewhat different administrative usage in relation to exercises like citizens' juries to which we shall return in Chapter Six) is essentially derived from the marketing process. This means that it is generally momentary, by which is meant that the research outputs describe how things are at a point in time in relation to opinion and attitudes. The purpose of the exercise is to modify some set of practices, the nature of products and the advertising of those products in marketing, the nature of policies and the presentation of policies in politics. This is very much part of the fabric of learning feedback by both the commercial and the political sectors in post-democratic capitalism.

However, it is possible to do more with focus groups and in particular it is possible to extend beyond the momentary. Byrne and Doyle (2005) used a focus group approach, primarily with groups which already existed as real social entities, to explore the way in which people in South Shields, a large formerly industrial coal mining and port town in the North East of England, responded to the very sudden and visually dramatic cessation of coal mining after some 200 years, which was accompanied by the destruction of almost all the physical structures and transport network associated with that activity in a town both literally and metaphorically 'built on coal'. This study combined the focus group approach with discussion stimulated in an unstructured way by visual elicitation. Participants were shown images of their town, of mining in it and under it, and of the building, operation and demolition of mining structures. What emerged were complex and interwoven stories – narratives which combined reflection on the past, the present and the future. They were stories of becoming – of people's understanding of their social world and their place in it. The underlying social issue being addressed both by the researchers, who themselves were products of the social world being investigated, and by the participants was the profound impact, and in particular the socio-cultural impact, of deindustrialisation. This has particular relevance in relation to the meaning of social exclusion in terms of cultural exclusion.

The use above of the word 'narrative' is important. A narrative is a story told in sequence where events follow each other. Structuralist use of the term 'narratology' extends this simple idea of sequencing to the provision of explanatory accounts, 'grand narratives'. Post-structuralism as one of the key elements of post-modernism dismisses the very possibility of such grand narratives in a turn to absolute relativism – Pawson and Tilley's hermeneutics II (1997) in which all accounts stand as valid since they are the construct of the maker of the account and have no necessary correspondence with reality. Here we are not concerned with this intellectual dead end, precisely because this book is written in a spirit of agreement with Pawson and Tilley's identification of the utility of hermeneutics I – realist interpretation as against the uselessness of extreme relativism. Rather we are simply interested in the validity of stories, of accounts, of the past, present and future of complex systems – of how they have been, of what they are, and of what they might become. Uprichard and Byrne (2006) discuss the way in which narratives can give us an understanding of the trajectories of complex systems though time, with a particular emphasis on how human intentionality can shape trajectories into the future. Mass Observation diaries have served primarily in publications as narratives of experience and in particular of experience of change. We want here to consider the role of narrative in understanding a particular kind of entity – the institution – in relation to the crucial significance of institutional memory for applied social science.

Blackman et al (2010) in the study of what has generated relative success in relation to closing health inequalities went backwards in time in order to identify management practices and practice styles in Spearhead locales at the time point three years before that of the actual measurements of health outcomes. The rationale for this was that it takes time for interventions to develop some effect. Byrne et al did the same thing with their much earlier correlational study of the relationship between educational expenditure and educational outcomes (1975) and found for example stronger relationships between the educational achievement of cohorts of children in local education authorities and the expenditure on primary education over the years when those cohorts had been in primary education than existed between the cross-sectional and simultaneous measurement of resources commitment and educational outcomes. Of course this appears obvious but the point is worth making.

It was relatively easy for Byrne et al (1975) to find accountancy data on expenditure for a period covering between 11 and six years before the date at which they measured educational outcomes. Such data was recorded in quantitative time series, then by the professional body of local authority accountants – the then Institute of Municipal Treasurers and Accountants, now the Chartered Institute of Public Finance and Accountancy. Blackman et al (2010) found it much harder to obtain qualitative descriptions of management and practice forms even just three years before the period at which they measured health inequality outcomes. In effect constant managerial and personnel change had destroyed much of the tacit day-to-day institutional memory of those practices and there had been no formal method of recording them in a systematic fashion. It might, through documentary and oral history, be able to reconstruct this kind of description on a case-by-case basis but we do not have any qualitative equivalent of the quantitative accounting and related administrative practices which make it so much easier to construct time-ordered quantitative surveys. There would be very considerable value in the construction of such systematic records.

Inspection records can, because they generally follow more or less similar templates, generate material which can be used to reconstruct qualitative descriptions as the basis for cross-case comparisons. For example, the reports on English schools by Ofsted – the agency responsible for ongoing school inspections – do provide systematic, more or less standardised, and since repeated at regular intervals, time-ordered accounts of schools as institutions which at least can be used to generate a kind of institutional memory through time.

The point of this chapter has been to demonstrate the value for any kind of applied social research of systematic description of what is and how it has come to be as it is. What is covers a very wide range of topics and issues, not just attributes which are more or less 'factual' in Bateson's terms (1984) but also opinions and attitudes. It also includes descriptions of entities other than individuals, firms or households – the usual objects of quantitative social surveying. We have to understand the nature of the survey in very broad terms with qualitative as well as quantitative components. We have to think in terms not only of the cross-sectional snapshot but also of how things have been in the past. We can also reach through people's own declarations forward to the future. This kind of information is fundamental to any social action for transformation. To reiterate Patrick Geddes' formulation – first we must survey.

## Notes

[1] The domain of the profession of 'chartered surveyor' – key players in the management of the interaction of humans and their environment.

[2] Of course human action can change hydrographical features and does so regularly, particularly in relation to the development of ports – Gerrits' account of policy in relation to complex systems (2008) is precisely concerned with the management of estuarine ports.

[3] For example, most contemporary or recent grand social theorists seem to operate in a state of woeful ignorance in relation to the present state and historical trajectory of any real contemporary society. Bourdieu was something of an exception although very much limited to the rather special case of France.

[4] For a full account, albeit one couched in terms of actor network theory, of the development of state-originating systems of enumeration see Desrosières (1998).

[5] This was changed in 2006, not without some informed opposition, to replace the emphasis on facts about society with an assertion that the key objective of the RSS was to develop and sustain statistical methods and their application. This is not a trivial issue.

[6] See www.rss.org.uk/PDF/1887Charter.pdf

[7] See www.statistics.gov.uk/socialtrends/

[8] Bateson made the important point that fact:value is not an absolute dichotomy – a strict either/or. Rather absolute fact and absolute value are the polar ends of a continuum and any real measurement of any real entity may be positioned at any point on this continuum.

[9] These points are developed further in Byrne (2009).

[10] Pathfinders are projects organised on a quango basis with the task of intervening in 'failing housing markets'. Their operations have been highly controversial, involving in brutal summary the confiscation of working-class assets to benefit private developers, and in any event have now been overwhelmed by the global financial crisis.

[11] It is often said that once an indicator which is a descriptive measure becomes a target against which the performance of agencies is assessed, then it becomes useless as an indicator since agency managers will manipulate activities to change that indicator in a positive direction. The way in which many English secondary school management teams focus on moving children who would attain a D in a GCSE subject towards the achievement of a C grade in order to up the percentage of children obtaining five grades A–C in that exam, a crucial indicator of school performance, illustrates this very well.

[12] See http://surveynet.ac.uk/sqb/about/introduction.asp

[13] The popularity of which derives, we might assert, in no small part from the fact that particularly unstructured focus groups are in essence artificially created ethnographic opportunities for the observation of conversations.

[14] For details see www.sussex.ac.uk/library/speccoll/collection_catalogues/
massnewprojectdate.html

# FOUR

# Evaluating: determining the worth of social interventions

Evaluating is the gerund of the noun 'evaluation'. The *Oxford English Dictionary* gives three meanings for that word. The second with first usage dated to the late 18th century is to do with estimating or establishing the magnitude of any general quantity, but particularly scientific and engineering quantities. The third with a first usage in the 1960s is precisely about the subject matter of this chapter: the study of methods of evaluating the impact of social interventions. The first, and now largely obsolete, meaning makes 'evaluation' an exact synonym of 'valuation' and has to do with saying what something is worth. Actually that original meaning seems very useful in grounding the discussion in this chapter. Evaluation can be understood as the process of looking at what has resulted from some action and saying whether or not that action (or set of actions in normal interventions) was worth doing – if it had any positive value. In an ideal world we would want to attach a quantity to that value, and as we shall see, efforts are made in that direction, but in general we want to know if things have simply got better than they were before. Of course we also have to do some basic economic thinking here. We have to consider the amount of resources devoted to a purpose, consider how those resources might otherwise have been utilised – the opportunity cost – and again, ideally, have some mechanism of establishing a rate of return on resources deployed – the ability to conduct some sort of quantitative cost-benefit analysis. Can we do any or all of these things? How might/should we do these things? Why are social scientists engaged in doing them at all? These are the questions we will attempt to answer here. Inevitably there is a considerable overlap between the themes of this chapter and those of Chapter Two which dealt with constructing evidence. Here we want to focus in on the specific sort of evidence which tells us whether or not something has worked, and of course the whole purpose of evaluation as a process for telling us what works is so that we can establish transferable knowledge – in other words we can do again somewhere and somewhen else what has worked here and now.

The easiest question to answer from those posed above is: Why do social scientists evaluate? Carl May in the passage quoted in the introduction, which was one of the stimuli for the writing of this book, has provided the socio-political answer. We operate as the outsourced workers of the evidence-based state in a world where politics are post-democratic and, perhaps for not much longer, post-ideological. The institutional consequences are acerbically and accurately portrayed by Ray Pawson:

> On a bad day, the ivory tower can look awfully like a shopping mall. In the UK, much, if not most, policy inquiry is conducted by units and centres that perch on the edge of mainstream university departments, and whose existence depends on the winning of the *next* contract. (2006, p 3, original emphasis)

As Pawson goes on to say, policy evaluation is not merely conducted by the marginalised contract researcher workforce of the academy but also by directly employed social researchers at all levels of government and quasi government, by charities and charitable foundations, by 'think tanks' and by the private sector ranging from the self-employed individual through to global accountancy and management consultancy firms. To use the term previously applied, all those who do this are 'technical intellectuals' working in distinctive social order. We do it because it pays. Of course many, and in the present author's view most, of us also do it because we have that old-fashioned modernist belief in progress and doing some good – seeing where we have been and being happy to look back on that work as decent work well done. Whether it is of course is precisely the question defining what Taylor and Balloch called *The politics of evaluation* (2005).

Pawson makes another important point about the actual reality of evaluation which should frame our discussion here. He identifies each evaluation as a unique social process based on a specific and unusual division of labour involving different assemblages of actors (and even, in actor network terms, actants).

> The key point is that these complex arrangements are assembled from scratch in each and every evaluation, with the result that there is a degree of improvisation about the team assembled, the approach chosen, the evidence gathered and the advice proffered. There are all sorts of interesting alliances between the parties, but none of them is really responsible for the cumulation of evidence findings; there is no job on the list whose function is to feed the evidence

steadily back into policy-making and then on to the design
of further inquiries. (Pawson, 2006, pp 10–11)

Pawson identifies this issue as a reason for the turn towards systematic
review and meta-analysis and we might add rapid review to the list. This
turn is important and we will return to the implications of it when we
explore the health inequalities example, but for now what matters is
the description of the social process of evaluation as a social practice.

The issues which surround evaluation will be pursued here through
an elaboration of examples. Three will be presented. The first will deal
with a UK attempt at an evaluation through experimental approaches
in a context and in relation to a style of intervention which might be
considered to at least have dealt with the practical if not methodological
problems which arise in social experiments. That is the Employment
Retention and Advancement Demonstration concerned with improving
job retention and advancement for low paid workers (see Greenberg
and Poole, 2007). The second is a linked pair concerned with 'urban
regeneration'. These are England's 'New Deal for Communities', the
latest in the palimpsest of urban initiatives developed to deal with the
consequence of post-industrial transformation in English formerly
industrial localities and neighbourhoods (see Lawless, 2006; Wright
et al, 2007), and the European Union's Urban Community Initiative
Programme (see Murtagh and MacKay, 2003). Here we are dealing with
complex multi-faceted and long-lasting social interventions. Finally
we will examine not a specific project but rather the issue which has
driven projects across the English-speaking world other than the US:
health inequalities and what might be done about them. Here we will
draw on a range of examples from the UK and New Zealand.

As always in this book the frame of reference of our discussion will
be complex realism. This position has been employed explicitly in
relation to evaluation by Sanderson (2000), Barnes et al (2003) and
Callaghan (2008). We will draw on all of them, and in particular on
Callaghan's very useful deployment of the idea of negotiated order in
relation to processes of evaluation and implementation in complex
social programmes. We will also draw on discussions of realist evaluation
which began with Pawson and Tilley (1997) and on 'theories of
change' (see Mason and Barnes, 2007), as well as the useful counter
posing of these two positions by Blamey and Mackenzie (2007). In
our view both of these approaches can be assimilated into a complex
realist programme. We will also draw on the traditions in development
practice and health interventions which are informed by the thinking
of Paolo Freire and which are associated with radical innovations in

participatory evaluation. Some themes which emerge from the synthesis of these positions need to be specified before we proceed.

## Setting the frame of reference

First let us draw on 'realism' as a social theory, that is as a general account of the nature of social reality and social processes including social change, in order to specify the context of all social interventions. To begin, let us assert the epistemic position. For realism all accounts will be theory driven. The theory is open to modification and even refutation in the course of the empirical investigation but we start from some notion of how things work and go out to see if this is the case, or even to what extent this is the case. Theories in this sense are not merely, and that word 'merely' matters a lot, testable hypotheses. They are much more like models since they involve complex and multiple interactions operating in context and at a range of levels. Theory-based evaluation is a common phrase but the ontological specification of realism means that we always are addressing how the world works, how generative mechanisms are expressed in context. *And* that context is always social. Pawson puts it like this: 'a critical feature of all programmes is that, as they are delivered, they are embedded in social systems. It is through the workings of entire systems of social relationships that any changes in behaviours, events and social conditions are effected' (2006, p 30).

Another way to express this is to say that social structure matters. Now 'structure' is a messy term – as Westergaard noted: '"structure" is only a metaphor, but useful to denote persistence and causal force' (2003, p 2).[1] Callaghan develops this idea very fruitfully in relation to the idea of 'negotiated order':

> The notion of negotiated order is premised in understanding of how systems are not only structural entities, but are also fundamentally shaped in the context of the forces and conditions pertaining at the 'bottom' of the hierarchy, being created and recreated by the actors located there. Straus et al (1933) developed the concept from fieldwork in organizations in response to the clash between the perspectives of Parsons (primacy of order) and Dewey (primacy of change). Strauss argued that within organizations order is negotiated and that this is an ongoing production of the actors involved. Organizational relations, therefore, although having a structural quality, are the product of this continued process of making and remaking. The existence

of structure is important in setting the positions from which individuals negotiate and, in turn, which gives these negotiations their patterned quality, but these products are historical and temporally shaped, always open to review and revision. The order that is produced is best described as negotiated because it relies on the daily decisions of actors within this context. ... In negotiated order we can understand the structures as created but also as creating the context for action. (2008, p 45)

We can extend this, as Callaghan herself does, beyond the level of the organisation to that of the social order as a whole. Anything we do we do in society. The interventions examined here happened within a particular post-industrial, post-democratic, consumer culture-oriented version of market capitalism. They happened in particular places with particular traditions and forms of social and political life. For instance the New Zealand examples in relation to action on health inequalities were influenced, very much for the better it seems, by contemporary social interpretations of the 'Treaty of Waitangi' which stands for a commitment to the incorporation of Maori world views and processes into the nature of social governance and social intervention. At the same time the interventions in the UK happened in the context of what Polanyi might have called a second 'great transformation' in which the industrial social base is disappearing – we might even say has been disappeared – along with the socio-political context of a Keynesian mode of regulation and the Beveridge-style universalist welfare state. The urban programmes were set in a context where urban regeneration was an important part of the whole process of social reconfiguration. The experiment in relation to worklessness reflected both the social creation of mass unemployment/worklessness and a major reordering of the basis of social security entitlements in the context of that transformation. Health inequalities are a product of the general inequalities of market capitalism and have been exacerbated by the increase in overall inequality in all its forms, consequent on post-industrial social transformations and the policy shifts which have both driven and reflected those changes. Key propositions in relation to complex systems are that they are 'nested' – systems are contained within systems, that they are intersecting with aspects of systems interwoven with other systems, and that the chain of causation is non-hierarchical with causality running in all possible directions. We certainly have social determination as an aspect of causality in relation to any system but with determination understood neither as absolute specification nor as permanent and always enduring. Instead we have to think of determination as Williams (1982) proposed in terms of the setting of limits of possibility and understand that even that bounding is time specific and open to radical change.

Certainly we have to understand any social process, the objects of our evaluations, in terms of the specific socio-historical *and* local contexts in which they operate but there is both variation of outcome possible within those contexts *and* the possibility of radical transformation of them. Moreover, the emphasis on negotiated order resonates absolutely with Pawson's account of the implications of the division of labour in any actual evaluation process. We can understand both process and the environment of process if we think in these terms. Callaghan's take on negotiated order helps us to relate structure and agency in real contexts. Let us turn to our examples.

## Evaluation through experiment and quasi-experiment – a focus on getting people into work and keeping them there

The Employment Retention and Advancement (ERA) Demonstration represents as close an approximation to a true randomised controlled trial as it seems possible to achieve in social interventions. Full descriptions are given in Greenberg and Poole (2007) and Walker et al (2006)[2] but in essence the programme involved the random allocation of clients of Advancement Support Advisors (ASAs) working from Jobcentre Plus Offices – that is to say as part of the UK Employment Service – to treatment and control groups. The targets were located in three groups: those eligible (usually required) to join the New Deal for the Long Term Unemployed targeted at people over the age of 24; those entering by choice the New Deal for Lone Parents; and single parents who were both working part time and claiming the Working Tax Credit.[3] The intervention took the form of cooperation between the ASA and the client in the development of an Advancement Action Plan. The control group of clients worked with their advisors to develop a plan for obtaining employment, but not for retention and advancement. In effect the scheme offered advice and support for those in the programme over 33 months and also offered financial incentives for those working at least 30 hours a week which could total £2,400 through the programme. There was also a financial incentive for participants to engage in training of up to £1,000 plus the payment of training course fees. None of these financial incentives were available to the control group.

This programme is based on the importation into the UK of the kind of large-scale social experiment which is common in the US. The role of the US Rockefeller Foundation in bringing together MDRC, a US not-for-profit research firm, and the UK Treasury was crucial in the development of the exercise. It seems that this was a case of a method in search of an issue – experiments are wonderful so let's find an issue which we can subject to experimental investigation. The evaluation components in relation to this experiment include an impact study, a process study, a cost study, and a cost benefit study (see Morris et al, 2004). The process study is concerned with how the actual research works out in practice. The impact study is the core effect study. It will be based on the formulation of a range of hypotheses which address the following issues:

> To what extent do services and financial incentives delivered through the ERA Demonstration improve the work retention and employment advancement, as well as other outcomes, of those assigned to receive them? To what extent do services and financial incentives delivered through the ERA Demonstration improve work retention and employment advancement among different subgroups of those assigned to receive them? To what extent does the impact of services and financial incentives for those assigned to receive them differ from site to site? These broad research questions lead to the formulation of specific hypotheses that can be tested. These specific hypotheses reflect different outcomes that are indicative of improvements in retention and advancement. (Morris et al, 2003, pp 34– 5)

The cost study will be an accountancy exercise determining precisely what resources have been devoted to the exercise. The cost-benefit study will, as always with cost-benefit, attempt to establish bang for buck, to determine just what has been achieved in relation to resources expended.

This study is the demonstration project of those civil service social researchers quoted in Chapter Two who assert that it is the RCT which provides the knowledge most useful to policy makers. Walker et al (2006) summarise the first phase of the process study in some detail with a particular focus on contamination of sample design in relation to recruitment to the study and allocation to treatment or control groups. It seems that the integrity of design and random allocation were maintained but only to a degree rather than absolutely. However, the real practical difficulties in a social RCT usually arise subsequent to this stage and we do not yet seem to have process accounts of how delivery and retention have gone. The issues in delivery are to do with standardisation of treatment. The issues in relation to retention are about having enough subjects retained through the life of the experiment in order to be able to make statistically significant decisions in relation to specified hypotheses at the end of the exercise. In this study the acceptable minimum level of retention – of achieved sample – was specified as 65% although there was a real intention to improve on this. This is a fundamental issue for long-term social intervention RCTs even if we accept the overall logic of the procedure. It is perhaps cruel to say that satisfactory achieved outcome sample sizes are plucked from the air, although they are, but we are always faced with a major problem, whatever matching processes are undertaken in comparing lost with retained cases and weighting to compensate. We cannot know what is different about the cases for which we have no data but we know that they are different because they have left the study. This simple issue alone renders any findings suspect unless very high retention rates are achieved.

If the technical issues were all that mattered then it is fair to say that this study has been very carefully thought through and designed in order to manage them. However, that is not the fundamental problem. The study was set up prior to the massive economic crisis which developed in 2007 and is still ongoing. To use a crude expression from the author's youth, any effort at addressing marginal employment in the face of this crisis is pissing to windward. In other words the fundamental theory underlying the intervention was that there was employment available for those who both desired it and were adequately prepared for it, coupled with a belief that those in low paid poor employment could improve their prospects by a mix of motivation and training. The faults were all in the unemployed and poorly employed. The problem was purely on the supply side. There was no sense of structural problems, particularly acute in some post-industrial regions and localities, which rendered the possibility of positive outcomes less likely. An additional problem, which may or may not be addressed in the cost-benefit analysis, is the potential displacement effect. The injection of resources into the intervention subjects may well result in better outcomes for them at the expense of worse outcomes for others who lost the employment and betterment opportunities which went to the subjects of the intervention. This is not a medical intervention where better health for subjects does not mean worse health for others.[4] The individualised focus of the intervention seems to wholly ignore the overall social context of employment markets.

One aspect of the New Deal for Communities evaluation which has adopted a quasi-experimental approach relates to worklessness and is based on the difference of differences method. This study (Gutierez Romero and Noble, 2008) seems to meet the objective proposed by Parry and Judge in these terms:

> even strong advocates of theory based evaluation recognize that, on their own, such approaches have limited capacity to predict all that could happen absent the intervention ... Consequently some researchers are seeking to integrate theory based program evaluation into more traditional quasi-experimental designs with the use of control groups. (Parry and Judge, 2005, p 627)

Actually Gutierez Romero and Noble did this in reverse by integrating a quasi-experimental design into a theory-based evaluation – although of course all interventions are theory based even if the theory amounts to no more than the belief that this thing might work. In any event they set out to use administrative data to explore the net impact of New Deal for Community (NDC) Programmes as a whole on transitions out of worklessness over a time period by comparing these transitions in NDC areas with transitions in matched non-NDC areas. This was very much a counterfactual – what happens absent the intervention process, which here was a complex mix of area-based activities more or less specific to NDC areas. There was also an effort to control for outcomes in relation to the individual characteristics of those covered by the enormous administrative data base. The logistic regression technique employed demonstrated an overall 1.01 odds ratio impact effect of being in an NDC area. The impact was statistically significant for men but not for women. A major limitation of the exercise in terms of its own logic was that all the data was able to show was that the person had moved off benefits to an unknown other state. To be facetious they might have been abducted by aliens.[5] However, a more important limitation arises from a failure to consider exactly this issue – what a move from benefit dependency actually means. In particular the authors did not address the issue described as *chômage d'exclusion* – the repeated passage from poor work to benefit and back to poor work characteristic of the dispossessed working class of marginalised post-industrial spaces. An enormous amount of electrons seem to have laboured to bring forth not very much that tells us anything of any great importance about the impact of NDCs in relation to worklessness in their areas. After all, with all the necessary caveats and real problems of cross-level inference, what we were left with was a one per cent effect. Let us turn now precisely to these very large and complex area-based initiatives typified by NDC and see what we might make of evaluation of them.

## Evaluating the urban – interventions designed to change the relative position of disadvantaged neighbourhoods *and* of those who live in them

Ray Pawson (2006, p 13) gives a first-person account of a conversation which seems to happen very often and almost everywhere in relation to New Deal for Communities – the most recent of the palimpsest of interventions in deprived neighbourhoods in England:

> Practitioner (often in these stories a cop):"What does NDC stand for?"
>
> Researcher: "New Deal for Communities."
>
> Practitioner: "No – it means 'No Discernible Change'."

Why palimpsest? The word means a parchment or papyrus which has been written on more than once with the later writings written over the earlier which to some extent are still legible through them. This is a good metaphor for British urban policy directed at redressing area-based deprivation. Pawson gives an actually incomplete list of area-based initiatives (ABIs) which have been deployed in British cities. I can go back further to the 1970s and run through Educational Priority Areas, Community Development Projects[6] and Comprehensive Community Projects before we get to Pawson's list which begins with Single Regeneration Budgets and runs through City Challenges, European funded interventions, Health Action Zones, Education Action Zones, Sure Start, Connexions and up to NDCs and no discernible change. Let us note something here. The statement – No Discernible Change – is an evaluation. We have done all this and it has made no difference.

Well, in doing all this we have been constantly engaged in evaluation. These projects all the way back to the Educational Priority Areas have been assessed to see how they worked or didn't and what consequences flowed from them. In this section we will examine those evaluations in terms of their logic and their process. We will focus on New Deal for Communities and the EU's Urban Community Initiative Programme. We could go right back in the US as well as Europe to the Ford Foundation Grey Area Programmes described by Marris and Rein (1967), to the interventions of the Johnson Administration's Great Society, or even to the New Deal itself, let alone run through the British palimpsest but the most recent may be the least decent so let us focus on them.

Before doing so let us remember something to which we will return in the conclusion to this section. ABIs directed at redressing deprivation do not function in isolation. Not only are they working alongside all sorts of other anti-deprivation programmes, for example, individual case-focused projects addressing worklessness; they also operate in relation to programmes of 'urban regeneration' which are directed at urban localities as a whole. In other words the system is the urban system and any changes in it will be the product of *all* the social interventions including massive infrastructural development through Urban Development Corporations and their ilk, cultural regeneration – City of Culture, cultural quarters and so on, and the overall processes of urban planning. All of these are informed generally by a sense of relative failure, perhaps not in a world city like London – Hamnett's (2003) *Unequal city* nonetheless – but certainly in the post-industrial conurbations – Tyneside, Manchester, Merseyside – as well as in the particularly derelict ex-coalfields of Durham, Yorkshire and so on. We will never be able to understand the effects of any complex social intervention in the form of an area-based initiative without taking all these things into account. Policy makers seem to take exactly the opposite view. Pawson notes that when he was:

> involved in a scoping study for the evaluation of NDC …
> it is interesting how little the client's expectations turned on the issue of the collective impact of these successive endeavours. If anything, the requirement was the other way around, one obsession being to design the evaluation for the nigh-on [no need for nigh-on] impossible task of separating out the effects of the NDC from those of other past and present initiatives. (2006, p 13)

There is a word for that client's sort of attitude and understanding and the word is stupid.

Before conducting a detailed examination of NDC and evaluation protocols developed in relation to it, it is useful to look at the EU Urban Community Initiative Programme (URBAN) as described by Murtagh and McKay (2003). This was intended to target EU Structural Funds at deprived inner-city areas through strategies implemented by local partnerships. The evaluation frame of reference was provided by MEANS (Means for Evaluating Actions of a Structural Nature). Murtagh and McKay described this as supporting:

> a largely systematic positivist model that links financial inputs to outputs, outcomes and results. This pattern is reflected in the evaluation guidance in the latest round of Structural Funds 2000– 2006 where the quantification of specifically defined indicators underscores the dominant normative paradigm and a concern for measurable efficiency in the way in which EU resources are used locally. (2003, p 194)

Their argument draws usefully on the distinction Marsden and Oakley (1991) made between instrumental – neutral, rational, objective, generally quantitative and concerned with clarifying objectives and reliant on quantification – on the one hand, and interpretative approaches which adopt in essence what amounts to a stand point epistemological stance. The essence of Murtagh and McKay's argument is in support of the interpretative approach and they tie this in to processes of research in relation to planning issues which have a participatory and transformative agenda. They consider that 'institutional audit' as proposed by Healey (1997) offers a means for achieving this. The elements of this approach as outlined by them are:

- identification of stakeholders and of the degree to which appropriate stakeholders are represented in governance arrangements;
- identification of the arenas in which meaningful discussion and resolution occurs, of who has access to these arenas, and of the actual form of debate, that is integrative across the range of participants or compartmentalised on the terms of governance agents;
- identification of the actual routines and forms of debate and discussion – are these predetermined in formal terms or open to different modes and alternative forms of knowledge?
- identification of the nature and character of power relations as expressed in policy discourses;
- identification of the modes through which agreement is reached and monitored and of the scope for disagreement and subsequent challenge.

This provides a rather good framework for the evaluation of complex urban social interventions through process tracing as proposed by George and Bennett (2005) and described in Chapter One.

Murtagh and McKay work through the actual evaluation of URBAN in Derry[7] in Northern Ireland. This combined the MEANS format which dealt with changes in quantifiable target indicators with an institutional audit based on Healey's framework. This is an interesting and well-presented example and certainly the authors demonstrate change across a whole range of quantifiable indicators and relate those changes to 'discourses and processes' in the context. However, it has to be said that there is no evidence here of any change in the qualitative experience of life of Derry's dispossessed working class, whether Protestant or Catholic. Instead there is a listing of what are at best throughput indicators – training places, capacity groups, use of health and culture, arts and leisure, alongside volume of new building which is the characteristic objective of property-focused urban regimes dominated by business objectives.

Carpenter (2006) reviews the evaluation process across the URBAN programme as a whole. She notes that this did not rely on quantified outputs, not least because these were not available in base line or even completion terms for many projects, but also because of the emphasis in the programme on process. This seems at odds with the MEANS format but each participating state defined its own outcomes, usually in processual terms. Carpenter was well aware of potential conflicts when social integration and equalisation are conducted in relation to urban regeneration but her account of outcomes in relation to examples from the projects is basically a description of experience rather than an overall review of power relations and their outcomes.

New Deal for Communities has been the English ABI which corresponds to the employment and benefit system 'New Deals' for individuals. A full description is given by Lawless (2006) and the programme is very firmly located in relation to New Labour's 'Evidence base for policy' agenda. The defining mantra was that of 'holistic' regeneration, of combining social and environmental infra-structural and programmed activity with initiatives defined in terms of changed attributes of the individuals resident in the NDC areas. Place-based outcomes were to do with crime, the community and housing, and the physical environment. People-based outcomes were addressed to health, education and worklessness. NDC is targeted at 39 areas only and this has been understood by those responsible for its evaluation, a consortium involving both academic and consultancy organisations and led by Sheffield Hallam University's Centre for Regional Economic and Social Research. The evaluation is data driven with survey work being done by the National Evaluation Team rather than individual partnerships. This very much accords with Freeman's prescriptions of the 1980s. A crucial instrument is a household survey conducted with a sample size of 500 in each NDC area and combining a panel and top-up cross-sectional element. About 25% of respondents had been interviewed in all three waves of the survey as of 2006. There is a 'control' element with a similar survey being carried out in comparator areas in the same local authorities which are matched in deprivation terms but are not adjacent to NDC areas. In addition a whole set of administrative data, including the benefit/workless data utilised by Romero and Noble, has been collected for the NDC areas, for the comparators, and the for local authorities containing them.

Two other sets of information are being collated in relation to NDC. First, accountancy management systems are being interrogated in order to elicit whatever they can deliver in relation to expenditure, outputs and project development. Second, there is a biennial survey of operations in all partnerships which takes the form of a data collection exercise describing both the operations of the partnerships and their engagement with other relevant agencies and overlapping ABIs. In effect data is collected on resource allocation, what is being done, and which agencies it is being done with. As is general in efforts to establish causal relationships in relation to outcomes, the NDC evaluation has employed regression modelling techniques. This simplistic and inappropriate approach to understanding complex and multiple social causation[8] demonstrates little here as usual. The trivial findings are that NDCs in less deprived local authorities seem to be improving more relative to their comparators but this is almost certainly because those authorities are much less deprived overall and are therefore better able to concentrate resources on NDC areas, and the more agencies operating, the better the outcomes seem to be. Of course a fundamental flaw in the whole exercise is the specification of outcomes in relation to a set of separate indicators. These indicators are quite useful if considered not as real variables with an existence separate from the cases to which they are attached but rather as variates traces (see Byrne, 2002) of the trajectories of real complex systems. They are attributes inseparable from the cases which they describe. Byrne (2005a) proposed that the appropriate way to measure real social change, that is transformative change of kind, would be to use cluster analysis or another method of numerical taxonomy to classify social areas at time one and then again at time two. A meaningful change would be a change of kind across the period of the intervention.

---

Technical issues of appropriate measurement are important but of course a complex realist approach to the evaluation of NDCs requires us to think about the wider socio-political systems in which they are embedded. Lawless et al remark that: 'Some NDCs, such as Newcastle, have worked closely with one ABI, in this case the local Housing Market Renewal Pathfinder, to influence the major redevelopment of a substantial part of the NDC area, a task for which the HMRP is far better funded than the NDC' (2010, p 267). Pathfinder projects are highly contentious. They involve the demolition of large amounts of housing in working-class communities in a bid to revitalise supposedly failing local housing markets. Allen (2008) argues that Pathfinders involve the disintegration of communities and the appropriation of working-class assets, including owner-occupied houses compulsorily purchased at prices which do not allow residents to relocate either to housing of equivalent quality or to purchase new stock built on cleared sites in their original neighbourhoods. They are in effect cleansed from their localities in order to facilitate 'gentrification' although in practice the real beneficiaries in the Northern English cities where Pathfinder operates are not the middle-income households who acquire new dwellings but the developers who make profits from the process along with, in the case of Pathfinder, private sector consultancies paid very large sums in order to undertake reviews and consultation exercises. In Newcastle 'Bridging Newcastle/Gateshead', the local Pathfinder, is a follow-on from the extraordinary local City Council 'Going for Growth' exercise (see Byrne, 2000; Cameron, 2003). In other words NDCs are operating alongside what are at the very least highly contentious policy interventions which may have negative consequences for the 'communities' which NDCs are supposed to serve. Any kind of serious evaluation of the exercises would have to take this into account. There is minimal indication that this is the case with NDC evaluation thus far.

## Reducing health inequalities

In the UK and some other English-speaking countries the issue of inequalities in relation to health outcomes now seems to be almost the dominant inequality issue. It has displaced concern with inequalities in income and wealth and seems to run ahead in policy terms even of the shibboleth of equal opportunity in relation to social mobility and ultimate destination in relation to educational experience. Since the Black Report of 1979 put 'Health Inequalities' back on policy agendas we have seen a range of health initiatives, including ABIs, directed at reducing the large differentials in premature mortality rates which are the usual indicators/targets associated with health inequality.[9] The salience of health inequalities in contrast to other inequalities is interesting. In part it reflects the re-emergent status of public health medicine. Public health doctors are now important clinical managers in relation to local health care systems and premature death is a dramatic event. Moreover, the prevention of premature death has been associated with a range of campaigns directed at behaviours which are health damaging and incur substantial health care curative or palliative costs, so avoidance of those behaviours is financially beneficial to health care systems. It is also the case that international development indices – for example the UNDP's (United Nations Development Programme) human development index – include life expectancy data. In this section we will review an effort at a quasi-experiment and an effort to assess the health impacts of NDC and then consider two sets of New Zealand programmes which worked in a very different way informed explicitly by a complex realist framework.

We can begin with a serious effort at something like a quasi-experimental approach in the form of 'the Well London Project'. This is described by Wall et al (2009) as a cluster randomised controlled trial, although with only 20 cases in the treatment and allocation groups, at least in the form of areas, there are issues with that designation. Outcomes will be assessed, inter alia, from survey data generated from a random sample of 100 adults within each neighbourhood and for 60 adolescents recruited from schools.[10] There is an interesting contradiction to the experimental logic in this exercise, which by the way, in terms of substantive content seems worthwhile and sensible. That is the building in of an element of participation. So we find that:

> The exact mix of activities in each area has been decided upon through priorities identified by residents and complementarity to the facilities and services already provided …. While the *approach* to the needs assessment, and intervention design and delivery, and the types of intervention delivered will be identical in each experimental cluster, the *exact content* of the interventions will be tailored to local needs. Recent literature on evaluation argues that this is valid as 'context level adaptation does not mean that the integrity of what is being evaluated across multiple sites is being lost. Integrity defined functionally, rather than compositionally is the key. (Hawe et al, 2004, p 1563, original emphasis)

Hawe et al draw explicitly on complexity theory in developing their argument but, to put it bluntly, they don't seem to grasp the implications of understanding social contexts in complex terms. We will try to make it as alike as possible but allow it be different all the same is the slogan here. Freeman and Sherwood (1970) would have kittens over this. If local variation and local development is allowed, as indeed it should be, then the whole RCT logic is abandoned, as indeed it should be. The 'Well London' project seems tailor-made for evaluation by systematic comparison based on careful process tracing with the emphasis on processes rather than short-term outcomes, however measured. Here it serves to illustrate a real crisis of confidence in their methods by those who often assert the superiority of scientistic abstraction.

The NDC initiative has been addressed in health terms by Parry and Judge (2005) and Stafford et al (2008). Parry and Judge were proposing a model for evaluation. Stafford et al have reported on an actual evaluation. The former focus on processes, identifying three key processes or pathways of change, namely the actual commissioning of relevant interventions, the process of selecting neighbourhoods for intervention, and the bottom-up participatory nature of interventions. This is a manifestly sensible guide to what should be a process tracing approach to ultimate evaluation of NDC in all its aspects. Stafford et al attempt a much more conventional evaluation which in form has much in common with attempts to evaluate the impact of NDC in relation to employment and employability. The essence of the evaluation was based on repeated survey assessment of the health of panels of residents in intervention and control areas. Multi-level regression modelling was deployed to demonstrate, yet again, not very much at all. The crucial issues in this sort of exercise remain. First, linear methods cannot address complex changes. Second, the changes that matter are changes of kind, not of degree.

Let us turn to two New Zealand based examples which were explicitly informed by a developed understanding of regarding complex social interventions and their social contexts in complexity terms. The first, described in Matheson et al (2009), involves exploring two community-based interventions through detailed case comparisons. The actual projects were one dealing with the health impacts of a home insulation project and one focusing on inter-sectoral community action. Very careful attention was paid to 'casing' (after Ragin, 1992), that is to the process of identifying precisely what were the cases which should form the substance of investigation. The form of account was absolutely resonant with the logic of process tracing and, without using that terminology, very much echoed Callaghan's emphasis on the negotiated order of this kind of social process. The first project also generated results which were based on a cluster randomised study with health assessments incorporated into the assessment process but what is most interesting is the description of processes in relation to the execution of the work. This is the replicable and transferable element. The outputs cannot be understood outwith the narratives of process.

The second New Zealand example reviewed the experiences of a project specifically targeted at examining the interactions among the food outlet environment of primary school children, the school-based efforts at reducing childhood obesity by promoting good nutrition, and children's behaviour (Walton et al, 2009). This involved doing research in order to build a model, in the sense of dynamic description, of the interactions among school food environment, school interventions, household resources, wider social policies, and the agency of children and their caregivers. The purpose of the model was that given its systems base it could be used to identify potential points for effective intervention in order to generate good outcomes. The model was itself the result of interaction between an overview of social contexts and agency informed by an understanding of complex systems, with empirical observation which developed and refined the description of the specific contextual model which could inform action in this sort of place at about this time. This kind of model building seems to be an essential pre-requisite of the kind of causal narratives which are the only possible basis for complex social interventions.

## Conclusion

Evaluation is necessary, no doubt about that. We need to learn from what we have done in order to do what works, do it next time, do it in the next place, and do it better. The problem is that the dominance of really a crude and – at this stage of our understanding of the nature of social processes and social structures – woefully ignorant and ill-informed positivistic approach to science gets in the way of doing these things properly. It is the pity of the world that good projects like 'Well London' get stuck with evaluative protocols which have never demonstrated anything very much because they can't – because they are not capable of looking at what is important within the context of the project itself and within the wider social context in which projects are operating. The last point has not been made all that much of in this chapter, other than with reference to the interaction of Pathfinder projects and NDC. It matters and we will pick it up with some force in Chapter Five.

# Notes

[1] The passage is quoted at length in Chapter One (see pp 26–7).

[2] The summary which follows is a paraphrase of Greenberg and Poole's description.

[3] For an account of the overall social context of New Deal and its successors see Byrne (2010).

[4] Other than in relation to the opportunity cost of alternative health provision: money spent in one way cannot be spent in another but that is not the same as costing others their jobs or promotion prospects.

[5] There is an intention to pursue the destinations of benefit leavers forward through integrating employment and benefit receipt records. If this is done what will be very interesting is a patterning of the actual dynamic relationships across benefit receipt, poor work and other work which could be done with such a data set.

[6] Employed me on a University Senior Lecturer's salary at the age of 27, which I didn't mind at all.

[7] My Bellaghy grandmother would use no other name and neither will I.

[8] Chapter Seven will develop a full account of the uselessness of linear modelling in applying social science.

[9] English health targets include reductions in the rate of teenage conceptions (girls under the age of 18 to be precise) but most indicators are to do with premature mortality from specific conditions, especially coronary heart disease and cancers.

[10] Interventions are area based whereas some effects will be measured on the basis of individuals. This might be considered to raise real issues within the logic of the RCT method.

# FIVE

# Legitimating: the *selective* use of social science in justifying policy and practice

> To affirm or show to be legitimate; to authorize or justify
> by word or example; to serve as justification for. (*Oxford
> English Dictionary* – meaning three)

This chapter is about the way in which governments and other large institutional actors in post-democracies use social science for the purpose of justification. If politics is no longer about ideological distinction or even competing material interests – because, as Crouch (2000) tells us, the most major political parties endorse the business interests of dominant forces in market capitalism, so there is no competition – then claims for electoral victory have to be based on something else. One such basis is 'character' – a risible and much reduced version of what Max Weber understood when he wrote about charismatic authority. It is now not so much a matter of charisma as of celebrity coupled with 'moral' status. However, character matters most where individuals are elected to sovereign power as presidents, however circumscribed or limited that power is. In parliamentary democracies, and especially in the UK which again is a prototype here, a major claim must always be demonstration of effective technical competence in relation to the business of governing. We might treat this as a special and developed case of Weber's notion that legitimate authority can derive from a rational/legal basis. Indeed we could consider it to be the apotheosis of that mode. The argument runs: 'We deserve power because we have shown you that we can use it well and the way in which we show you that is through the reporting of evidence derived from the practices of social science.'

Evidence does not merely support post hoc claims to demonstrated competence. It also justifies the pursuit of particular policies. Whereas the rational Whig version of the political use of evidence asserts that policy is framed on the basis of truth in the form of evidence – evidence-based policy – we might consider that evidence is often framed in order to sustain policy decisions – policy-based evidence.

This chapter will focus on the politics of evidence. It will examine the political factors in the construction, publication and use of evidence generated by applied social science. It will show how political factors always enter into these processes and review the implications of this for applied social research in general. Particular attention will be given to the way in which governments selectively, and often inaccurately, present the results of applied social science investigations in order to justify policies and defend their record in relation to the technical efficiency of their administrations. These issues have arisen especially in the use and abuse of official statistics but also in the ways in which academic studies have been seized on to 'demonstrate' effectiveness in the achievement of policy outcomes. Examples include UK assessments of changes in social mobility, arguments about the relative effectiveness of schools provided other than through traditional local governments, and a range of discussions relating to the relative efficiency of private versus public provision in health, welfare and education. We will also find 'evidence' playing a crucial role in the management of service reorganisation and examine how this has worked out in local health service reconfiguration processes where there has often been sustained opposition to the withdrawal of services in the name of efficiency and improvement. Many, but not all, academics have 'willingly' enlisted in the presentation of policy-based and practice-based evidence, sometimes in terms of ideological assertion (this is particularly true of economists), sometimes in relation to funding opportunities. However, some civil servants and in particular statisticians, have an honourable record in resisting the pressure for 'good news and only good news'. We will consider how the examples of statistics commissions[1] and professional codes provide a basis for 'honest' applied social research.

The issue of privatisation, of the re-commodification or even commodification for the first time of services provided by government or related agencies on a not-for-profit basis, is a crucial theme underpinning many of the arguments about evidence being used to justify policies. The only rational argument for handing over public not-for-profit provision to private for-profit providers[2] is that there will be improved efficiency to such a degree that the services will be provided at a better level for less cost – there will be more bang for the public buck. Two issues arise immediately. The first is truthful accounting – do the business plans and cost estimates produced in advance of such transfers actually demonstrate any real possibility that there will be efficiency savings and better services? This is the pre-transfer issue. Will hospitals or other public facilities delivered through the Private Finance Initiative (PFI) actually end up costing the public purse less for the same output value as the public sector competitor? Post-transfer there are issues about the quality of service provided as measured by appropriate output and outcome indicators. Do academy schools actually perform better than schools still under conventional local authority control? There is a plethora of evidence around these particular issues and it provides little in the way of comfort for the political and academic ideologues of privatisation. The way in which government ministers, spokespeople and academic allies have sought to discredit uncomfortable evidence here is a particularly blatant illustration of how legitimation is by no means always founded on rational and objective truth.

The argument will be carried by examples and it is to these that we now turn.

## Social mobility

In unequal societies the promise of social mobility is of crucial significance. Leisering and Walker tell us why:

> Individual mobility is crucial to modernity. It is a functional prerequisite of change in social structures ... Mobility is also a powerful means by which people drive forward their ambitions in life. Irrespective of the actual mobility that occurs, the idea of mobility is fundamental to the legitimization of Western Societies. The promise of mobility allows 'open societies' to maintain a system of firmly established structural inequalities. The optimism about macro-dynamics, the belief in societal progress, translates at the micro-level into the belief in individual progress. (1998, pp 4–5)

The form of social mobility for which governments have responsibility is inter-generational mobility. Movement within one's own adult life course, intra-generational mobility, can be understood as primarily a function of one's own abilities, efforts and luck – although government may have some role. Movement across generations is a function in large part of the opportunities offered by educational systems. At the school level at least, and in most developed countries even at the tertiary level of higher education, those systems are to a very considerable degree the responsibility of the state. Let us examine how the UK New 'Labour' government has sought to legitimate its role in relation to inter-generational mobility. We must note that this has particular saliency because of the way in which New 'Labour' has moved its political agenda away from redistribution, a traditional social democratic objective. If we are to be, as Peter (now Lord) Mandelson asserted 'comfortable about people being filthy rich' then we have to allow others some opportunity to become so. Although the 'filthy rich' are always going to be a tiny minority, movement into more modest but comfortable positions serves a legitimating purpose. Given that inequality in the UK as measured by the Gini coefficient rose very substantially during the 1980s and has basically flat-lined during the period in office of New 'Labour' since 1997 (although its current trend is upwards from a post Second World War historic high of nearly 0.40)[3] then inter-generational social mobility matters a lot.

It was therefore something of an issue for New 'Labour' when a research report funded jointly by the Department for Children, Families and Schools and the Sutton Trust[4] appeared to show that there was less social mobility displayed in a cohort of children born in 1970 than was the case for a cohort of children born in 1958 (Blanden et al, 2005). The technical basis of this study has been challenged in severe terms – see Gorard, 2008 – but as that author observes it has had a great deal of policy salience. The same point was expressed by the editor of *Prospect*, a respected UK current affairs monthly, as having had:

> arguably, more influence on public debate than any academic paper of the past twenty years. Every commentator and politician who 'knows' that mobility has fallen of a cliff in recent years is almost certainly basing his or her assumption on the Sutton Trust report. Yet it is a highly controversial and contested piece of work. (Goodhart, 2008)

While Gorard's criticisms can in brutal summary be described in terms of the representativeness of the sub-samples of the two cohorts which were the basis of the calculations underpinning the original findings, Goodhart picked up on the argument in social mobility studies between economists who focus on income and sociologists who focus on occupationally defined social location and suggested that work using the latter frame demonstrated that there was more social mobility than income-based studies suggested and that the UK was not a low mobility society. Both approaches have severe flaws, not least in the treatment of mobility as a matter for individuals without taking account of the households to which individuals belong in adult life, but the sociological studies as traditionally organised seem to have a far too general and in many ways inappropriate conception of occupational hierarchies as a specification of social position. Be that as it may, this study and others, for example evidence prepared by Macmillan (2009) as evidence to 'the Panel for Fair Access to the Professions' which was set up in the wake of the concerns about mobility, seem to suggest that with the coming to an end of the absolute social mobility[5] which was a consequence of the UK's transition from an industrial to post-industrial economy, there has been a closure of relative social mobility particularly in terms of access to high status and well-remunerated professions. Given increasing inequality this was obviously a serious issue for a governing party which had a history of social democratic concern with equality but had replaced that with an emphasis on equality of opportunity.

It is therefore no exaggeration to say that when subsequent research emerged which seemed to say that things had got somewhat better since 2000, government ministers and spokespeople seized on it and publicised it widely. For example in the 2008 document *Getting on: Getting ahead* it was claimed that: 'What is now clear is that although social mobility did not fall between 1970 and 2000, policy did not succeed in increasing it ... recent academic research shows that there have been positive changes since 2000' (Cabinet Office Strategy Unit, 2008, p 6).

The basis of this claim lay in a single graph with just three points on it reported by Blanden et al (2005) which showed a statistically significant but still small reduction in the degree of association between family income and attainment in GCSE – the examination which UK secondary school children take at age 16. *Getting on: Getting ahead* reproduced this graph and claimed: 'These findings, therefore, suggest that family background will have less of an impact on the income of these children when they reach adulthood, than those born in 1970. They are likely to experience higher social mobility' (Cabinet Office Strategy Unit, 2008, p 36).

Of course they show nothing of the kind. Dorling (2008), acting as a very useful public intellectual, responded to this in a think piece for the left-wing think tank Compass making the important point that results at different time points had very different implications for life course. Obtaining good GCSE scores in the mid-1980s meant something quite different from obtaining such scores 20 years later because the relative significance of good scores had changed. Indeed one of the original paper's authors, Gregg, was quoted in the *Financial Times* making exactly this point:

> 'If more and more people are getting good GCSEs – and they are – then GCSEs may be less important than they were

as the key to future life chances. People may need A–levels, or a degree or even a masters to really get on. It is a little like literacy, which was a huge advantage 200 years ago but became less so as more and more people could read.' The clutch of policies Labour has introduced may indeed have a lasting impact on social mobility for children born after 2000, he says. But it will be years before the evidence is clear. And right now, he says, 'it is a bit premature to claim a big success'. (Timmins, 2008)

This particular episode had a whiff of desperation about it. Things had to be represented as looking good in relation to some part of government policy. True, the original researchers and other academics weighed in quickly with qualifications, reservations and downright dismissals of government's interpretation. The argument presented in Liam Byrne's (the Minister for the Cabinet Office responsible for this area) blog to the effect that:

There's some good news – and some powerful lessons from the past. It seems that despite the huge economic, social and political change between 1970 and 2000, social mobility didn't get better. It stayed the same. Now, finally it could be getting better. Early evidence from Bristol University shows that parental income could be beginning to have less of an influence on the exam results of kids born in 1990/91. That hasn't happened by accident. Investment and reform in early years services, schools, vocational education and work–based training are all vital for the future. But our task is two fold. Investing in a more mobile society. And second capturing a big chunk of the high value jobs that come with the doubling of world wealth over the next 25 years, so there's more high paying jobs to go round. Tory confusion and cuts won't deliver that,[6]

just doesn't hold up but the claims were made without much engagement of brain or, more importantly, without checking with the researchers to see if their research sustained them.

## Policy-based evidence – health service reconfigurations and the 'clinical' case

Health service reconfiguration in the UK but particularly in England involves major reorganisation of existing health care services. This can take a multiplicity of forms. It can involve the transfer of services from secondary providers, traditional general hospitals, into the primary care sector – for example through the development of polyclinics. It can involve concentration of services into large secondary providers – bigger hospitals. Both processes can threaten the financial viability of existing hospitals and hence lead to hospital closures. This has been a threatening issue in UK politics since Richard Taylor, a retired consultant physician, defeated a sitting Labour minister in a campaign organised around the single issue of the closure of Kidderminster Hospital.

Here we do not have a case of the misuse of a particular study. Rather we encounter a campaign of representation to the effect that, in very crude summary, bigger is better. This began in 2006 when the think tank the Institute for Public Policy Research (IPPR) published a briefing note summarising a report which was not actually published until January 2007. The case was being made for concentration of services, particularly of Accident and Emergency services, into larger units. That coincided with an interview with the newly appointed Chief Executive of the National Health Service (NHS) in which he announced that consideration was being given to:

> up to 60 'reconfigurations' of NHS services, affecting every strategic health authority in the land. Some changes will try to squeeze out overcapacity that contributed to the NHS's £512m deficit in the last financial year. But most will be aimed at redesigning the NHS to improve care by concentrating key services in fewer hospitals. Mr. Nicholson identified A&E departments, paediatrics and maternity services as areas where provision would have to be overhauled. (Carvel, 2006)

In December of that year the Prime Minister, Tony Blair, made a speech arguing that hospital reconfiguration would save lives. This drew on both an IPPR press release and two reports issued from the Department of Health (Boyle, 2006; Alberti, 2007). The term 'clinical change' is particularly significant. These reports were deployed in order to say we can do better if we reorganise, although neither report contained any referenced evidence. For that we had to wait until the publication of the full IPPR report in January 2007, *The future hospital: The progressive case for change* (Farrington-Douglas and Brooks, 2007). This was not a systematic review – indeed the nature of the evidence base on the relationships among size of unit, amount of work done by unit and by clinician, and the general outcome volume debate is so confusing that no systematic review seems possible. However, overall it argued that the evidence supported concentration. This was simply not the case. Posnett summarised the actual state of the evidence thus:

> It is tempting to think that larger hospitals are more cost-effective than smaller ones because of the operation of economies of scale. However, the evidence does not back up this belief. While increasing hospital size can cut costs for some specific procedures, such economies are exhausted at a relatively small size. Many people also believe that patient outcomes improve with hospital size. Unfortunately, most studies of this relationship are poorly controlled for differences in prognosis, if at all. When such differences are taken into account, the correlation between outcomes and size turns out to be relatively minor or even absent.

> *Findings:* The literature on hospital economies of scale suggests that they are fully realised in facilities of 100 to 200 beds. Yet, in many countries, the concentration of hospital services continues to be a major policy aim, especially through mergers. In private health care markets, mergers are undertaken primarily to reduce competition and enhance profits. In public systems, two other justifications predominate. First, when hospitals operate at less than full capacity, mergers are a way of eliminating excess capacity and cutting costs. Second, a merger can address performance issues for particular units or services. However, concentrating hospital services often reduces patient access because it increases social and economic costs for many patients. Research suggests that these increases have the greatest impact on the use of diagnostic, outpatient and screening services in primary care. Evidence of the impact on secondary and tertiary services is mixed; some studies suggest that patients who live further from a hospital have lower referral and intervention rates, while other studies show no difference.

*Policy considerations:* Bigger hospitals are not necessarily better. Research shows that they rarely result in lower costs or better patient outcomes. A good deal still needs to be understood about how to achieve better clinical results, and common size indicators, like hospital activity volume, are too crude to be useful in planning clinical services. Optimal hospital size depends on local health care needs and the availability of complementary services. The burden of proof for any proposed merger ought to lie with its proponents, who should be able to quantify the expected benefits and costs and explain how the benefits will be realized. (WHO/Europe HEN, 2003; see also Posnett, 1999)

The role of the IPPR is of interest. Although often described as a 'left wing' think tank, it has in fact had a history of endorsing neo-liberal and pro-privatisation policies in relation to public services and has been a particular cheerleader for the PFI. This was clearly identified by Allyson Pollock and colleagues in the appendix to their Catalyst Working Paper, *Public services and the private sector: A response to the IPPR* (2001). This followed the publication of the IPPR's major report *Building better partnerships* (Commission on Public Private Partnerships, 2001) which purported to provide a philosophical and evidence base for greater commercial involvement in welfare. Pollock et al noted that:

The commission represents a striking coalition between big business and government. Commission members have direct links into many of the key government departments. A growing share of the sponsors' revenues and profits are built on the billions of pounds of public funds and government contracts' (2001, p 41)

The reason this matters is that reconfiguration and the development of new and larger hospital sites could only be carried out on PFI terms. Indeed the driver in many instances seems to have been the development of a PFI-led scheme rather than the improvement of health services per se.

Hospital reconfiguration as a principle is an interesting example of a coalition of voices from inside and outside government coming together to push a line. There was a rapid rejoinder to all of this – Byrne and Ruane's *The case for hospital reconfiguration: Not proven* (2007), published by the campaign group 'Keep our NHS Public' (KONP), and the argument has not been deployed in quite this form again at a national level but major reorganisation schemes have gone ahead at a local level. The interesting thing is that clinical voices, if not really in any proper sense clinical evidence, were brought into play in order to legitimate what was proving to be a deeply unpopular set of processes. A good example is provided by two major and interrelated health service reconfiguration exercises in Greater Manchester.[7] These were Making It Better: Making it Real (MiB) and Healthy Futures (HF) proposed in 2006 by consortia of PCTs in Greater Manchester. The first, which dealt with services for children, young people, parents and babies, covered the whole Greater Manchester area. The second, which covered all other secondary (hospital-based) health services, referred to a smaller part of the Greater Manchester Area in the north east of that territory. We will come back to this exercise in Chapter Six when we review consultation and participation as applied social science processes. Here the focus is on the 'clinical case for change', which provided a crucial rationale for both exercises. Ruane (2007) shows how the assertion that 'bigger is better' formed a crucial element in this with repeated but un-evidenced statements to this effect:

> 'the health professionals who gave us their views were in no doubt that many specialities will benefit from a reduction in the number of sites where inpatient treatment is offered. (HF, *Criteria and Methodology for Selection of Options*, 2005, p 2, quoted in Ruane, 2007, p 5)

> There is evidence that sick children, young people and babies do better in larger units than in smaller units. There is a huge benefit in concentrating more specialist skills into fewer, larger units rather than spreading the skills and experience more thinly across a large number of smaller units.' (HF, *Criteria and Methodology for Selection of Options*, 2005, p 18, quoted in Ruane, 2007, pp 5–6)

> There is now acceptance of a 'critical mass' whereby clinicians – doctors, nurses and those involved in providing health care – need to see and treat a particular number and type of patient in order to maintain their clinical skills.' (MiB, Appendix G, 'The need for change and the clinical model', 2006 quoted in Ruane, 2007, p 6)

These statements run quite contrary to the logic of evidence-based policy. The first is a matter of collection of opinion rather than of any evidence. The second and third really misrepresent the complex and essentially unresolved debate surrounding the relationship between volume and outcome in health provision which has been going on since the 1980s. They certainly accord with Nicholson's (the NHS Chief Executive's) desire for national and local assertions of a 'clinical case for change' in relation to health service reorganisation but they are not proper evidence in any meaningful sense of that word. It is interesting to reflect on their purpose in relation to legitimation. We might consider that a crucial audience for the argument was in fact the senior managers, clinicians and members of health governing bodies who were the drivers of the reconfiguration process. Certainly they wanted to convince others, lay publics and the health scrutiny committees of local authorities – the only democratic element in the process. But perhaps the first and most important group they had to convince was themselves. They had to believe that what they were doing was for the public good and that the rational evidence demonstrated this. Self-delusion is an important part of contemporary governance.

## Truthful numbers – the role of official statistics

If we recognise that any organised state needs to know about itself and the territories and activities it governs, then we will immediately recognise that it requires systematic flows of ordered information and that much of that information will necessarily be quantitative. This is the role of statistics in the meaning of that word which derives from the German *stadt* – state, information about the state and society. In cybernetic terms we can regard this as the necessary learning feedback loop in the system. Such information will not be useful if it is not in some way related to the actual reality it describes. Whatever our views on the social construction of statistical information, there has to be a means by which we know what is going on. However, who are we? Can the state confine the flow of information to its own internal bureaucracy? Can it keep information which is embarrassing to it out of the public domain? Here interestingly we see one advantage of market-oriented complex societies. Markets cannot function effectively without open information flows. Economic data which is of relevance to financial markets has to be presented in a form which can inform those markets. If it is not, then that in itself will be a source of suspicion and a negative factor in relation to the way in which market makers regard, for example, the credit rating of states in relation to public sector borrowing. There are times when market makers and states seem to collude in mutual self-delusion. The run-up to the financial crisis of 2007 certainly was one of them. However, in general financial statistics need to be 'true' or at least, and this is not quite the same thing, fit for purpose.

The same is not necessarily true of more purely 'social' statistics. A good example is provided by the way in which unemployment has been counted in the UK during the 20th century.[8] Opposition parties constantly accuse governments of fiddling unemployment figures so as to undercount the extent of unemployment. In the early 1990s the Labour opposition accused the Conservative government of massively undercounting the unemployed. More recently the Conservative opposition with Liberal Democrat support accused the Labour government of exactly the same offence. This has never been a matter of falsifying actual numbers once collected. It has always revolved around the way in which unemployment is actually defined and counted in the first place – around the issue of operationalisation. A working party of the Royal Statistical Society investigated this issue (Bartholomew Working Party on the Measurement of Unemployment in the UK, 1995). They observed that: 'It is clear to us that the general public, many politicians, the media and various pressure groups do not trust the unemployment figures or find them convincing' (1995, p 389). They recommended that basing unemployment estimates on the administrative count of claimants for an unemployment benefit was unsatisfactory because it depended in very large part on changing eligibility criteria for benefit receipt. Instead counts should be based on the Labour Force Survey – that is on the results of a specific investigation of the character of the labour force.

This is now done. Since 2003 the Office for National Statistics (ONS) has based estimates of unemployment on a count using the International Labour Office definition of unemployment. This has not made the issue go away. Beatty et al (2007) estimated the real level of unemployment in the UK at 3.4 million compared with a claimant count of 1.6 million and a Labour Force Survey count of 2.47 million. The major reasons for the discrepancy were the disappearance of significant numbers of NEETs (young people Not in Employment, Education or Training, and not in receipt of benefit) from any count, and the presence on long-term sickness benefits – Incapacity Benefit – of about a million people who could work.[9] During the late 1990s and the early 2000s UK government ministers regularly made comparisons between the flexible employment base in the UK and the more highly regulated employment system in Germany to the detriment of Germany by claiming unemployment was much higher there. In fact worklessness rates in Germany and the UK were broadly similar and this despite the costs to the German economy of reunification and the collapse of the former East Germany's industrial base. The collapse of the UK's manufacturing base had had much the same effect but the consequences were concealed through classifying people as unfit to work rather than as unemployed.

The furore over unemployment counts is one of the background factors behind the development of a relatively independent Statistics Authority in the UK. In their 1995 piece, the Bartholomew Working Party on the Measurement of Unemployment in the UK noted that a previous Royal Statistical Society Working Party (Moore, 1991) had argued for a centralised statistical service with a degree of evident independence in order to maintain public confidence in statistical products as true representations of social and economic conditions. In the 1990s the Labour opposition made a manifesto commitment to introduce an independent statistical body accountable to Parliament as a whole rather than to government. This was done in 2000 with the establishment of the Statistics Commission. In 2007 this was replaced by the Statistics Authority, which was given substantially more powers in relation to ONS and the responsibility for the independent monitoring and oversight of all UK official statistics.

The Statistics Authority has not been frightened to bite if vexed. In 2008 the Home Office published a press notice and fact sheet. Claims were made in relation to achievements of the 'Tackling Knives Action Programme'. These figures were released despite the opposition of the National Statistician – the professional head of ONS – and the statisticians who had produced the data, since the data had not gone through a full checking process. The Chair of the UK Statistics Authority, Sir Michael Scholar, made a considerable public fuss and the Home Secretary was obliged to apologise to the House of Commons. This was not seen as an isolated incident since the Home Office had published other figures which did not meet the requirements of the Statistics Authority's code of practice. In February 2010 Scholar laid into the Conservative Shadow Home Secretary, Chris Grayling, for using figures on violent crime in a way 'likely to mislead the public'. Again this revolved around a measurement issue. Scholar pointed out that a new method of recording violent crime which had removed front-level police discretion was responsible for an apparent increase of more than a third over one year. He unequivocally criticised the misuse of figures by Grayling as he had previously rebuked the New

'Labour' minister Harriet Harman for exaggerating the pay gap between men and women.

The Statistics Authority seems to be capable of showing its teeth in relation to the quantitative products of official government data collection. However, other forms of evidence seem to lie outside its remit. It has no responsibility for claims made in relation to research conducted by the 'outsourced [academic etc.] labour force of the evidence based state' (May, 2005). Likewise it seems not to have a real function in relation to audit-style claims made about the effectiveness of particular government programmes. That is in principle, and to some degree in practice, the job of the National Audit Office, which is an explicitly independent non-civil service body directly accountable through the Public Accounts Committee to the House of Commons. The Audit Commission has a similar function in relation to local government and there are equivalent bodies in relation to the devolved governments of Scotland, Wales and Northern Ireland. The Audit Commission is being scrapped by the Conservative/Liberal Democrat coalition government and its functions will now be carried out by private sector accountancy firms that have a direct interest in extending the general private sector provision of public services.

## Evaluating academies – claims versus reality

Academies

- Today's statistics also show that academies are leading the way in reducing low attainment – and so are a key element of the National Challenge.
- For the 63 academies which have been open long enough to have results in both 2008 and 2009, there has been an increase of 5.0 percentage points in the number of pupils gaining five A★ to C grades at GCSE including English and maths – double the national increase and an increase on last year's improvement rate of 4.3 percentage points.
- Comparing the 101 academies with results in 2009 to their predecessor schools in 2001, there has been a 16.4 percentage point improvement in the percentage of pupils achieving five A★–C including English and Maths from 17.8 per cent in 2001 to 34.2 per cent in 2009. This compares to an 11.9 percentage point improvement nationally from 38.8% in 2001 to 50.7% in 2009.

(DCSF, 2010)

The academy programme was introduced in England by New 'Labour' in 2000. It involves the transfer of secondary (and now some primary) schools from the control of local education authorities – the elected local governments which traditionally have managed state education in the UK – to an independent status with private sponsors nominating the majority of the governing body. Originally sponsors were intended to be drawn from the business and commercial sector but the remit has widened and sponsors now include universities, the Church of England and private schools. The original commercial sponsors were a mixed bunch. The sponsors of academies in the north east of England include on the one hand a foundation run by an evangelical Christian car dealer who has required the teaching of creationism alongside evolutionary theory in biology, and on the other a Scottish (there are no academies in Scotland) Monaco-resident tax-avoiding multimillionaire and self-declared sex addict – it definitely takes all sorts!

Academies were introduced to replace poorly performing schools in deprived areas. The whole point of academies was to improve the performance of the children going to them. We can see from the quote above that the DCSF certainly asserts that they have but does the evidence support this contention? Three investigations come to rather different conclusions. The National Audit Office carried out a review which reported in 2007. This examined a range of aspects of the academies programme but in relation to improvements in performance it concluded: 'the rates of improvement in GCSE results between 2005 and 2006 ... for academies were greater than for comparable schools and for all schools. Academies' rates of improvement were also greater than other schools between 2004 and 2005' (National Audit Office, 2007, p 18, para 2.10).

Another evaluation of the academies programme has been undertaken on a continuing basis by the transnational accountancy and consultancy firm, PriceWaterhouseCoopers LLP. The preamble to this report contains the following passage which is worth quoting since it illustrates the difference between the views of the academy (which nonetheless is also moving in the direction of owning intellectual property rather than free academic exchange) and the commercial world.

> Proposals, tenders, reports together with working papers and similar documents, whether interim or final and other deliverables submitted by PriceWaterhouseCoopers LLP, contain methodologies, models, pricing information and other materials and work product, which are proprietary and confidential to PricewaterhouseCoopers LLP, or which have

been provided to PriceWaterhouseCoopers LLP by third parties who may have made such information available on foot of confidentiality agreements, either written, implied, or under the law of confidence. PriceWaterhouseCoopers LLP clearly identifies all such proposals, tenders, reports and other deliverables as protected under the copyright laws of the United Kingdom and other countries. Such documents, presentations and materials are submitted on the condition that they shall not be disclosed outside the recipient's organisation, or duplicated, used or disclosed in whole or in part by the recipient for any purpose other than that for which they were specifically procured, pursuant to our engagement letter. In the event that, pursuant to a request which the DCSF has received under the Freedom of Information Act 2000, it is required to disclose any information contained in this report or any deliverable prepared by us, it will notify PriceWaterhouseCoopers promptly and consult with PriceWaterhouseCoopers prior to disclosing such information. The DCSF agrees to pay due regard to any representations which PriceWaterhouseCoopers LLP may make in connection with such disclosures and the DCSF shall apply any relevant exemptions which may exist under the Act to such information. (PriceWaterhouseCoopers, 2008)

Actually this report includes a perfectly reasonable and useful account of the way in which the research in it was done. Obviously the declaration is applied to all outputs but it does show a difference in ways of thinking and is worth noting.

There are some very interesting elements reported in this study. In relation to the social background of pupils in academies it noted:

There were almost 8,000 pupils from socially deprived backgrounds attending Academies in 2007 – just under a third of the total. The *absolute number* of pupils from such backgrounds has grown by around 1,400 since the first Academies opened but the *proportion* has declined at a faster rate than other schools, with a fall in the FSM percentage of nearly 6pp compared to 2pp in control schools and 1pp in England as a whole (though it should be noted that Academies started from a higher base and have on average a higher proportion of pupils from

socially deprived backgrounds than their catchment area).
(PriceWaterhouseCoopers, 2008, p 62, para 3.34)

There has been some considerable debate as to whether academies are recruiting fewer pupils from deprived backgrounds than their predecessor schools and some clear evidence in the PriceWaterhouseCoopers report that they exclude more pupils. In other words the question arises, are they doing better because they have a better intake? None of the available research has modelled achievement in a way which enables us to present an answer to this question. In relation to improvement in performance the conclusion of the PriceWaterhouseCoopers report was that:

> The average Academy improvement (8pp [percentage points]) exceeds that of the Comparison Groups (4pp) and, to a greater extent, England as a whole (2pp); and when achievement including English and Maths is included in the analysis, the average Academy improvement reduces (to 5pp), though it still exceeds the Comparison Group (2pp) and England (1pp) averages. (2008, p 211)

However, an independent academic study came to a rather different conclusion: 'changes in GCSE performance in academies relative to matched schools are statistically indistinguishable from one another. The same pattern emerges if all state schools in the academy's local authority are used as the comparator group' (Machin and Wilson, 2009, p 8).

There are important differences in method among the three studies. Machin and Wilson's approach of careful local matching and consideration of the full range of academies seems the best overall, but all three studies report carefully on research approach in an entirely appropriate fashion. The key point, however, remains. The most independent study – the academic one – shows no difference, arguing that in effect what we are seeing with very much underperforming schools in general, including academies as they were established, is that over time they regress towards the mean performance. In other words the claims in the 2010 *DCFS News* do not stand up. Government has selected the evidence that suits it in order to assert that what it has done has worked.

## Conclusion

Governments, and particularly the UK's New 'Labour', do not like criticism. The ferocious response by New 'Labour' to the work of Allyson Pollock and her colleagues (summarised in Pollock, 2005) illustrates this. The New 'Labour' MP Julia Drown, a former NHS manager, actually got a section dismissing this body of work included in a report of the House of Commons Health Select Committee despite the opposition of the Chair of the Committee who thought such action wholly inappropriate. It was of course in practical terms not merely inappropriate but entirely counter-productive since it raised a storm about the fiddling of calculations in allocating new hospital development schemes to PFI rather than the public sector and brought to wider public notice the enormous long-term costs of this disastrous method of financing public capital projects. They minded a lot. They made the public relations mistake of attacking instead of ignoring. And yet they still ignored. That perhaps is the crucial point. Much of this chapter has been concerned with examples of government making legitimating claims on the basis of unclear evidence – health service reconfiguration exercises claiming bigger is better, DCFS claiming academies are doing better. In those cases the reality is that we don't know, and we don't know in large part because the actual methods used to deliver evidence are inappropriate for understanding outcomes in relation to change in complex systems. In relation to PFI and related schemes like the development and operation of health Independent Sector Treatment Centres, ITSCs (see Player and Leys, 2008), the evidence is absolutely unequivocal. These things are not good. They cost more and they do less. Actually both those studies and the related work underpinning them take the form of careful process tracing-based investigation of specific cases rather than quasi-experiments. They are good evidence. And they are ignored, although not in the arena of public and especially specialist and informed debate where they receive good coverage. The *British Medical Journal* has been exemplary in relation to the attention it has paid to these arguments. Rather they seem to have no impact on political processes.

So we are left with an intriguing question. If a government – UK New 'Labour', which has constantly asserted that it is in the business of rational decision making based on good evidence – so blatantly ignores reality shoved in its face, what are we to make of this? At one level we simply return to Colin Crouch and the character of post-democracy. In post-democracy the interests that are served are business interests, and certainly PFI and ITSCs serve business interests by opening up the non-commodified operations of particularly English health care to for-profit operators. However, why the fuss about evidence and the anger about contradiction? One plausible explanation is that these people really want to believe that they are doing the right thing and do not like being told they are not. If we look at local health service reconfiguration where key players are the organic intellectuals of the health system, clinicians and health managers, then we can see that they work best if they believe what they say. The establishment of 'evidence bases' for practice is not only a means to public legitimation but also to personal reassurance. It seems this goes all the way to the top and we have to include very senior civil servants *and* politicians in the set of organic intellectuals and recognise that they too want to believe what they say even when it is not just ain't necessarily so but is definitely not so.

Is there an alternative? The example of the Statistics Authority shows that it might be possible to have an independent and honest process for the resolution of evidence. However, statistics is perhaps a special case in two ways. One relates to the nature of the evidence. The substance of the argument in relation to the examples dealt with by the Statistical Authority has resolved around counts – actual specific measurements. We have seen in relation to unemployment that operationalisation changes counts. This was a major factor in the dispute over crime statistics. Still at least operationalisation rules are clear and given in relation to publication of data. There is an element of simplicity in relation to the products of surveys of what is, which is not present and cannot be present in relation to evaluation of complex social interventions.

In the case of statistics there is another factor. This is the continued existence in the UK of that wholly admirable[10] survivor of the radical science movement of the 1970s, *Radical Statistics*, which defines its nature thus:

> Members are 'radical' in being committed to helping build a more free, democratic and egalitarian society. Members of Radstats are concerned at the extent to which official statistics reflect governmental rather than social purposes. Our particular concerns are:
>
> • The mystifying use of technical language to disguise social problems as technical ones

- The lack of control by the community over the aims of statistical investigations, the way these are conducted and the use of the information produced
- The power structures within which statistical and research workers are employed and which control the work and how it is used
- The fragmentation of social problems into specialist fields, obscuring connectedness

Radstats members believe that statistics can be used as part of campaigns for progressive social change – just as they were used to support measures that led to improvements in public health in the 19th century. (www.radstats.org.uk/about.htm 2010-03-10)

Radstats is a superbly democratic and low key – in the sense of administrative simplicity and clear sense of purpose – organisation of organic intellectuals of the Left. It has served a useful purpose in keeping statistics honest, with the assistance and active participation of many senior figures in both the technical and professional arms of the statistics profession. Long may it flourish and it does provide an example of non-careerist and engaged work on the side of truth and justice – a statement way too pretentious to appeal to most of its members but this author is allowed a Celtic flourish. It has, in that useful Churchillian expression, 'kept buggering on'. We will now turn to how that kind of work can feed outwith academic and policy debate by engaging with social science's role in political process in relation to the post-democratic political modes of consultation and participation.

### Notes

[1] In the UK now the Statistics Authority.

[2] Some transfers from the public sector of governance are to the 'third sector' of charitable or other voluntary/co-operative providers. However, given the turn of this sector towards business models and the level of remuneration of senior management in much of it, it is difficult to distinguish many third sector operators from their openly for-profit competitors.

[3] Below Average Income, DWP (1994/95 onwards) and the Family Expenditure Survey (earlier years) obtained via data published by the IFS; UK; updated August 2009.

[4] An educational charity which promotes high educational achievement by children from relatively deprived backgrounds.

[5] Social mobility which happens because there is an expansion in the proportion of more desirable occupational roles and/or better remunerated occupations in the employment structure. Relative social mobility in contrast is to do with social fluidity – with the degree to which the social location of children is independent of the social location of their parents.

[6] See http://liambyrnemp.wordpress.com/, 2 November 2008.

[7] I am grateful to Dr Sally Ruane of De Montfort University for much of the information in the following section. See Ruane (2007) for a fuller account.

[8] Before the introduction of unemployment insurance and benefits in 1911 and the recognition, to quote the title of Beveridge's book that preceded this measure, that *Unemployment [is a] problem of industry* it was not meaningful to regard unemployment as a distinctive economic status. Under-employment was far more the normal condition in an almost wholly casualised labour force.

[9] The government responded to this by changing assessment processes in relation to the non-employed who were in receipt of Incapacity Benefit or single parents and forcing them towards Jobseeker's Allowance, which requires an active search for work. This was done in the teeth of the most severe recession since the 1930s. The outcome can be awaited with interest for those of us fortunate enough not to be subject to these benefit regimes.

[10] In the opinion of an active member of it who regularly audits its accounts, namely the present author.

# SIX

# Consulting: the role of social research in relation to new modes of governance

Consult, v.i. To seek another's approval of a course already decided on. (Ambrose Bierce *The Devil's Dictionary*, 1911)

Arnstein (1969) proposed, explicitly as a heuristic device, the idea of a ladder of participation:

> The bottom rungs of the ladder are (1) Manipulation and (2) Therapy. These two rungs describe levels of 'non-participation' that have been contrived by some to substitute for genuine participation. Their real objective is not to enable people to participate in planning or conducting programs, but to enable powerholders to 'educate' or 'cure' the participants. Rungs 3 and 4 progress to levels of 'tokenism' that allow the have-nots to hear and to have a voice: (3) Informing and (4) Consultation. When they are proffered by powerholders as the total extent of participation, citizens may indeed hear and be heard. But under these conditions they lack the power to insure that their views will be heeded by the powerful. When participation is restricted to these levels, there is no follow-through, no 'muscle', hence no assurance of changing the status quo. Rung (5) Placation is simply a higher level tokenism because the ground rules allow have-nots to advise, but retain for the powerholders the continued right to decide.
>
> Further up the ladder are levels of citizen power with increasing degrees of decision-making clout. Citizens can enter into a (6) Partnership that enables them to negotiate and engage in trade-offs with traditional power holders. At the topmost rungs, (7) Delegated Power and (8) Citizen Control, have-not citizens obtain the majority of decision-making seats, or full managerial power. (Arnstein, 1969, p 216)

Under her scheme consultation allows some sort of voice for those who are 'consulted' but no real influence on the outcome of events – in Bierce's sarcastic terms, they are asked their views after crucial decisions have already been made. And yet consultation/participation – the two terms represent points on a continuum – are crucial to contemporary governance and policy implementation. They are key features of post-democratic systems of political administration. And social science provides the essential framework through which they are actually done as social practices. We need to consider carefully just what this involves and implies.

Arnstein was very specific about the limitations of consultation understood as such:

> Inviting citizens' opinions, like informing them, can be a legitimate step toward their full participation. But if consulting them is not combined with other modes of participation, this rung of the ladder is still a sham since it offers no assurance that citizen concerns and ideas will be taken into account. The most frequent methods used for consulting people are attitude surveys, neighborhood meetings, and public hearings. ... When powerholders restrict the input of citizens' ideas solely to this level, participation remains just a window-dressing ritual. People are primarily perceived as statistical abstractions, and participation is measured by how many come to meetings, take brochures home, or answer a questionnaire. What citizens achieve in all this activity is that they have 'participated in participation'. And what powerholders achieve is the evidence that they have gone through the required motions of involving 'those people'. (1969, p 217)

There is an extensive literature on the limitations of participation in relation to the diffusion of power and the ability of 'the masses' to have any impact on decision making by bodies of governance and in particular on strategic decisions as opposed to matters of detail in relation to implementation. An early and apposite example is Dennis's *Public participation and planners' blight* (1972). The focus in this chapter will be in large part on the role of research *in* processes of consultation and participation but we must consider the actual experiences of participation as a social practice as well. We have to establish the context in which research becomes an actual part of the day-to-day processes of governance themselves.[1] So let us begin by attempting to understand what is meant by that term 'governance'. Newman provides a useful definition:

> Originating as a way of capturing shifts in the character of political rule, governance as a concept has been stretched to encompass a range of different transformations including the increasing emphasis on 'governing the social': drawing citizens and communities into the process of collaborative governance and constituting new forms of governable subject. (2005, p 1)

The context of this shift is one in which nation states have been 'hollowed out' because conventional hierarchical modes of government seem incapable of dealing with a whole set of social issues relating to the interaction between increasing inequality in all its forms and processes of policy and practice across a range of activities, from the detail of health care provision through to the regeneration of city region urban systems. The conventional literature sees this as a competency problem – conventional governments just can't manage these tasks and have had to shift mode towards what Newman calls 'co-production' with other agencies and with citizens themselves. Bang (2002) sums this sort of argument up: 'democratic states lack governance capacities simply because they are more attuned to coping with abstract problems … and conflicts of interest in the democratic regime … than to handling concrete policy and identity problems [project politics and politics of presence]' (Bang 2002, quoted in Newman et al, 2004, p 204).

There is another way of looking at these sorts of developments and that is to see the move of power away from local representative democratic institutions, and in particular elected local government, as a way of concealing policy and practice developments which serve major material interests and in particular the business interests who profit from re-commodification of both health and welfare services and business-oriented urban regeneration. The operative word in much of this process has been modernisation.

> Overall, two features of political modernisation stand out. One, the most obvious, is the seemingly irreversible commitment to the market as an efficient, resourceful and effective means of securing the provision of public services; the other is the elaboration of forms of partnership and governance that stress collaboration. The so-called modernisation project rests on a belief in the ability to

> secure cohesion within society and to remove or reduce ideological and social conflict. This essentially apolitical narrative assumes the solution of problems through the compatibility and complementarity of public and private sectors. (Blowers, 2002, p 72)

It is precisely because the democratic mode allows for a reasonably clear expression of conflicts of interest that it has been so reduced in significance at the local level. This is particularly the case in the UK where, as Newman (2001) has noted, New 'Labour' has built on the pre-existing quango state – what has been called the 'New Magistracy' drawn in large part from unelected and strongly networked local elites – and added a whole series of 'partnerships' operating at the neighbourhood level and in relation to specific functional areas. At the same time the scope for local initiative and variation has been reduced by the introduction of centrally determined quantitative targets. We will return to the vital significance of targets in relation to research processes.

One important factor, again particularly and pre-figuratively in the UK, is that traditional democratic local government has become part of this governance process. This is a consequence in part of it being stripped of functions, for example, it has lost all control over further education and through the academy process over many schools. At a crucial period in many conurbations planning and development powers for key areas were transferred to unelected Urban Development Corporations. It also reflects the engagement of the *leadership* of elected local government in the new partnerships and other institutional forms of the quango state. Of particular significance are Local Strategic Partnerships (LSPs), which have a crucial role in shaping the future trajectories of whole localities but must do so in relation to centrally imposed targets. The emphasis on leadership of elected local government is important. The change in the political administration of UK elected local government from a mode in which all councillors sat on service and overall authority management committees to one in which a minority of councillors are 'cabinet leads' in an executive ministerial role and the majority simply have a scrutiny role in relation to service operation is of the greatest significance for post-democratic politics at the local level.

The point being made here is that the erosion of traditional democratic local government, which had many faults and failings, is closely associated with a re-commodification of both services and urban planning and development processes. But that poses a problem. For all its faults democratic local government based on mass political parties served a crucial role in relation to local governance understood as a system. It was a vital mechanism for feedback both in relation to details of administrative practice and to wider issues relating to social conditions and social attitudes. Local councillors were, in the Leninist expression, transmission belts between the realm of the social and realm of the state in the form of local government. Of course local councillors still exist but the party structure which stood behind them has been massively eroded in the UK which again, as so often in this text, serves as a pre-figurative example in relation to post-democracy as a whole.

It is highly functionalist, but functionalist explanation is often entirely adequate, to say that social research's role in relation to consultation through to participation is in some considerable part as a replacement for the political processes and institutions of a more or less functioning mass democracy. That democracy did not die of its own volition. It, in the UK at least, was helped on its way by policy decisions and changes in practice which began under Thatcher's conservative government and continued with increased force under New 'Labour'. At the same time the institutions of industrial democracy, in the form of strong industrial trade unions, which had a significant interface with social democratic politics in local government, were also swept aside. Significantly organised labour has no as of right presence for example on English Local Strategic Partnerships (LSPs). Of course many of these issues existed when elected local government was much more powerful than it is now. Dennis's (1972) account is of planning processes undertaken by an elected Labour local authority, although even then regional and national spatial policy outwith local democratic control played a big part in developments. In any event local democratic politics no longer operates effectively at the crucial local level where most policy decisions actually take shape in relation to development and implementation in specific contexts. So what is social research doing in relation to this? Again we will proceed by examples.

## Consulting whilst reconfiguring – the case of health

There has been a legal requirement for bodies in the English NHS to consult in relation to major service reorganisation since the NHS as a whole was very substantially reorganised in 1974. The legislative background to this is currently provided by sections of the Health and Social Care Act 2001 and the NHS Act 2006. Originally a crucial element in consultation was provided by local Community Health Councils (CHCs), which had representation from elected local government and bodies in civil society, but these were abolished in England (but not in Wales) in 2003. Community Health Councils had a multiple role including investigating individual complaints but also addressing the issues surrounding all aspects of NHS work in their localities. They were accused of patchy performance but a factor in their abolition by Alan Milburn, who has been an enthusiastic supporter of private sector engagement in the NHS both in office as Secretary of State for Health and out of it as a backbench MP with close connections to the private health sector, seems also to have been motivated at least in part by the role that some of them played in opposing privatisation and in particular PFI schemes. Part of their function has been transferred to health scrutiny committees of local authorities. There are also now Local Involvement Networks (LINks) established to replace the Patient and Public Involvement Forums (PPIFs) that replaced CHCs but themselves had started to become rather stroppy in relation to major reconfigurations with a substantial privatisation element within them. LINks are geographically based and have a range of powers relating to access to information and consultation with the public.

There have been many health service reorganisations which have involved consultations with the public and other 'stakeholders' – to employ a key term in the vocabulary of post-democratic governance. A good example is provided by the overview of consultation in relation to the 'Healthy Futures' reconfiguration described in Chapter Five. This was carried out by various staff from the University of Salford organised through that university's 'Market Intelligence Unit'. That title is a good indication of the developments of the role of the academy in relation to social research which were identified by Ray Pawson and cited in Chapter Four. This is a useful case to consider, not least because it seems to have been conducted in a competent and professional fashion.[2] A summary of the process is provided by the *Final report: Public response to the Healthy Futures consultation* (Farrall, 2006). The actual consultation process was carried out by the Healthy Futures Team but the analysis of the results was done by the Salford University Team. The consultation included a mix of distribution of consultation documents with responses sought, meetings with both the general public and special groups within civil society, meetings with staff including the general staff of the institutions and senior clinicians/managers, and the reception of representations from a range of relevant organisations.

The document makes interesting reading. Here are some quotations from reported selections in its qualitative component:

> "The consultation has been very selective. It has failed to address the matter of whether or not the people of Rochdale actually WANT to have A and E at the Infirmary. The issue

has been omitted and the proposals fail at any point to include A and E in Rochdale. It appears that the decision has already been made to exclude A and E at Rochdale. Selective points have been brought forward to exclude Rochdale from a full package of services. The proposals are based on preset criteria. We are being asked to approve of criteria/ proposals already decided." (Rochdale)

"I think it is an absolute disgrace that a blatant cost-cutting exercise, arising from gross mismanagement of local health services over the past few years, is being dressed up as 'the way forward, to improved and safer healthcare'. The proposal that a town the size of Rochdale with 100,000 inhabitants, and possibly another 50,000 in the suburbs and surrounding areas, are to be left without an A and E unit, maternity service and the like is a criminal act." (19–40, Rochdale, British)

"LIFT is just another way of privatising the NHS just like PFI and foundation hospitals. LIFT transfers ownership of primary care premises from the public sector or GP practices to private investors. This is nothing but the commercialisation of primary care. The real reason why hospitals and services are being closed is the high cost of introducing market mechanisms into the NHS." (Male, 41–60, Rochdale, British)

"There is a limit for providing local and community health services. All the services can't be provided at community level. For a defined geographical area (like Rochdale), there should be a specialist centre which was catering the needs of people until now. By scrapping these essential services, I don't know what you people are going to achieve. After all, if these changes are made in the best interest of the locals, then convince them before you implement changes. Otherwise it amounts to bullying and nothing less than that. I am sure you agree with me!" (Male, 19–40, Rochdale, Indian)

"I do not feel it is fair for me to vote on the future of people who work and use the facilities of Rochdale and Bury." (Male, 31–60, North Manchester, English)

"If I lived in Rochdale, my answer would be different."
(Female, 31–60, North Manchester, British)

"I live in Oldham and it seems Oldham will not lose any
major services, from a week point of view it suggests that
I would be working in Rochdale, I do not have a problem
with that but I am glad that I don't live in Rochdale!! I
feel very much for the staff and more for the public of
Rochdale." (Male, 31–60, Oldham, White British)

"This was not a consultation but a 'done deal' and we are
given the choice of the least worse options for Rochdale
which is not acceptable or safe practice. Recent financial
mismanagement by the Pennine Acute Trust and the
subsequent treatment of staff and patients adds further
concerns that our NHS management have [sic] poor control
of the local budget and will place their own personal
interests first not the people they are supposed to be serving.
How can a pay-off of over £400,000 to the chief executives
be justified when he presided over the mismanagement."
(Not specified)

"It is good to see so much effort going into consultation
but it feels tokenistic. The trusts have made their preferences
clear – I would have preferred to be given a wider range of
options to choose from." (Male, 41–60, Rochdale, British)

The selection has been made to illustrate an argument but is not
unrepresentative of an important strand in the public response.

The report as a whole consists of a mix of quantitative tables dealing
with responses to structured questions and qualitative snippets of the
kind quoted above. There are serious problems with the quantitative
element in this kind of consultation. Characteristically, and this was
the case in this example, the respondents are not selected through any
sort of random sampling process but instead comprise simply those
who reply to questionnaire requests in various publicly distributed
documents. The pattern of respondents in terms of facesheet attributes
– age, gender, ethnicity, locality, but not often class – can be compared
with census data in an effort to assess how representative the achieved
opportunity sample is of the population as a whole but that is all. Much
more seriously the structured questions necessarily simplify and reduce
very complex issues into crude agree/disagree options for response. In

particular people were asked to choose among a set of pre-determined options which had been arrived at by 'the experts' prior to consultation. This kind of marketing simplification is completely inadequate for dealing with public views on issues of this kind and the tables presented do very little more than provide a very crude reductionist legitimation of complex issues. Norman Dennis dealt with this sort of thing back in the 1970s (Dennis, 1972) although in the North Manchester case there was a large minority of individual respondents who rejected the preferred option and a majority of group respondents that rejected it.

In contrast, the qualitative comments, which are reproduced well in the Salford report, are far more capable of expressing the complex responses to complex issues. Here one has a real sense of people having their say. The comments do not confine themselves to single issues but draw in the wider national and regional political context, argue on the basis of need and location, and even, and rather refreshingly, display a sense of equity and traditional fair play. The other theme which emerges here, and in other comments not quoted, is a real sense of the inadequacy of the consultation process. And so we find in North Manchester, as in many other examples, that far from legitimising change, consultation simply seems to anger people who feel that key decisions are taken despite them. In North Manchester the Rochdale local authority as a democratically elected body was able to challenge the decisions of the Strategic Health Authority and forced a referral of the proposals to the 'Independent Reconfiguration Panel' but this panel simply endorsed the original proposals. If we read over this material we might find it difficult to consider that the consultation process could be identified as having any real effect on the final outcome.

One crucial issue in this instance as in many others was the development of options which then become the basis for a consultation exercise. It is difficult to have any kind of expert shaping of governance procedures in relation to major service change without expert and perhaps political input into the construction of options.[3] That said, we have already seen that in the case of health service reconfigurations a crucial aspect of the expert case – bigger is better in relation to secondary health services – was deeply flawed. There were a whole series of background factors in relation to the reorganisation which are detailed in Ruane (2007). These included the impact of the European Working Time Directive on junior hospital doctors' allowable working hours, which had substantial cost implications for the local health economy in Manchester, and concerns in relation to training opportunities in smaller hospitals. An important element in relation to the cost issues was the continued underfunding in relation to health care needs across the whole of Greater Manchester. Ruane concluded that this amounted to an underfunding of some £270 million over a five-year period. And of course the estimates of underfunding are a product of the interaction of accountancy information and a needs formula constructed through the application of social indicators. What this raises is the whole issue of budgeting – of the implication of resource allocation and use in relation to any kind of participatory exercise at any level.

## Consultation in the processes of governance – the example of English Local Strategic Partnerships

The health examples involve what we might consider as 'reactive consultation'. In other words a problem was identified through expert governance and options were developed in order to deal with it. Let us turn to how participation is addressed as part of ongoing processes of governance with special reference to how UK local strategic partnerships work as shapers of what we might consider 'urban futures'. We can begin with a definition:

> A Local Strategic Partnership (LSP) is a single non-statutory, multi-agency body, which matches local authority boundaries, and aims to bring together at a local level the different parts of the public, private, community and voluntary sectors. LSPs are key to tackling deep seated, multi-faceted problems, requiring a range of responses from different bodies. Local partners working through a LSP will be expected to take many of the major decisions about priorities and funding for their local area. (Office of the Deputy Prime Minister, 2001)

The word 'strategic' is significant here. This adjectival derivative of strategy contains elements which together comprise planning for a purpose over the longer term. In local governance 'planning' in the UK we can make a clear distinction between development control – negative feedback – which is clearly tactical, and the long-term specification of objectives in a range of inter-related domains – 'joined up government' in the contemporary jargon – together with the development and implementation of means of achieving them, which is clearly strategic.

The other key term is 'partnership'. This is a highly contested notion. Balloch and Taylor (2001) show the term to be unclear and contradictory: 'Partnership reflects ideals of participatory democracy and equality between partners. It assumes overarching common interests between different players and it can underplay the difficulties in bringing together different interests and different cultures'(2001, p 2). Geddes has been even more critical:

> while the discourse of 'partnership against social exclusion' is one of a holistic response to a multidimensional problem, this is a discourse based on weak rather than strong conceptions of exclusion. With few exceptions, local partnerships studiously avoid engagement with the question of 'who are the excluders?', and with the structural, social, economic and political implications of a thoroughgoing assault on social exclusion, preferring easy assumptions about the possibility of an inclusive society. The dominant practice of local partnership – as opposed to some of its rhetoric – enshrines elitist, neocorporatist or neopluralist principles, and excludes or marginalizes more radical egalitarian and solidaristic possibilities. (2000, p 797)

The historical context in relation to participation which seems characteristic of LSPs is quite accurately described by the consultant engaged by the Environment section of the Newcastle LSP:

> Over the last decade in Newcastle there has been a gradual change concerning participation in decision-making processes. Using Ms Arnstein's ladder [Sherry Arnstein's 1969 ladder of participation] it can be argued that this process of change has involved the provision of information, the introduction of widespread consultation processes, plus various forms of placation [activities which involve conciliation and appeasement of the public]. However, there have been few real examples of partnership involving the wider public in Newcastle. (Energy Intelligence and Marketing Research, 2003)

A web search using the key words 'LSPs, consultation, research methods' yielded an interesting set of approaches being deployed by a range of LSPs. These included the conventional methods of survey research, consultation through public meetings and focus groups. A special version of the latter is the citizens' jury, in which evidence is presented to a group which can cross-examine the witnesses who appear before them somewhat in the mode of a court, although in practice the method has more in common with the practices of a typical public inquiry or parliamentary select committee.

In relation to data construction – the actual making of information – several issues emerge in relation to consultation practices in LSPs. As with other consultative processes, there seem to be generally quite fundamental flaws in relation to the generation of original quantitative data. While perfectly adequate use is made of reasonably reliable secondary data generated by survey and administrative processes, the sampling basis of many consultations seems to be almost non-existent. Questionnaires are distributed and returned on a basis which can best be described as arbitrary. When opinion is sought, as opposed to simple background information being collected, the issues being examined are generally so multi-dimensional as to be inaccessible through any structured quantitative research process.

Qualitative information is generated in a much more interesting set of ways and in terms of quality seems much better suited to representing public views on complex multi-dimensional issues. The emerging preferred method would seem to be focus group extending into citizens' jury forms of collective discussion and deliberation. The former UK Prime Minister Gordon Brown is on record asserting the value of the citizens' jury:

> I'd like to have what are called citizens' juries, where we say to people, look, here is a problem that we are dealing with – today it's housing, it could be drugs or youth services, it could be anti-social behaviour – here's a problem, this is what we are thinking about it, but tell us what you think. And let's look at some of the facts, let's look at some of the challenges. Let's look at some of the options that have been tried in different countries around the world, and then let's together come to a decision about how to solve these problems. This is not sofa government, it's listening to the people. (Speaking on BBC Today Programme, 7 July 2007)

However, there has been very little in the way of methodological examination of the material produced by these approaches. We are of course faced with a fundamental of social reality. Given the nature of the social causal nexus, that the social is made by actors in accord with their purposes and that things are real if they are real in their consequences, then whatever is generated and acted from through qualitative consultative procedures becomes socially real. However, that does not allow us the kind of automatic out in relation to methodological critique which would be available to a relativist in full post-modernist garb. Rather we have to ask how we might consider the products of exercises like citizens' juries to be in some way representative. Of course representation should never be thought of in this sort of context, that is to say in the management of political administration, as something which can be captured in a snapshot survey as a once and for all truth. It must always be something which emerges in social actions, but that said, then what emerges is a product of the actions from which it emerges. So what can we make of what emerges from these sort of consultative processes?

We might compare them with the processes which inform traditional democratic debate and resolution in mass political parties – say, for example, with the local operations of the UK Labour Party as it was as recently as the 1980s. The key mechanisms for deciding on action then were through debate on resolutions. These could originate with an individual member of a local party or trade union branch (although a seconder was always required) who would propose something, argue for it using a mixture of evidence and principles, and if passed on a majority vote it would then move up the hierarchy of party organisation perhaps even to Annual Conference to become party policy. When New 'Labour' decided it was vital to keep politics out of politics it replaced this process with consultation with policy forums. Although the party's website claims that these involve more members in policy formation than ever before, this statement has to be considered in a context where the local organisation of the party has collapsed in many of its heartland areas and membership is at a historic low. Remaining members seem somewhat sceptical as to the influence of the forums on real decision making.

Of course political parties even when they had mass memberships were essentially minority affairs. However, they were open in terms of membership and clear in terms of formation. Even if citizens' juries do have any influence on policy formation – and there is remarkably little evidence of this – then they cannot have the social status of genuine collective political actors. Let us turn to one process in which consultation might be considered to have real consequences – participatory budgeting.

## Deciding on priorities – participatory budgeting

Participatory budgeting is a mode of governance rather than a mode of social science. However, it is closely linked to practices which form the basis of participatory action research – the subject of Chapter Seven. Moreover, while it is a mode of deliberation it is a mode which requires information and much of that information comes from social scientific investigation and reporting. Essentially participatory budgeting involves processes of engagement in resource allocation. It began in Porto Alegre in Rio Grande de Sol in Brazil, a city then under the control of the Workers' Party. The Workers' Party itself is a political force which emerged out of the resistance to military dictatorship in Brazil in the 1960s and 1970s. It is a coalition across the Left in general involving trade unionists and community groups, many of whom encountered liberation theology in the basic Christian communities, and assorted leftists with a variety of backgrounds. Freire, who coined the phrase 'dialogical research' and is a key figure in relation to participatory action research, was one of its founders. So the Workers' Party is a product of groups in civil society and the intersection of civil society with the economy (trade unionists) who coalesced around resistance to an authoritarian and undemocratic state. In this respect it has a good deal in common with the African National Congress (ANC) in South Africa but it has retained more of its civil society character, particularly at the state and municipal levels, than is true of the ANC which has become a rather traditional statist political party.

Participatory budgeting is one of the buzz phrases of the industry – no other word will do – which stands at the intersection of the state and civil society in relation to problems of governance and social inclusion. A simple Google web search employing the term yields a massive set of links including links to elements in this network including both UK central government and the European Union. A key player in the UK is the Participatory Budgeting Unit funded by the Department for Communities and Local Government. Whereas in Porto Alegre participatory budgeting dominated the resource allocation process in the city, in the UK and elsewhere in Europe it has involved relatively marginal sums (marginal in relation to the full budgets of local government and associated quangos). The UK examples given in the document on participatory budgeting prepared by the Neighbourhood Renewal Unit (2006) seem to have had a maximum commitment of less than £1 million and some were risible in scale being of the order of £15,000.

Participatory budgeting is often associated with claims that various initiatives involve 'empowerment' but experience shows that this is seldom if ever the case. Wright et al, in a review of New Deal for Communities, a key area-based initiative (ABI) with a partnership frame and a rhetoric of empowerment, concluded that:

We found that the NDC's potential for 'bottom–up community-led' regeneration is limited.... The practical tasks of partnership, perception management, vision and mainstreaming tightly confine resident activities within government priorities. Furthermore, the thesis of democracy and citizenship requires residents to accept the government's analysis of the causes of deprivation and prevents them from conceiving alternative explanations. Finally, while the existing hierarchy of urban governance severely restricts partnership autonomy, the 'what works' agenda and 'PM' technique enforce the government's own methods of policy development upon communities, thus controlling its day to day working. We conclude that if NDC is a 'bottom–up community-led' programme, it is community led in the sense that the government decides how the community will be involve, why they will be involved, what they will do and how they will do it. (Wright et al, 2006, p 349)

There is no discernible evidence that partnership, consultation, call it what you will, operates anywhere or in any scheme or in any service, in England other than in this fashion.

## Consultation and social science

What then is the role of social science in relation to consultation? One entirely proper role is external inspection and critique – the position of standing outside the tent pissing in. Name it for the dross it is. But is that role enough? If that is all we do then we ignore the role of social science and social scientists in managing processes of consultation and meaningless participation. It is not so much that academics, even many insecurely employed researchers, are engaged themselves in consultative forms of collaboration of very varying quality. That does matter and the legitimacy lent by academic location to processes of management of dissatisfaction is far from a trivial matter. However, rather more important is the role of those with a social science training in the actual processes themselves. Academic disciplinary-based social scientists sometimes seem to forget that in many advanced post-industrial countries we have been turning out thousands of people with social science degrees and/or professional qualifications with a substantial social science content since the early 1970s. They are out there and what are they doing? One of these things is managing processes of consultation/participation within the systems of post-democratic political administration. And they do this at every level. There is more than one former street level community worker with a sociology or related first degree who has taken their career to very senior levels in various agencies of local governance and acted there as a combination of prophet and enforcer of the New Public Management and its modes of popular engagement.

Social science provides the bodies of knowledge which inform the organic intellectuals of the neo-liberal post-democratic state in its interrelationships with contemporary civil society. It provides the techniques from the management of secondary data in the processes of target setting and measurement, through quantitative survey work of varying but usually low degrees of quality, through often rather interesting and well-conducted modes of qualitative engagement right on through to apparently participatory modes surrounded by a rhetoric of empowerment drawn from Freire, who, poor man, must be turning in his grave at this sort of debasement of his ideas and ideals. Is there an alternative? That is to say, is there any possibility of modes of engagement in participatory processes which are not some sort of combination of engagement of potential opposition and legitimation of process with the target of legitimation primarily being those who do these things themselves?

One response would be a rather empty-headed pseudo radicalism which dismisses any sort of role for social science, understood in the terms set by the Gulbenkian Commission as organised empirical knowledge about the social world. Instead we should turn to the authentic and unpolluted popular knowledge of the dispossessed and subordinated themselves, AND ONLY that knowledge. The popularity of that sort of banal nonsense with the lackeys of the socialising state ought to be enough to raise not only our suspicions but also our hackles. There is indeed an alternative and it is one which brings all the tools of social science understood as constituting a body of expertise into dialogue with the knowledges of all others in the social contexts with which we engage in applied social science, with practitioners, with people as the popular masses (to use a good old expression), and including ourselves. The massive proletarianisation of academics in relation to erosion of relative living standards and effective abolition of most of our professional autonomy means that we are now pretty well in this grouping even if we are among the better-paid members of it. But then coal miners always earned good money as well, so no problems there. The issue remains of how we do this sort of thing. That will be the subject of Chapter Seven where we will pass from what has become a sustained whinge of critical protest and discontent into perhaps a more positive set of assertions about how we might do things that are both useful and, in the best sense of the word, scientific as well.

## Notes

[1] There will be some considerable and necessary overlap between issues covered here and those addressed in our examination of action research in Chapter Seven because research which occurs in the context of social change always involves action and has action implications. However, for working purposes we will consider as action research only work which is specifically identified as such while recognising that the theme of participation by research subjects is the underpinning essential of dialogical research practice.

[2] Many consultations undertaken both by private consultancies and by academically based units are thoroughly incompetent and unprofessional – but no citations, no libel suits.

[3] One of the major political victories of the present author in a previous existence as a municipal councillor was, in association with other elected colleagues, to force a change in the patterning of catchment areas for secondary schools in relation to a major reorganisation of secondary education in Gateshead in the north east of England. The original officer proposals would have, in our view, created a set of inner-city schools with a more deprived set of pupils on the one hand, and a set of more suburban schools with the opposite composition on the other. The proposals actually involved the removal of one inner-city primary school's pupils from access to their existing secondary school. Up to this stage the decision-making process lay in the hands of officers and elected council members. When the revised proposals went out to consultation a group of middle-class parents launched a judicial review of the consultation process on the basis of the way in which options had been specified with one preferred. Ultimately this case was dismissed on appeal but the process dragged on and seriously disrupted the reorganisation process. However, this was a much more explicitly political process than is generally the case in relation to consultation exercises in current governance processes.

# SEVEN

# Modelling: representing the world in order to understand how it works

**Model** as verb: To devise a (usually mathematical) model or simplified description of (a phenomenon, system, etc).

**Model** as noun: A simplified or idealised description or conception of a particular system, situation, or process, often in mathematical terms, that is put forward as a basis for theoretical or empirical understanding, or for calculations, predictions, etc; a conceptual or mental representation of something. (OED)

So models are representations of the world but are necessarily simplified. Something has to be left out. Bradley and Schaefer put it like this: 'Modeling is the process of *formalizing* our framework for understanding the world around us by *abstracting* from a reality that is otherwise too complex for us to understand. In fact modeling is the central intellectual method that characterizes most empirical and mathematical approaches to the social sciences' (1998, p 23, original emphasis).

Immediately we have to identify a problem. If we are dealing with social reality composed of complex systems can we ever model by simplifying? If we leave anything out is it not the case that our representation – re-presentation, presentation again – will be inherently flawed because in complex systems everything matters in interaction with everything else and to omit anything means that we will have a model which cannot function to describe a system? So do we give up? Not at all. Let us return to Paul Cilliers' wise remark already quoted in Chapter One:

> The most obvious conclusion drawn from this perspective is that there is no over-arching theory of complexity that allows us to ignore the contingent aspects of complex systems. If something is really complex, it cannot be adequately described by means of a simple theory. Engaging

with complexity entails engagement with specific complex systems. Despite this we can, at least at a very basic level, make general remarks concerning the conditions for complex behaviour and the dynamics of complex systems. Furthermore, I suggest that complex systems can be modelled. (Cilliers, 1998, p ix)

The question is how? In this chapter we will examine the ways in which social science has sought to model reviewing general statistical approaches which derive from regression techniques, the special application of such techniques in econometric approaches, the development of a very different approach through simulation, and the potential of neural net-based representations. The whole point of modelling, despite some wise reservations which we will note here, is to predict. In other words we want tools which might tell us what will happen if we do this. If we think of ourselves as scientists instead of as engineers – and we will return to this distinction as developed by Crutchfield (1992) – then we will perhaps also be concerned with the degree to which our models actually represent the nature of reality itself. As pragmatists, of which more in Chapter Eight, we might just want to know if these methods actually work.

## Statistical modelling

Let us begin then with statistical models. What is a statistical model? Krzanowksi provides us with a very clear account of the nature of specifically statistical modelling:

> Analysis ... assumes inter alia that the available data forms only a subset of all the data that might have been collected, and then attempts to use the information in the available data to make more general statements about either the larger set or about the mechanism that is producing the data. ... In order to make such statements, we need first to abstract the essence of the data-producing mechanism into a form that is amenable to mathematical and statistical treatment. Such a formulation will typically involve mathematical equations that express relationships between measured 'variables' and assumptions about the random processes that govern the outcome of individual measurements. That is the statistical model of the system. Fitting the model to a given set of data will then provide a framework for extrapolating the

results to a wider context or for predicting future outcomes, and can often also lead to an explanation of the system. (1998, p ix)

Statements relating to 'the larger set that is producing the data' are in essence statistical inference. That is to say, they are about what we can say about a population on the basis of a sample from it. Note that while conventional statistical approaches almost always deal with samples, with parts that stand for the whole, in the social sciences we often at least have data about all the cases in a population even if we do not have all possible measurements of those cases. Statements about the mechanism that is producing the data which can be used for generalisation and/or prediction are causal models. In order to predict outcomes we must have some means of relating measurements of elements, usually considered to be variables, which are causal to the outcome, and a description of how they are causal. That description is the model. We should note that despite the usual function of statistical models being to predict, some authorities balk at claiming predictive power. For example Everitt and Dunn were far more cautious, and logically correct, when they stated that: 'In this text ... a model is considered to be a way of simplifying and portraying the structure in a set of data, and does not necessarily imply any causal mechanisms' (1983, p 5).

Immediately from a complexity perspective we encounter a difficulty. In the tradition of Newtonian science the causal power is assigned to 'variables', to disembodied forces existing external to real cases. Discovering causality is understood as a matter of abstracting from cases by measuring variables and describing relationships among them in relation to outcomes specified as values of a variable which is considered to be dependent. Abbott (1988) has challenged this notion of variable as possessing causal power. Ragin expressed the same position:

> For causation, the main contrast is between the conventional view of causation as a contest between individual variables to explain variation in an outcome and the diversity-oriented view that causation is both conjunctural and multiple. In the conventional view, each single causal condition, conceived as an analytically distinct variable, has an independent impact on the outcome. In the diversity-oriented view, causes combine in different and sometimes contradictory ways to produce the same outcome, revealing different paths. (2000, p 15)

Byrne (2002), while continuing to endorse measurement, has argued that the products of measurement should be understood not as variables possessing independent causal powers but rather as 'variate traces' which help us to understand the state of a system. We can take this further if we start not from causes but from effects. In conventional modelling an effect is a value, ideally measured on a continuous ratio scale, of a dependent variable. So, for example, in econometric modelling a model might input a set of variables describing various aspects of economic process, in order to predict the outcome value of a particular operationalisation of the rate of inflation. Models have been developed which derive from the original linear regression technique which is the basis of such prediction but which measure outcome in terms of ordinal or categorical values. The best known in relation to the latter are binary and multi-nomial logistic regression. Here the outcome is defined either in terms of the presence or absence of a category, for example, someone has or has not reoffended (binary), or in terms of a specific value on a categorical variable which has more than a present/absent value available. A good example of the latter would be the cluster membership of secondary schools when clusters have been constituted on the basis of sets of variables describing the achievement of cohorts of children passing through the school.[1]

Although these modifications of regression techniques depend on linear modelling, the actual specification of outcomes in terms of membership of categories has implications which are not generally appreciated by those who employ them. If we think of an outcome in terms of membership of a category then we are understanding outcome not as some sort of incremental change in the value of a continuous variable which stands outside a system, but rather as a description of the whole state of a particular system. This should obviously be the case when the outcome is membership of a category constructed from multiple variate traces through some process of numerical taxonomy but it is just as much the case when we are dealing, for example, with whether or not a person has reoffended after some form of penal programme treatment, the subject of Dyer's interesting research (2006). Here the outcome is membership of the radically different categories of offender versus non-offender. Ragin and Rihoux have noted that

> policy researchers, especially those concerned with social as opposed to economic policy, are often more interested in different kinds of cases and their different fates than they are in the extent of the net causal effect of a variable across a large encompassing population of observations.

After all, a common goal of social policy is to make decisive
interventions, not to move average levels or rates up or down
by some miniscule fraction. (2004, p 18)

Exactly – if we read articles using linear regression techniques in relation
to policy issues we find 'partialling out' in relation to the separate
influence of specific variables on outcomes measured at a ratio scale
level but very little in the way of what this actually means for causation
and even less in terms of policy implications of the findings. Logistic
regression procedures which are commonly used in the literature at
least recognise the qualitative character of an outcome. However, here
causality is represented by 'the' model which fits the data with additional
commentary on the strength of the specific contribution of particular
variables as components of that model. Interaction terms which describe
complex relationships among variables are seldom fitted and almost
never interpreted. Note 'the' model. In other words the overwhelming
tendency is to have a single model which describes causality. The
problem is that in the social world outcomes can, and indeed mostly
do, have causes which are not only complex but also multiple. QCA
with its formulation of 'configurations' – arrays of factors which are
present or absent in crisp set QCA or present to a degree in fuzzy set
QCA – can cope with the real nature of the social world.

One additional problem with conventional statistical modelling
is that it is generally linear in form. In the technical language of the
procedures themselves linear models assume super-position. That is to
say, change in an effect is proportional to change in causal inputs. In
non-linear systems this is not the case. Essentially inputs at given points
can have disproportionate effects. This is always the case with complex
models. There are various approaches to handling non-linearity, some
of which in engineering, for example, work well. However, in the
social sciences things are trickier. For example consider the Merton-
Scholes model for which the authors won the Nobel (actually Swedish
Central Bank) prize for economics in 1997. This model underpinned
the operations of Long Term Capital Management which collapsed
in 1998. This model and others related to it were fundamental to the
flawed risk assumptions which were causal to the great financial and
hence economic crash of June 2007.

There are some interesting examples of non-linear modelling,
particularly in the application of Baysian techniques to issues in health
'economics'. The inverted commas indicate that it is difficult to identify
much in the way of economic theory informing this work. Rather it
is careful quantitative work which examines resource allocation issues.

It certainly deals with economic issues but not within the central theoretical paradigms of neo-classical micro-economic theory, at least not in any fashion discernible to this author. Let us be clear. This is not a criticism of the work, far from it. O'Hagan and Luce's lucid *A primer on Baysian statistics in health economics and outcomes research* (2003) provides an excellent introduction to Baysian methods both in general and in policy contexts. There is a section in this dealing, very usefully, with economic models but the models in question are cost-benefit in character rather than theoretical models in micro-economics. Much of the work in this area has been done by statisticians and economists at the University of Sheffield. Tappenden et al (2004) provide a good example of the genre. This is plainly interesting work but at an impressionistic level at least it sometimes seems to make heavy weather of handling complex non-linear developments by insisting on continuous levels of measurement. That is to say, there is an argument to be had with it in relation to the primacy of understanding change in terms of category change rather than change of degree. Be that as it may, there seems to be considerable potential in these sophisticated approaches which have the great advantage of drawing on real data, in other words engaging with empirical reality, in exploring complex processes and outcomes.

The examples cited above could be considered to be instances of work within the tradition of econometrics, defined by the OED as: 'The branch of statistical theory concerned with the analysis of economic phenomena, in particular the application of statistical methods to economic data'. That seems absolutely fine but we should note that the Wikipedia article covering the topic of econometrics adds to this both a recognition that econometrics is interested in causality in contexts where that cannot be established by experimental methods and that it deals with equilibria. The contentious issue here is the specification of economic systems at whatever level as equilibric. Economic systems as recent events have demonstrated only too clearly are actually far from equilbric. They change in terms of kind not degree, however stable they may appear over the short or medium term. The non-linear Baysian models in health economics do seem to be moving away from the equilibric consensus. It is certainly worth noting that Tinbergen, one of the founders of modern econometrics, was interested in radical social change and its consequences, which concern derived from his lifetime commitment to social democracy.

There is one further example of statistical modelling which requires attention here. That is multi-level modelling, a set of approaches which displays one great virtue but in practice seems to be constrained by the general limitations of linear modelling as a whole. Multi-level modelling starts from a recognition of something about social reality which jumps out from our data sets – the world is hierarchical.[2] Goldstein put it like this: 'the multilevel modelling approach views the population structure as of potential interest in itself, so that a sample designed to reflect that structure is not merely a matter of saving costs as in traditional survey design but can be used to collect and analyse data about the higher level units in the population' (1995, p 5).

That is an important point but it is not enough taken on its own. We have to ask: what is the nature of the elements in the hierarchy? In the classic illustration of multi-level modelling the elements would be individual pupils and the levels of the educational system which 'contain' them – classes, schools, LEAs and so on. Multi-level modelling, in common with all analytical techniques, treats these elements as 'bundles' of variables and focuses on the significance of the variables at the different levels. It is true, and this is a major advantage, that multi-level modelling does facilitate exploration of interaction effects – Goldstein's example (1995) being exploration of the extent to which schools differ for different kinds of students. However, the approach is still variable centred and results in models which treat the elements in the hierarchy as mechanistic atoms moved in a probabilistic way under the influence of variables – an approach essentially identical to that of statistical mechanics.

Certainly multi-level modelling deserves serious attention in relation to applied social research but it is not a panacea and without modification it is seriously flawed in relation to the way in which it represents social reality. Duncan et al sum the situation up very well:

> [W]e do not wish to over-valorize the technique as it is still open to many of the criticisms that may have been made of traditional quantitative methods. It remains crude, reductionist, and mechanistic and does not authentically capture the complex way in which health-related behaviour is embedded in the flow of situated daily routines. Nevertheless, within these limitations, multilevel modelling techniques constitute a considerable improvement on existing quantitative methodologies. Furthermore, they offer the possibility of delivering a reconciliation with qualitative research. Since they consider both the general and specific they can reveal the broad patterns of health related behaviour whilst also disclosing the situations in which these patterns do not hold. (Duncan et al, 1996, p 820)

To conclude this discussion of statistical modelling we can say that it certainly has its uses and that moves, particularly Baysian moves, which address non-linearity and the multi-level (which in complexity terminology we would express as nested systems) of social reality, are moves in the right direction. However, it remains predominantly linear, trapped in a view of causality which defines effects as incremental changes in disembodied continuous variables rather than state changes in whole systems, and too often fails to recognise that modelling of complex and emergent social reality is not a second-class substitute for experimental approaches to a seldom available simplicity. Other than in the all too seldom attention paid to interaction, conventional modelling cannot really handle complex causation and the emphasis on 'the' model which fits the data is a serious distraction from the generality of multiple causes of interesting and social significant outcomes in the social world in general but in the domains of interest to applied social science in particular.

## Simulation – restricted complexity in action

> Simulation: The technique of imitating the behaviour of some situation or process (whether economic, military, mechanical, etc) by means of a suitably analogous situation or apparatus, esp. for the purpose of study or personnel training. (OED)

This is the third meaning of the word 'simulation' given by the OED. It is worth noting that both the other meanings contain implications of false representation! The Wikipedia article dealing with simulation identifies it in terms of imitation but with the implication that is an imitation which works in the same way as the thing being simulated. The key to simulation in the social sciences is the availability of computing resources which enable researchers to process lots of things very quickly. Simulation is modelling but not all modelling is simulation. Specifically, as Troitzsch (1998, p 27) points out, simulation has to be distinguished from the forms of mathematical modelling which can be resolved analytically. Those can be resolved elegantly (as mathematicians understand elegance) in formal terms. Simulations attempt to deal with the kind of situation in which we have to have recourse to the crude (as mathematicians understand crudity) approaches of iterative numerical solutions. If we come to simulation by way of mathematics that is what it is. However, Troitzsch, following Ostrom (1988), suggests that there is another way to understand simulation. That is as natural language descriptions translated into programming systems. Considered like this, simulation offers a third approach to description of the world which is different both from formal mathematical representation and from natural language. We should recall that Hayles (1999) called this mode the Platonic Forehand and distinguished it from the Platonic Backhand of the experimental method which has dominated science since Plato. Her discussion is focused on the use of simulation in science. That is to say, she identifies it with attempts to discover the underlying structure and processes which together constitute reality itself. Crutchfield is more sanguine, noting that:

> the epistemological problem of nonlinear modeling can be crudely summarized as the dichotomy between engineering and science. As long as a representation is effective for a task, an engineer does not care what it implies about underlying mechanisms; to the scientist though the implication makes all the difference in the world. The engineer is certainly concerned with minimizing implementation cost ... but the scientist presumes, at least, to be focused on what the model means vis-à-vis natural laws. The engineering view of science is that it is mere data compression; scientists seem to be motivated by more than this. (Crutchfield, 1992, p 8)

The engineering conception is essentially that of pragmatism, a philosophical tradition which we will discuss in more detail in Chapter Eight but which we can very crudely summarise here as saying what matters is that it works and it doesn't matter how it works. Certainly some economic modellers have asserted this position. So we have understandings of simulation which on the one hand see it as a way of understanding the structure of reality which would then allow us to intervene in that reality through technology, and on the other are not concerned with scientific causality but only with practical predictive value. It is important to deal with these fundamental issues which tend to be either ignored or elided before turning to simulation in application. We will return to fundamentals at the end of this discussion but for now let us consider how simulation approaches are actually used in applied social science.

One longstanding and entirely useful approach *in a period when there is no radical social change* is that of micro-simulation. The International Micro-Simulation Association defines this method thus:

Microsimulation (a.k.a. microanalytic simulation) is a modelling technique that operates at the level of individual units such as persons, households, vehicles or firms. Within the model each unit is represented by a record containing a unique identifier and a set of associated attributes – eg, a list of persons with known age, sex, marital and employment status; or a list of vehicles with known origins, destinations and operational characteristics. A set of rules (transition probabilities) are then applied to these units leading to simulated changes in state and behaviour. These rules may be deterministic (probability $= 1$), such as changes in tax liability resulting from changes in tax regulations, or stochastic (probability $<=1$), such as chance of dying, marrying, giving birth or moving within a given time period. In either case the result is an estimate of the outcomes of applying these rules, possibly over many time steps, including both total overall aggregate change and, crucially, the distributional nature of any change. .... Given the emphasis on changes in distribution, microsimulation models are often used to investigate the impacts on social equity of fiscal and demographic changes (and their interactions). Modelling of the distribution of traffic flows over a street network is another increasingly important use of the approach. (www.microsimulation.org/IMA/What%20is%20microsimulation.htm)

Micro-simulations may be static in which case the behaviour of the units is assumed to remain static over time, or dynamic in which case behaviour can change. Examples of micro-simulation in practice include Pensym2, a dynamic micro-simulation deployed by the UK Department for Work and Pensions to simulate the income of pensioners. It is important to recognise that micro-simulations are tied to empirical reality through the use of real data describing real cases, for Pensym2 this includes for example data from the British Household Panel Survey. An interesting example of the significance of assumptions in relation to dynamic micro-simulations is provided by arguments based on micro-simulations in relation to the actual tax yield achieved by increasing the rates of tax on higher incomes. This necessarily involves assumptions about the behaviour of those in receipt of such incomes in relation to tax avoidance. That in turn requires assumptions about the political and legislative capacity for minimising such tax avoidance both within states, by for example ensuring that it is not possible to transfer what should be income to capital gains taxed at a lower rate, and internationally, by aggressive targeting of tax havens. The recent willingness of the Federal German government to use its secret service to attack the tax haven activities of Lichtenstein and Switzerland is an interesting move in that direction. The point is that the yield depends both on the actions of tax payers and the actions of tax-collecting governments and the results of any analysis using a micro-simulation depend on assumptions in relation to both sets of agents.

There is one major qualification to make in relation to micro-simulations. That of course relates to the assumption sets which underpin even dynamic models. These can cope quite well with the conditions that prevail in a complex social system during the 'torus attractor' phase of behaviour of that system. That is to say, they can cope with systems which while not equilibric do not stray so far from equilibrium that they undergo phase shifts. When there is a phase shift, as is the case in relation to the 2010 ongoing world financial and consequent economic crisis, then all bets are off and things are very different. And that is not even considering the impact of volcanic eruptions and the long-term consequences of those![3]

The other main simulation approach which has implications for applied social science is agent-based modelling (ABM). Drogoul and Ferber define this:

> Multi-agent simulations are used primarily to represent situations in which there are many individuals each with complex and different behaviours and to analyze the global structures that emerge as a result of the individual's interactions. The purpose of such simulation is to take into account both quantitative and qualitative properties of the situation, as opposed to traditional simulations which only link properties to quantitative parameters. (1994, p 130)

As Drogoul and Ferber (1994, p 31) explain, in a multi-agent simulation the model does not consist of a set of simultaneous equations but rather is composed of entities including the agents, passive objects, the general environment defined as the topological space in which agents operate around objects, and the communications which enable relationships among agents. A key aspect of multi-agent simulations is that there is emergence. Things develop in the system which are not explicable in terms of the properties of the entities but rather arise from interactions among them. However, this approach – Hayles' Platonic Forehand – in which complexity emerges from simplicity has been characterised by Morin (2006) as constituting only 'restricted complexity'. This is important. It is not that some aspects of social reality cannot be legitimately understood in terms of emergence of the complex from simple interactions, but rather that only a restricted set of aspects of reality can be understood in those terms. Those like Holland (1998) who assert vigorously to the contrary are just plain wrong.

There are an increasing number of examples of the use of agent-based models in applied social science. An example in relation to criminology is provided by Bosse and Gerritsen (2010), who examine the interaction of 'offenders, targets and guardians' in relation to spatial 'hot spots' for crime using an agent-based approach. Oswaldo et al (2007) present an example of an agent-based approach in relation to ecological management, an important policy area which has been explored often by this kind of approach. The best recourse for applied social scientists interested in social simulation is to the online *Journal of Artificial Societies and Social Simulation* (JASSS).

An important distinction can be drawn in ABM between those models which simply state the properties and relations of agents by fiat – that is have no empirical basis – and those which incorporate real empirical information as all micro-simulations must. Alam et al (2007) draw out the implications of this difference:

> Evidence-driven agent based modelling constrains agent and mechanism design by independent evidence about the behaviour of the actors represented by the agents. This approach has been a niche activity in the social simulation research. In the year to May 2007, only a single paper (Xiong and Ma, 2007) in which agent behaviour was built on descriptions of specific and identifiable actors has been published in this journal. And the number published in the whole nearly eleven-year history of JASSS is certainly less than ten. JASSS' sister journal, *Computational and Mathematical Organization Theory* has not reported a single evidence-driven agent based model in at least the past four years.... Experience and knowledge of the social simulation community indicates that the scant presence of evidence-driven agent based models in the leading journals in the field is a fair reflection of the balance of social simulation research. We also note that to produce such models requires the modellers to engage deeply with the evidence and frequently to go back to expert informants as issues are identified in the course of the

modelling process. This is a much more time consuming process than the implementation of models driven by prior theoretical considerations or developed *ad hoc* on the basis of introspection and/or speculation. Consequently, the rate of production of models (and therefore articles) produced per author is necessarily smaller than the rate of production of theoretical or methodological papers. (Alam et al, 2007)

This distinction is extremely important. Alam and his co-authors develop their argument in relation to issues surrounding AIDS in a fashion which moves towards participatory engagement in the context of a real social problem. As they say, this is unusual in relation to ABM. Their approach would seem to have real potential as applied social science.

That said, there remains a fundamental problem. Agent-based modelling is a technique which remains within the boundaries of what Morin has called 'restricted complexity' in contrast to the 'general complexity' which is the most appropriate mode in relation to most of the social world.

Restricted complexity made it possible important advances in formalization, in the possibilities of modeling, which themselves favor interdisciplinary potentialities. But one still remains within the epistemology of classical science. When one searches for the 'laws of complexity', one still attaches complexity as a kind of wagon behind the truth locomotive, that which produces laws. A hybrid was formed between the principles of traditional science and the advances towards its hereafter. Actually, one avoids the fundamental problem of complexity which is epistemological, cognitive, paradigmatic. To some extent, one recognizes complexity, but by decomplexifying it. In this way, the breach is opened, then one tries to clog it: the paradigm of classical science remains, only fissured. In opposition to reduction, complexity requires that one tries to comprehend the relations between the whole and the parts. The knowledge of the parts is not enough, the knowledge of the whole as a whole is not enough, if one ignores its parts; one is thus brought to make a come and go in loop to gather the knowledge of the whole and its parts. Thus, the principle of reduction is substituted by a principle that conceives the relation of whole-part mutual implication. (Morin, 2006, p 7)

Essentially the problem with ABM is that it sees emergence only in terms of developments which occur from simple interaction. There are attempts to move beyond this and some, primarily those like Alam and his colleagues who have a real empirical engagement, are fully aware of this issue. One way to express the problem is to say that ABM cannot deal with the Durkheimian social, with a social reality which has an existence over and beyond the elements within the system. We must not fall into the error of holism. We need to consider elements in systems but while individual entities are an important set of those entities there are also sub-systems and nested/intersecting systems. All of these along with the system as a whole, however defined, have causal potential in relation to outcomes.

## Data mining and beyond

Data mining is not modelling although it is often dealt with in texts which describe social modelling procedures in general. In essence 'data mining' is a generic term describing the search for patterns in large data sets. The development of computing technology has made this an important activity for two reasons. First, very large amounts of data are now held in electronic form. Massive amounts of data can be mined for patterns. Second, the development of computing power means that ever more sophisticated classificatory and networking techniques can be deployed to search for those patterns. The two main objectives of data mining are the establishment of typologies, of classifications which assign cases to kinds which can then be targeted in particular ways, and the description of networks of connections among cases. The first is of prime interest to marketing, the second is important inter alia for surveillance by security agents. Garson (1998) gives a good account of the potential of data mining approaches in applied social science.

One possible objective of data mining, which informed for example Dyer's work (2006), is the tracing of the trajectories of cases through time through systems. Dyer worked on people passing through a system intended to divert people with mental health problems who had committed offences from custody. She established a data base recording characteristics of cases on entry, all processes through which they passed, and some exit characteristics. She then cluster analysed at time one on entry, at subsequent time points through the process, and on exit. She was therefore able to describe different trajectories of cases through the system and relate these to outcomes in terms of reoffending and the nature of any reoffending. This approach, particularly when coupled with QCA-style methods of establishing causal configurations, is a quantitative form of process tracing. It would seem to have very considerable potential in relation to any application of social science which is concerned with relating the trajectories of cases through social care, educational and health systems to outcomes, although there are ethical issues which arise in relation to these sorts of detailed explorations of large volumes of personal data. Marketing uses seem not to be too bothered by these and anonymity should be enough but the issues cannot be disregarded.

The reference to process tracing is an indication of the causal method which has been proposed as an alternative to modelling throughout this book. That is to say, what has been suggested is the retroductive exploration of causation through a combination of careful process tracing through case histories and systematic comparison of the trajectories established, using for example QCA, in order to establish configurations, even if in the first instance exploratory configurations, which enable us to understand what has been the causal path (including of course descriptions of what complex combinations have 'worked' in complex social interventions) towards given outcomes.

## Conclusion

Modelling is important in applied social science but there are real issues in relation to its use. All forms of quantitative modelling currently available to us have limitations. Sometimes these limitations, as with conventional regression modelling limited both by its linearity and its reification of variables, are so considerable that the models have only very restricted value in practice. They do not have no value, but it is seldom as more than a tool in exploration. Micro-simulation works quite well, subject to arguments about specification of dynamic regulation, within the boundaries of 'much the same sort of thing going on' systems. Agent-based models, particularly that class of ABMs which incorporate real empirical data, have considerable potential but cannot as yet get beyond the stage of 'restricted complexity'. The overall verdict must be some useful tools here but no ultimate resolution. That said, all forms of model in relation to any kind of complex social process are superior to randomised controlled trials. This is because they all, even if only in the form of interaction terms inserted into regression equations, can make some sort of allowance for complexity and emergence.

One issue remains and we will expand on it in Chapter Nine but it must be raised here. Models are useful if they are deployed with a very clear sense of their limitations. They are worse than useless, that is to say they are actually negative in their impact, if they are asserted as some proper 'scientific' account of complex social reality which should be the basis of social interventions and/or the general approach of governance to policy and practice. The most pernicious example here is provided by the absurd and erroneous claims of mathematical economic models as deployed in financial affairs. These were not only wrong, in that they could not cope with phase shift and non-linear transformation of state: they have actually provoked a major world crisis.

That issue is not just a matter of scientific accuracy and adequacy. It is profoundly ideological. The assertion of the rationales of restricted complexity, most elegantly expressed perhaps by Von Hayek in his Nobel Prize Lecture (1974), has been fundamental to the intellectual discourses of neo-liberalism. The mess we are in is due to greed, incompetence and cowardice on the part of social democratic governments but it is also in part a consequence of very bad science making claims that were downright wrong. There is more to good science than saying just that. We need practice as well. Nonetheless, all that said, modelling has its place. We must not throw out the baby with the bathwater.

## Notes

[1] Cluster analysis is the term for a generic set of techniques which utilise quantitative measurements of cases to assign the cases to categories. See Everitt and Dunn (1983) for a full account. They are one of the major ways in which data can be used to constitute taxonomies.

[2] This is an illustration of the obduracy of the world. Contemporary epistemology worries deeply about how we know the world. Sometimes we should think about how the world makes itself known to us.

[3] The author is currently working in his brother's spare room in Melbourne, Australia, when he should be back in the north east of England but UK airspace is closed to all traffic.

EIGHT

# **Acting**

**Action research**, chiefly *Sociol.*, research which leads to
the establishment and implementation by project researchers
of methods designed to alleviate the (esp. social) problems
under review; hence **action researcher** (OED)

The OED defines action research in terms of objective – it is not
about contemplative understanding of the social world but rather is
about changing it. That is to say, it fits the specification Marx made
in Thesis XI on Feuerbach – the point is not merely description but
transformation. If we think of research as intimately associated with
transformative action then we have to develop a radically different
methodological frame of reference and a set of research approaches
which fit with that frame of reference. Unlike the experimenter we
are not abstracting from the world in order to establish how it works
so that we can develop knowledge which can be applied elsewhere
in order to achieve desired outcomes. In that mode the knowledge
exists separately from context and can serve as the basis for action in
general. It is nomothetic. Does that mean that all action research is
inherently ideographic? That is to say, can it only describe the unique
and specific instance and that it lacks any potential for the development
of transferable knowledge? The argument here will be very much to
the contrary. We can develop transferable knowledge based on careful
process tracing and systematic case comparison but in the best realist
tradition we have to see that knowledge as bounded in terms of the
range of its possible application. Determining, which in this usage means
delimiting, the boundaries of the range of transferable application of
any processual and causal knowledge will be one of the key elements
of the action research process.

Let us consider an extension of our definition of the nature of action
research.

*Action Research* is social research carried out by a team
that encompasses a   professional action researcher and
the members of an organization, community or network
('stakeholders') who are seeking to improve the participants'

155

situation. AR promotes broad participation in the research process and supports action leading to a more just, sustainable, or satisfying situation for the stakeholder. (Greenwood and Levin, 2007, p 3)

So we find another aspect to action research: the necessary inclusion of the social actors naturally present in the social context in which the research is being carried out. Note that both the OED and Greenwood and Levin agree on the necessarily progressive character of action research (which is not at all a universal position). What has been added with the second definition is first the engagement of the other already present social actors in the research process itself – the essence of participatory research. This is not simply participation in governance. It is participation in the construction of knowledge. Second we now have the researchers engaged in the social action. They are not separate but in the thick of things. We have to go back to Freeman and Sherwood (1970) or to commentaries like that of Payne to find action research described in terms which separate the action and research processes:

In its strictest sense action-research is a process which utilizes sociological ideas and research techniques to formulate and subsequently, continuously to monitor, evaluate and modify actions to a specific problem. The separation of research from action and the reduction of research to a subsidiary role, which was evident in the CDP programme is not action-research. (Payne 1981, p 178)

Payne contrasts the CDP (UK Community Development Projects) approach with earlier action research projects conducted by the Tavistock Institute in industrial settings where the researchers accepted the terms of reference for the project set by sponsors who were the employing firms and agencies and stood back from the process. For Payne, as for Freeman, if research is to be able to produce generalisations then it must not mix the action and research processes.

The central point is that almost all contemporary discussions of action research would insist, completely contrary to Freeman and Payne, that it necessarily involves an integration of action and research processes. However, a central issue remains – if research and action are mixed and in consequence research as it is conducted is itself action (particularly, of course, participatory research in which the existing social actors in context are themselves producers of knowledge), then how can we in any way generate knowledge transferable out of specific context? We will proceed to examine how action researchers who have seriously considered this issue have attempted to deal with it. The general conclusion will be that most have not done so in a satisfactory fashion but have instead taken refuge in relativist positions of very varying degrees of sophistication. Only the most developed of these will be considered here. Many consist of little more than a simple re- or denunciation of traditional research approaches as oppressive, masculine, colonialist, and so on. This will not do. At least those who take that route recognise that there is an issue to be confronted, which is a lot more than can be said for those who are now attempting to assert an experimental scientism as the methodological mode for applied social research. However, we do need to have some basis for our knowledge claims. It is pertinent to note that Freire, who is often invoked by re/ denunciators of traditional research processes in a woolly and imprecise fashion, insisted on a *dialogue* in social practices. Everybody teaches and everybody learns. This certainly requires a respect for non-traditional and popular forms of knowledge and their expression on the one hand. On the other it equally requires a respect for knowledge created in the mode of science broadly defined.[1] In a dialogue both parties have something to say.

All that said, the main purpose of this chapter is not to criticise action research methodologies but rather to propose a solution to the problem through the development of process tracing and systematic case comparison as methods, with both set within a complex realist methodological framework. There remains one central issue. We can identify it plainly in terms of the question, whose side are we on?

> Participatory research promotes empowerment through the development of common knowledge and critical awareness which are suppressed by the dominant knowledge system. Participatory research is also about praxis. It recognizes the inseparability of theory and practice and critical awareness of the personal-political dialectic. Participatory research is grounded in an explicit political stance and clearly articulated value base – social justice and the transformation of those contemporary sociocultural structures and processes that support degeneration of participatory democracy, injustice and inequality. (Sohng, 1995, p 4)

Critical realism as proposed by Bhaskar (1979) has no problem with this engagement with praxis. Simple scientific realism would stand back from it. The position taken here will be a critical engagement with the rhetorical aspects of participatory action research which nonetheless is grounded in a commitment to transformative social practices. Sohng's account of the background to participatory research is coherent and thorough but her assertion that 'The concerns and claims of participatory research also bear a striking resemblance to the historical values and mandates that shaped social work in the United States' (1995, p 3) is only one side of the story. While there was always a radical tradition in some aspects of social work practice it has been far outweighed by the role of social work as part of the social control mechanisms of a dominant social order – social work and to a considerable extent community work in practice are both primarily about the maintenance of social order. Of course the maintenance of that very order is often desired precisely by the disempowered themselves, in that individualistic anomic actions create a state of social chaos which makes poor people's lives a deal worse – the essential position of the realistic criminology of the 1980s. Nonetheless we have to recognise that participatory action research just as much as participatory governance is not by any means necessarily emancipatory. Perhaps a recognition of the dominated character of social researchers' own role as the outsourced labourers of the evidence-based state helps us here. The proletarianisation of the academy and academics goes a good way towards demystifying the character of our own enmeshed roles as technical rather than traditional intellectuals. That should help us to clear the air on the nature but also the potential of our own work understood as a social practice.

## The methodological arguments

The literature on the methodological basis of action research is immense, varied and to a certain extent contradictory. This reflects the tension between consensual action research developed primarily in organisational settings and transformational agendas developed in relation to community-based interventions. It also reflects an issue as old as western philosophy itself, which in brutal summary might be expressed as the contempt of the philosophers for the demos. That said, there is one common point of agreement. Action research stands against the positivist norms of the hypothetico-deductive method which we can see represented almost in ideal form in the triple blind randomised controlled trial. It is well worth noting that one very strong exposition of this position can be found in the work of those with an engineering/management background who are associated with Checkland's arguments for a soft systems understanding of organisational process and objectives (see Checkland, 2000). That is to say, technologists – not 'mere artisans' but those who, like the architect Gaudi, apply scientific knowledge to practical purposes – reject in practice the methodological position which is asserted as the basis of that very understanding by those whe argue for *the* scientific method. We have already encountered an elision around the scientific method in Chapter Seven in relation to the generally tacit acceptance of the validity of simulation as a description of reality – something which, as Crutchfield (1992) if not many others has recognised, is fundamentally antithetical to hypothesis testing based science. Here we have an outright rejection. The issue is what alternatives have been proposed by those who have given serious attention to the methodological foundations of action research.

There seem to be two positions which have been adopted although often they are expressed simultaneously. Let us be clear – it is perfectly possible to take both of the views which are about to be delimited. The insistence on analytical purity in the Anglo-Saxon tradition is misconceived in relation to a complex world. We are not in the business of developing purity of school but rather of getting together a way of working which does the job. And to say that is to express the essence of one of the methodological positions which action researchers have taken up – pragmatism. Greenwood and Levin (2007) develop their discussion of epistemological foundations of action research in relation to an endorsement of the pragmatist programme as it has developed since its original 19th-century formulation. A distinction is often drawn between the common English use of 'pragmatic' and the philosophical content of 'pragmatism'. To the extent that 'pragmatic' is understood in terms of the dismissal of any theoretical foundations for knowledge then that distinction is appropriate. However, pragmatism remains essentially about outcomes. Of course given the significance of educational practice as a domain for action research the turn to pragmatism is often associated with an endorsement of the work of Dewey, who developed an educational programme for the enhancement of democratic action in society as a whole. This is entirely fair enough, so far as it goes, but it does not go far enough. The problem is that the pragmatic turn is a turn away from any kind of non-contextual knowledge, however limited the bounding of application of that knowledge. We lose structure when we take this turn.

This vital point is rather well illustrated by Greenwood and Levin's synthesis, more or less after Rorty, of pragmatism with the 'practical philosophy' developed by Gadamer in *Truth and method* (2004). We have already encountered elements of 'practical philosophy' in our discussion of phronesis in Chapter One and we will develop an argument with it in this chapter. First let us identify the essential elements of Greenwood and Levin's position. They note Rorty's:

> ... repudiation of what he calls 'the epistemological project'. Though Rorty defines this project in a variety of ways, at base he means to criticize modern philosophy's pretensions to create a system of analysis that would permit philosophers to distinguish between 'correct' and 'incorrect' knowledge – a view of philosophy as a kind of self-appointed supreme court of knowledge to which everyone would have to submit.... Rorty counters the epistemological project by distinguishing between *systematic philosophy* as the search for an absolute reality determined by philosophical experts and *edifying philosophy* which he views as an ongoing conversation involving methods and debates that attempt to bring people into some kind of state of communicative clarity. (Greenwood and Levin, 2007, p 71)

To this Greenwood and Levin add an endorsement of Gadamer's version of the hermeneutic turn which emphasises the provisional and never completed character of interpretation in the constitution of the social. Gadamer also serves as the basis for Carr's (2006) rejection of the very search for a methodological foundation for action research at all. Carr outlines his project as drawing:

> in Gadamer's powerful vindication of the contemporary relevance of practical philosophy in order to show how, by embracing the idea of 'methodology', action research functions to sustain a distorted understanding of what practice is. The paper concludes by outlining a non-methodological view of action research whose chief task is to promote the kind of historical self-consciousness that the development of practice presupposes and requires. (2006, p 421)

Carr outlines what he admits is a rather partial history of action research[2] and concludes that:

> while this way of writing the history of action research undoubtedly shows why we now debate questions about the kind of methodology on which action research should

be erected, it does nothing to illuminate the logically prior question of why we now assume that a mode of inquiry concerned with the development of practice needs to be erected on the basis of a research methodology at all. (2006, p 421)

He takes us through a thorough and important discussion of the classical distinction between techne and praxis, turning like Flybverg to phronesis as the appropriate mode of engagement with the social world. The whole argument is profoundly influenced by Gadamer's dismissal of the possibility of a science-based social science which in any way stands outside the experience of our own immersion in the world. Carr's conclusion is worth reporting in full:

Interpreted in this way, action research would no longer be understood as a social science 'research paradigm' that can achieve what conventional social scientific research has conspicuously failed to achieve. Rather it would be regarded as nothing other than a post-modern manifestation of the pre-modern Aristotelian tradition of practical philosophy. As such, it would be a mode of inquiry whose chief task was to reclaim the sphere of praxis from its modern assimilation to the sphere of techne – by fostering the kind of dialogical communities in which open conversation can be protected from the domination of a research methodology. This is not an easy task to achieve. Within the dominant culture of modernity, the concepts of phronesis and praxis have been rendered marginal and now face something approaching total obliteration. But it is only by seeking to ensure that the void created by the demise of practical philosophy will not be filled by a research methodology that action research will be able to defend the integrity of praxis against all those cultural tendencies that now undermine and degrade it. (2006, p 434)

Like Flybverg, Carr takes us back to Aristotle for an account of praxis. This of course requires a major body swerve in terms of intellectual history past the towering figures of Hegel and in particular Marx. There is little to quarrel with in relation to the notion of praxis as intended towards the achievement of the good but much if we think of this in relation to the classical conception of the good life. Not only was this very much an exclusionary exercise – the practice of philosophy as praxis was only accessible to a tiny exploitative elite – but it operated entirely outwith the enormous body of understanding generated by modern science understood in its widest sense. The distinction made in Chapter One between the classical conception of techne and the modern notion of technology is illustrative here. We can apply science. The Greeks could not, or certainly could not in terms of the massive extension of the range of human possibilities open to us. Although Gadamer was not classified as a Nazi sympathiser at the end of the Second World War[3] much of his programme derives from his relationship with Heidegger and the notion of '*dasein*' – with the renunciation of modernity and the assertion of the need to immerse in the world. The phenomenological programme's insistence on a return to the things themselves has served as a necessary corrective to the overly abstractive tendency of reductionist science but it can be taken far too far. If we accept Freire's understanding of a dialectical relationship in the research process we certainly will not be prepared to abandon the notion of a realist scientific programme as part of the action research exercise. Carr makes an interesting argument but by counterposing an essentially positivist version of science against practical philosophy he ignores the way in which a bounded and cautious realism can bring science, understood in the broadest terms, into the arena of action. We do indeed need a methodological programme in action research but we need one that neither seeks to impose a positivist straitjacket on practice nor abandons the tasks of scientific description and hunting for causes as the research part of action research. The argument here is, of course, that complex realism offers the possibility of precisely such a methodology.

An important move in the direction of complex realism is provided by Burns (2006, 2007). Essentially Burns makes a complexity move by explicitly deploying the vocabulary and frame of reference of systems theory in relation to the processes and objectives of action research. There is much to commend this turn but it is not fully realised in that Burns, while seriously engaging with methodological issues, does not fully develop the implications of complexity in relation to complex causation. His examples are generally about unintended consequences of single factors in chains of systematic processes. So he describes how a whole systems approach to the trajectory of elderly patients through from domestic competence to high dependency care identified how this derives from catheterisation while in hospital for what are supposed to be short stays in relation to health needs. This is entirely convincing and appropriate but it is not engaging with complex and multiple causation, although his account of the way in which the Welsh government is managing its equivalent of NDC — that is by allowing much more local autonomy and developing an evaluation strategy which fits well with the idea of process tracing — demonstrates the potential for work which might address complex causation.

The proof of course is in the doing and the remainder of this chapter will be devoted to the translation of the complex realist methodological framework into the practice of action research and the learning of lessons from that practice.

## Acting and research and learning and translating – the doing of and learning from action research

What are the roles of action in action research? Note that plural – 'roles'. So far our discussion of the application of social research has focused on research as a generator of knowledge which can be somehow abstracted from the real social contexts and processes within which the research is being conducted. We have emphasised, indeed asserted, that it is crucial to delimit the boundaries of application of any abstraction, but we have taken limited generalisation to be the task of applied social research. It absolutely is *one* of the tasks but not the only one. The implications of this can best be developed in relation to a real example and here we can draw on the author's own engagement in the 1970s as a researcher on the North Tyneside CDP. The CDPs had been established by the Home Office, the English (and then Welsh as well) department of state historically concerned with the management of social order. A senior Home Office civil servant had encountered both the Ford Foundation research projects described by Marris and Rein (1967) and successor developments under the aegis of the Johnson administration's Great Society programme and the 'War on Poverty'. Urban disorder in the US in the 1960s seemed to prefigure the possibility of similar disorder in UK cities. The Conservative politician Enoch Powell had made his infamous speech in which he declared in typical style that, like the ancient Roman, he saw the Tiber foaming with blood.[4] The threat came in consequence of large-scale immigration in the 1950s and early 1960s into the UK from former territories of the British Empire, which for the first time introduced a large 'non-white' population into what had previously been understood, however erroneously, to be an ethnically homogeneous white population. In fact the only rivers of blood which flowed through any UK cities flowed through Belfast and Derry in ethno-cultural conflicts between two populations – catholic and protestant – which are distinctive solely in terms of religious observance and otherwise are ethnically identical.

Actually the Home Office was quite prescient in recognising the profound implications for social order and governance of massive social change, even if when the CDPs were established there was no real sense of the actual character of the driver of that change – extensive deindustrialisation in the sense of loss of industrial employment consequent both on globalisation and on the increasing technical efficiency of industrial production and transport systems. In any event CDP projects were established with two teams appointed to each project – an action team employed by the relevant local authority but located within what after local government reorganisation in line with the Bains Report (1972) was the central Chief Executive's department rather than any specific service department, and a research team located in a university or polytechnic. The CDP action teams were a very early example both of an ABI and of neighbourhood-level joined-up governance. Their task was to intervene, with the general model being that of community organising. Some reference was made to the work of Saul Alinsky's identification of the role of 'community organiser', a role undertaken on his way to the White House by Barak Obama. In any event the task of the action teams was to develop organisation and participation in neighbourhoods where this was thought to have been eroded by social change. It was evident although not explicit that UK central government senior civil servants considered that the existing structures of local government were not functioning properly in relation to deprived neighbourhoods. Equally they considered that conflict was both inevitable and functional in relation to CDP action initiatives. However, this was not spelled out to the local authorities concerned. Conflict was an inevitable aspect of CDP work.[5]

The role of the research teams was much less well defined. There seemed to be a kind of assumption that the teams would function as external evaluators but even that was fuzzy in part because the only UK precedent for the CDP style of intervention was provided by the Educational Priority Area (EPA) interventions established in response to suggestions made in the very influential Plowden Report (1967). EPA research teams had engaged with their action teams in a support role and CDP teams were more or less expected to do the same. In North Shields we resolved this issue immediately by agreeing that the research and action teams would function as a single team with researchers engaging in action and action team members engaging in research. This concordat reflected the fact that both research and action team members were all people with social science degrees and experience of community action and all in their late 20s or early 30s. The confusion between the accountability of action team members to the local authority managerial structure and the 'academic freedom' of the researchers was often very useful in relation to controversial practices.[6]

In this way of working, research immediately acquired a 'service' function. It took on what Payne (1981) labelled as a 'subordinate role'. Actually that label is wrong. It implies that research and action can somehow be separated and ranked. The mode of working employed in North Shields involved research being conducted to inform action, as part of action, and as a description of action. The first two elements were 'service research', the last was the basis of evaluation as it was what we might now call process tracing. The very large housing element of the CDP team's work provides a good illustration of how this worked out. A large part of the CDP territory of action was provided by the Meadowell – a big social housing estate with some 2,000 dwellings and a population at the time of the 1971 census of more than 8,000 people. The team, informed initially by Meadowell residents, rapidly came to realise that the history of this estate from its building in the 1930s was crucial to understanding its contemporary status and set of social problems. It had been built under legislation in the 1930s which allowed for the construction of social housing to replace cleared slums and to reduce overcrowding. This was in marked contrast to the basis of provision of both earlier and later estates which had been built for general housing needs and had not been explicitly tied to slum clearance programmes. The Meadowell estate had originally consisted almost entirely of accommodation in low rise flats. What looked like a pair of large semi-detached houses was actually a structure containing four flats (apartments). About two thirds of the estate had undergone or was undergoing a modernisation programme which involved converting the four apartments into two largish semi-detached houses. The CDP team realised that the history of the estate *and* its historical and contemporary relationship with the whole of the rest of the housing system in North Tyneside were crucial to understanding both its present situation *and* the potential for social action in relation to that situation. In complexity theory terms we had to establish its present state system, the character of its trajectory towards that state, the nature of the intersections of the system with other relevant systems and the potential set of future states which might be possible for it to achieve.

Of course it was never possible in practice, nor should it have been, to separate research's role in establishing a basis for action and as part of action. The historical accounts of the development of the Meadowell estate drew on documentary materials but they also drew on the oral testimonies of Meadowell residents. That process of developing an oral history in dialogue with documentary sources (which included secondary data sources drawn both from decennial censuses and housing records) was itself part of the community development process. This was associated with a census of the estate undertaken by members of the community groups with CDP team support which sought to establish all of the structure of households then resident on it, the problems that they felt existed in the area, and what they wanted done about them. The products of the survey were processed by the research team and presented to the community organisations. After discussion the community groups then formulated a set of proposals for the future structural improvement and management of the area. Actually this process caused little difficulty with the local authority, in contrast with similar processes in areas of private housing nearer to the centre of North Shields. The Director of Housing responsible for the management of the municipal stock was perfectly happy to see the whole of the estate modernised – a key demand of the residents – and collaborated with them in making representations to central government for the allocation of resources so that this could be achieved. In central North Shields resident demands were for the improvement of areas of late 19th-/early 20th-century Tyneside flats rather than their demolition, which was the current local authority policy. Here there was real conflict but eventually, and in response to a shift in central government housing policy from clearance to improvement, most of these areas were retained. They now are seen as desirable places to live.

The CDP team's evaluation of its work took the form of a series of final reports documenting context and process. The housing work in particular actually demonstrated considerable success in changing policy, implementing it and achieving relatively good outcomes if outcomes are understood in terms of resident satisfaction and a developed mutual engagement of local governance and residents. In contrast with much of the experience of say NDCs, North Tyneside Council and CDP, residents actually managed to work together to some purpose. That said, the most controversial aspect of the team's work was not a consequence of local conflicts. They were actually resolved in a way which reflected the Home Office's original notion that conflict could shake things up in a way which was ultimately functional and beneficial for all concerned. Rather they arose from the role a group of CDPs collectively played in defining the nature of deindustrialisation and proposing action in response to it. This was done through the CDP 'Political Economy' collective and the production of a series of reports coloured both by a Marxist explanation of developments and the proposal of radical socialist responses to them. When the International Monetary Fund imposed cuts in public expenditure on the Labour Government in 1976 the CDP teams produced a report documenting the impact of these on the areas in which they were working. Labour cabinet ministers, particularly Barbara Castle, responded angrily. Likewise reports documenting the impact of the Bains Report (1972) on the accountability of local governance and critical pieces on the future of the car industry in the West Midlands (there were CDP teams in Coventry and Birmingham) were highly controversial. There was an interesting contradiction here. The CDP teams were the first social science informed group in the UK to identify the crucial significance of deindustrialisation. Although they were accused of exaggerating its impact at this time, in fact their prognosis was for a less severe change than has actually occurred. The emphasis on deindustrialisation as a source of social problems was not fundamentally contested. In fact senior civil servants found it persuasive and drew on the material in policy development. What was at issue was the way in which the CDP teams assigned the origins of these changes to an unregulated capitalism and asserted that the solution to problems lay in socialist policies. This was done when the UK was governed by the Labour Party which was still formally committed – through clause IV, part 4 of its constitution, which was printed on every party membership card – to the socialisation of the economy as a whole. Actually the CDP teams were associated with local initiatives which reflected moves in this direction, in particular in response to the Industry Act 1975, which seemed to prefigure a move towards a more planned industrial policy with substantial trade union engagement on the lines which had prevailed in joint production committees in the Second World War. The CDP teams had almost all come to the end of their life by the time of the election of the Thatcher government in 1979. Their relationship with the Wilson Labour government and with Labour local government was uneasy but not impossible.

What the work of the CDP Political Economy Collective illustrates is the implication of praxis for action researchers. If there is a serious commitment to real transformative social engagement it is impossible to confine work to the immediate local context. Essentially in specifying the ultimate cause of the problems emerging in their locales in the late 1970s, the CDP teams were saying they lay in the nature of the capitalist social order. While 'old' 1970s Labour was actually founded as a political party around precisely that proposition, it had entered into a not always easy set of accommodations with a capitalist social order characteristic of all social democratic parties and even of 'Euro' communist parties from the 1970s onwards. The CDP research outputs, which were meticulously grounded in careful and detailed work, served as an uneasy reminder of the consequences of that engagement. Nonetheless the Labour and trade union movement did exist as a potential institutional audience for this work and it did have some influence in relation to it. That is a most important point. One of the key things we have to consider in relation to applied social research is the character of the audience. The assumption of the traditional intellectual is that the audience for new knowledge is everybody and that knowledge will have effect in relation to its validity as an account of what is and of the causal mechanisms which have generated that condition. The CDP teams were functioning as organic intellectuals and did have a specific audience with a specific set of interests. However, that audience itself – the Labour and trade union movement – while overlapping in interests with the dispossessed working class people of places like North Shields, did not have exactly the same interest set. Things are always messy and fuzzy in the reality of action research both as process and in relation to the way in which the products of the research can have any sort of real impact for transformative social change.

## What can we learn from action research?

The answer to this question must of course be qualified by noting that it all depends on what we want to learn from action research. In terms of the programme most elegantly formulated by Freire in recent times we will always learn that the ultimate resolution of the problems we face requires a transformation of the overall social order. That might turn us towards revolutionary action although the history of the outcomes of revolutionary action will not encourage us in that direction. It might turn us towards a practical technical pragmatism in which we are prepared to engage with process tracing and careful case comparison with a recognition of the absolute significance of path dependency as the basis for the generation of transferable good practice to other contexts of work which resemble those – if we use the comparative method then the plural is crucial – in which the original work was conducted. Certainly that is the mode of understanding which underpins consensual policy and practice research. Of course that ignores the reality of conflict and the absolute continued existence of non-commensural interests in almost all domains in which we might deploy action research. If we ask if there is an alternative, then we have to consider both the technical issues and the politics of praxis.

Let us turn first to the technical. Complex realism gives us clear guidance here. In action research as virtually always in social interventions we are seeking to achieve a change of state, to make the whole relevant system or systems different in terms of kind rather than degree. So our first principle again is that outcomes have to be considered in terms of system transformation. In terms of method we must always have a full and careful narrative of process. Here we are faced with the reality that we may have different narratives. Different actors will have different and even possibly contradictory stories to tell. Somehow we have to achieve a synthesis. This synthesis will not be a matter for compromise. Complex realism requires a severe insistence on the possibility of the establishment of a 'truthful' narrative, one which corresponds to the actual reality of experience. All voices must be heard but not all versions can contribute to the final story. What this implies is that all those engaged in constructing narratives must have a firm commitment to rational account. The notion of positional versions as all truthful in their own way goes out of the window here. No single position can dominate other than the overall commitment to getting it right. Conflicts become a matter of record rather than the determinant of the narrative.

Multiple narratives of multiple instances – sets of case histories – provide the basis for systematic comparison using QCA or related approaches. These will always be at least in the first instance exploratory. Most of our configurations will be contradictory until we look further for more differences. Nonetheless the careful exploration of differences among 'near neighbours' should give us guidance in relation to our fundamental question – what works where and when and to what end. Here sometimes we will of course be interested not in final state condition but in the direction of a trajectory. The health inequalities examples after Blackman et al (2010) were about direction of movement rather than final achieved state. Exploring for direction of movement is perfectly appropriate but the really interesting things will always be to do with fundamental change of state. Here of course the definition of outcome, *which definition will emerge during process rather than being defined in advance,* is absolutely vital. To say that definition of outcome will emerge during process is not to say that projects will commence with no conception of intended outcome. Of course there will be a broad original understanding of what the whole exercise is intended to achieve. However, in absolute contrast to experiments in hypothetico-deductive mode, that outcome must be plastic. It may indeed be completely transformed although less drastic revisions are likely to be more common. In summary, process tracing and systematic comparison can provide us with causal accounts in relation to action research processes.

When we turn to the politics of praxis, the account of the emergence of the modern capitalist order provided by Karl Polanyi in his seminal *The great transformation* (2001, orig. 1945) is very helpful to us. Polanyi emphasises something which was succinctly expressed by Marx himself – the importance of the transformation of quantity into quality, an idea which resonates absolutely with the complexity frame of reference. The accumulation of changes can lead to a new form of social order. Significant change is not achieved simply by a capture of the state by the revolutionary party. As Bahro (1978) observed the 'Great October Revolution' seems to have involved just as much or even more a capture of the Bolsheviks by the structural necessities of the Russian State as a revolutionary transformation of the state itself. Rather it requires change in all of the interlinked systems of the economy, civil society and the state.

Let us consider this in relation to issues of health inequality. Westergaard in his prescient review of the limits to redistributive welfare reform (1978) noted the exceptional character of health policy in relation to inequality. Uniquely the UK NHS as established in 1948 and some other European health care systems sought explicitly to achieve equality of outcome. However, Westergaard noted that:

> Even within the field of health, the goal of substantive equality has receded into elusiveness, both as the pressures from the contextual inequalities of the larger society have made themselves felt; and as the institutional devices to secure equal access have proved inadequate or, in some respects indeed, have been stripped down. Still more noticeably, neither in Britain nor elsewhere has the implicit notion of 'selective equality of condition' been extended from health to other possible spheres. (1978, p 91)

The evidence on health inequalities unequivocally supports Westergaard's pessimism. How, we must ask, can action research projects in this least contentious of areas in relation to objective actually achieve their goals? Let us reflect for a moment on that statement – least contentious of areas. We do not find equality of outcome accepted as a social goal in any other area of social life even in the most radical of social democracies. In education we find instead an emphasis on equality of opportunity, equal opportunity to become unequal. In relation to income distribution we find, even in an era when the parasitic and useless character of financial elites has been demonstrated for all to see, that there is a marked policy resistance to stiff redistributive taxation even when this is argued for on the principle that the polluter pays as a way of resolving the acute fiscal crises of most western democracies. Health is, as Westergaard put it, exceptional.

The key thing is participation. If we are to address health inequalities in any effective way, of course we can and should develop forms of practice which work better than others. However, in so doing we must also inevitably raise the consciousness of two fuzzily intersected groups of the general population. In Freire's terms we are bound to engage in conscientisation. Usually this is understood in terms of developing a consciousness of the source of their position on the part of the most deprived and dispossessed groups in society. They matter but they are not the only people who matter. Health inequalities are a product of inequality itself. Every medical, nursing and para-medical student writing an essay on health inequalities will reproduce that statement. Every practitioner working in relation to health inequalities knows it to be true. Every intervention in relation to health inequalities runs into the issues which occur because the systems in which they operate are profoundly unequal. We must address both the community at large and health workers as health workers.

This is particularly the case in relation to contemporary area-based initiatives. These operate in an overall social context of profound economic crisis and in relation to local contexts where urban regeneration strategies, driven overwhelmingly by the interests of business and capital accumulation, have actually contributed to increased social inequality on the ground. Strategies of economic regeneration which sought to substitute for lost industries financial jiggery-pokery and credit-based over-consumption with a greater or less colouring of 'culture' as the base of local economies have manifestly failed. This is quite literally in the face both of poorer urban residents and of all the organic intellectual practitioners, themselves employees of a fiscally challenged state system or indirectly employed from tax revenues in the third sector, who engage in interventions in 'partnership' with them. Of course this will by no means inevitably lead to coherent social action of a transformative kind. A major obstacle is the weakness of the traditional institutional bases of such action in the form of social democratic/labour parties and even the trade union movement. To describe their current status in the vernacular of industrial Tyneside, they seem to have lost their knackers in the flood. In other words the neo-liberal hegemony, associated particularly in the case of UK New 'Labour' with capture by a neo-liberal entryist clique, has led to a complete failure of both intellect and will on the part of the traditional transformative institutional forces in market capitalism. That said, in the context of crisis there really does seem to be no alternative. Of course this will require a reshaping of political forces and the re-emergence of a belief in the transformative potential of radical reformist social policies but, as Edward Thompson put it we are in a period when 'experience walks in the door without knocking'. Let me quote the relevant passage in full:

> Many contemporary epistemologists and sociologists, when they hear the word 'experience', immediately reach for experience II. That is, they move directly to what Marx called social consciousness. They then go on to show that experience II is a very imperfect and falsifying medium, corrupted by ideological intrusions, and so on. ... Historians within the Marxist tradition – as well as many without – have for so long been using the term 'experience' in a different way that in *The Poverty of Theory* I did not adequately explain it.... What we see – and study – in our work are repeated events within 'social being'– such events being indeed often consequent upon material causes which go on behind the back of consciousness or intention – which inevitably do and must give rise to lived experience, experience I, which do not instantly break through as 'reflections' into experience II, but whose pressure upon the whole field of consciousness cannot be infinitely diverted, postponed, falsified or suppressed by ideology.... Experience I walks in the door without knocking.... Experience I is in eternal friction with imposed consciousness, and, as it breaks through, we, who fight in all the intricate vocabularies and disciplines of experience II, are given moments of openness and opportunity before the mould of ideology is imposed once more. (Thompson, 1981, p 406)

It seems evidently clear that we are at a moment of openness and opportunity. How we might make use of it is a topic to which we shall return in the conclusion to this book. For now we can conclude our discussion of action research by saying it is praxis or it is nothing.

## Notes

[1] In the present author's not inconsiderable experience such views are never expressed by community groups, labour movement organisations or any other element of the 'popular masses' but are often expressed by community workers and others working in roles best defined as in and for the state and

in consequence 'educated' to a level of imposed ignorance and stupidity. Most practitioners are much more sophisticated and aware of the contradictory nature of their own roles but some are not. In contemporary young teenage argot, such people are really annoying.

[2] His account of the US history of action research is correct, as is his identification of the problems that tradition encountered in relation to the positivist hegemony over US social science from the 1960s onwards. However, he neglects the continued existence of that mode in US business school work and locates post-positivist action research almost exclusively in relation to educational research practice ignoring its role in development studies in the widest sense. That said, he makes no claim for full coverage.

[3] He seems to have kept his head down. It required enormous courage to do more than this so no fault there.

[4] This was too erudite altogether for the UK press and the speech is usually described in terms of the threat of 'rivers of blood' flowing through UK cities.

[5] Actually in North Shields although there was plenty of conflict, much of the time the CDP team and local senior council officials got on reasonably well. People who had come up through the traditional bureaucratic structures of UK local government were not used to loose cannon activity by people who although on quite senior salary grades (a far from trivial aspect of CDPs in a context where pay grade mattered) were outwith the traditional system. That said, after initial conflict quite often both sides got together for a common purpose. Local elected councillors were much more threatened but that reflected a political change in relation to the local Labour party.

[6] The head of department in Newcastle Polytechnic to whom the research team were responsible invariably backed us up when we cited this justification.

# NINE

# The academy and beyond: applied social research in the real world

The Gulbenkian Commission Report on the Future of the Social Sciences, *Open the social sciences* (1996), reviewed the historical development of the social sciences as a component of the modern academy with the intention of seeing where they had come from as a foundation for seeing where they might be going. One crucial aspect of this review was the identification of disciplinary divisions within the social sciences as both relatively recent and to some considerable degree both contingent and artifactual. None of the social science 'pure' disciplines – sociology, psychology, economics, anthropology, and more fuzzily, geography – have an independent history dating back further than the middle of the 19th century. Most of the rest of what constitutes the social science academy consists of fields – some like political science emerging from a synthesis of philosophy, history and statistical methods, others like education and business utilising the methods of social science – in relation first to the vocational education of practitioners and then as the basis for distinctive research programmes. Then there are fields defined by area of interest. The Gulbenkian Commission discussed these in terms of 'area studies' – Middle East studies, Latin American studies, Soviet studies, even American studies – that is, the multi- or even interdisciplinary study of a geographical or politically defined region drawing on all of the social sciences, on history with its ambivalent position straddling the social sciences and the humanities, on literature and even on theology as the basis for a kind of external understanding of other complex and literate social orders. The model here was the pre-modern development of 'oriental studies' in a Europe which was by no means necessarily superior to the Islamic, Vedic and Chinese world orders it was confronting or encountering before the 18th century and the achievement of Euro and Euro-American global hegemony.

What is missing from the Gulbenkian review, which is generally comprehensive in its coverage and persuasive in relation to forward argument, is any real attention to the fields which are the domain of applied social science. If we think of 'health', 'urban studies', 'social policy' (which has tended to focus to a considerable degree on social security systems in interaction with fiscal systems), criminology, and indeed 'development studies' then we are again in the realm of the multi- and indeed interdisciplinary investigation of complex problems embedded in complex systems. The Gulbenkian Commission recognised the application of geographically defined 'area studies' in relation to the statecraft of hegemonic political units, especially the United States in the post Second World War world. The emergence of 'international relations' as a distinctive field in the academy reflected that. What they, mostly, missed was application in relation to the basal social systems, and especially health, education and welfare systems, of nation states and even, in urban and development studies, of the global social order as a whole.

In terms of forward project the Commission argued for a post-disciplinary future explicitly informed by complexity theory. Ilya Prigogine was a member of the Commission and while the European 'General Complexity' frame of understanding informs its prescription in an entirely appropriate fashion, it was perhaps less applied to backward review. The Commission asserted that:

> the most severe problems have been with the three more nomothetic social sciences [economics, sociology and political science]. In taking the natural sciences as a model, they nurtured three kinds of expectations that have proved impossible to fulfil as stated in universalist form: an expectation of prediction; an expectation of management; both in turn premised on an expectation of quantifiable accuracy. (Gulbenkian Commission, 1996, p 50)

This was absolutely correct in diagnosis but did not get into the aetiology of the issue. That is to say, the problems of the quantitatively oriented social sciences, including much of US and European sociology if not of British sociology, derive from an attachment to fundamentally false posited premises and a reliance on linear modelling, both of which ignore the non-linear and complex character of real social orders and processes. Complexity theory can be used to rebuke as well as prescribe. When the UK Academy of Social Sciences (AcSS) Commission reviewed the state of social sciences as a whole in the UK, it rejected in a distinctly huffy fashion the Gulbenkian Commission's verdict on the nomothetic social sciences:

This Commission accepts that the 'academic division of labour' in the social sciences causes a number of problems. ... But we are not sympathetic to the draconian opinions about the failures of economics, sociology and political science as expressed above. We take as axiomatic that good social science will often embrace both quantitative and qualitative approaches and that prediction is an important element of some work. All such work must however be done to high standards, as judged at least by experts in those domains. (2002, p 27)

The crucial issue is that 'experts in those domains', having built careers within them and being committed to existing academic discourses as sources of prestige and power, are perhaps the last people to judge their overall real worth. Oddly the AcSS Commission had actually used this quotation as an epigraph to its report:

The social sciences today are in a serious crisis which gets less attention than it should. It is threatened on several fronts. One danger is that it becomes trivial and mechanical ... An opposite (although related) danger lies in the purposeless sophistication one finds within parts of mathematical economics ... However, the most serious danger for the social sciences is a tendency to become pretentious and uncontrolled. The abstractions start living their own lives. (Elster, 1989, pp 11–12 (imperfectly translated from the Norwegian by H.O. Melberg))

Nonetheless they proceeded to disregard the essential message of this wise comment. Subsequent events have demonstrated the uselessness of conventional quantitative neo-classical 'positive economics' both in practice and in theory. Ormerod has recently, and justifiably, remarked that his account of the failings of economics as an academic discipline, which he presented in *The death of economics* (1994), has been entirely borne out by the utter failure of the discipline to predict or even to understand the current financial and hence global economic crisis. Her Majesty Queen Elizabeth II (of England, and so on, but I of Scotland), who is a distinctly wise old bird, said much the same on a recent visit to the London School of Economics and Political Science, which, despite being founded by Fabians who had some critical understanding of the capitalist social order and its ideologues, has been a temple of the high priests of an utterly fallacious economic orthodoxy. We have dealt with much of this in Chapter Seven in relation to economic modelling and its gross inadequacies. In assessing the value of contemporary mainstream economic theory Ormerod is blunt:

> [O]rthodox economics is in many ways an empty box. Its understanding of the world is similar to that of the physical sciences in the Middle Ages. A few insights have been obtained which will stand the test of time, but they are very few indeed, and the whole basis of conventional economics is deeply flawed.... Good economists know, from work carried out within their discipline, that the foundations of their subject are virtually non-existent. (1994, p ix)[1]

We will return to neo-classical positive economics' ideological role in the review of the role of disciplines in application in this chapter.

Let us clear up some terminology. What do we mean by the expressions multi-, inter-, and post-disciplinary? Of course there is no general agreement about the implications of these terms but it is worth specifying what is meant by them in this text. Multi-disciplinary work is work in which researchers bring to bear the perspectives of their particular discipline in relation to some problem in the social sciences defined in the widest sense of 'problem'. So for example economists, political scientists, sociologists, and anthropologists have all worked in relation to problems of 'third world' development. We can even use the word 'development' as a preface and talk of development economics although the other disciplines tend to be subsumed into the more interdisciplinary field of development studies.[2] Development studies in which the boundaries among disciplines have become much fuzzier typify interdisciplinary work. Here there is a much more eclectic mixing of the intellectual apparatuses of disciplines and the construction both of work and careers outwith the publication and departmental boundaries of the original disciplines. Post-disciplinary work in effect returns to the original position of the human sciences before the development of disciplinary boundaries and academic and intellectual empires. It rejects the distinctive intellectual and methodological programmes which have been built up over the last one hundred and some years. Very often the post-disciplinary position is explicitly founded in a complexity influenced frame of reference. Of course these terms are fuzzy. While work is often described as multi- or interdisciplinary in character, the term 'post-disciplinary' is seldom explicitly employed. That said, a good deal of actual research is really post-disciplinary in form. This is particularly true of participatory action research but most applied research has a definite tendency to draw on a range of tools and deploy them in a way which would be anathema to the more pretentiously methodologically specific disciplines of psychology and economics. We will work through the role of disciplines in a subsequent part of this chapter. Let us first consider how the academic social science world, as represented by the AcSS Commission and another report prepared for the British Academy, *Punching our weight: The humanities and social sciences in public policy making* (2008) has addressed these issues in the recent past.

Both reports agree on one key issue. That is the tendency in government at all levels to look to the short term and desire immediate responses when issues are long term and require consideration on that basis. The British Academy report puts this well:

> Government departments need to enhance mechanisms for anticipating, and responding to, future challenges and uncertainties. Our findings show that a high proportion, often as high as 60%, of departmental research budgets is being allocated to short-term projects to meet current political and administrative demands. This is contrary to the Government's own guidelines on the use of scientific research in policy making, which state that government departments should 'think ahead' and 'should broaden their advice'. (2008, p x)

This is absolutely correct but the short-term nature of central government interests in the UK, although not necessarily in all other post-democratic states, reflects the imperatives of the electoral cycle in interaction with the first-past-the-post electoral system. It is evident that the devolved administrations in Wales and Scotland where proportional representation generally produces governing coalitions seem to be able to think forward rather more clearly. In any event *Punching our weight*'s specification of the issues of globalisation; competitive innovation; life chances, talent and social mobility; an ageing population; personal responsibility and changing behaviour; welfare and well-being; and 'participatory politics for learning and resilience' does present an interesting set of long-term complex and at the very least interdisciplinary issues. Of course the very framing of the list matters. Why mobility and not equality? Why personal responsibility and not corporate responsibility? Why competitive innovation and not re-ordering of priorities away from ecologically damaging unrestrained economic growth and consequent resource depletion? The British Academy report provides us with an answer when it observes that:

> Studies have shown that policy makers want research findings that: are relevant; are timely; are robust (and the methodology is relatively uncontested); are applicable to the issue of concern; are accessible to wider audiences; bring together relevant expertise from a number of disciplines; have champions and advocates; involve the users of research in the research project from the outset – the 'co-production model'; support existing ideologies and are uncontentious. (2008, p 3)

The last element – 'support existing ideologies and are uncontentious' – is of course deeply contentious if we are in the business of, however pompously, speaking truth to power. What is required from applied social science is work which accords with the hegemonic status quo. The AcSS report expressed a similar position (and perhaps an even more supine one since, to be fair, the British Academy group were simply saying what policy makers wanted), when it identified the stakeholders for the output of social of the social sciences and listed last in its specification: 'The citizenry – which can benefit from rigorous social science research underpinning democratic debate and the availability of skills carried into the workplace by new graduates' (2002, p 3, Box 2.44).

The citizenry whose taxes support the great bulk of social science in the contemporary academy come ninth well after less than worthy special pleading, that is the whinge directed at certain professional accreditation bodies which make things difficult for university senior management by insisting on minimum staff–student ratios on courses they accredit. Even then, informing democratic debate is lumped in with the training of the workforce. It is not that social science should not inform governance and the other constituencies, the stakeholders which preceded the citizenry in the listing. It is rather that the notion of a critical social science is wholly absent in this somewhat abject catalogue.

## The failure of the disciplines in application – how and why

Why have the foundational disciplines of the social sciences performed so miserably in the application of the social sciences? The answer to that question requires consideration both of the inadequate at best and wholly erroneous at worst framing of some disciplines, notably economics and psychology,[3] and of the politics of the academy since the mid-1970s in terms of the relationships among the academy, civil society and the state. Let us deal summarily with economics. The contribution of economics as a discipline since around the early 1980s – which has to be carefully distinguished from work done by economists as social scientists working outside the frame of their discipline usually as quantitative social scientists in a general sense – has mostly been worse than useless in relation to understanding the issues that should concern applied social science. We have dealt with the fundamental inadequacies of economic modelling in Chapter Seven. Here we are dealing not so much with the erroneous individualism which underpins both the original notion of economic man and the maunderings of rational choice theory, as with the ideological assertion of market superiority in relation to resource allocation which has informed so much of the privatisation agenda in relation to public services since the 1980s, particularly but not exclusively in the UK.

We might begin here with the relabelling of the UK's Social Science Research Council (SSRC) as the Economic and Social Research Council in 1981. This followed on from the Rothschild (!) Report (1972) undertaken at the behest of Sir Keith Joseph, who considered that of the social sciences only economics had any claim to be scientific. Since the dominant neo-classical positive micro-economic tradition is the least scientific, in the sense of having any foundation in real empirical research into social reality, of all the social sciences, this was profoundly ironic but very much fitted the Thatcher government's *weltanschauung* as a pre-cursor of general neo-liberal hegemony on a global scale. Horrified by the prospect of losing grant income, the UK social science community in general, instead of urging Sir Keith to practise the art of cranial fundamental self-insertion in search of diurnal illumination, rolled over and accepted this gross insult to their whole foundation and set of practices. Economists in general, excluding some often reviled exceptions who understood the meaning of the term 'political economy', even welcomed this development, as did those psychologists who committed their discipline solely to a scientistic individualistic reductionism. At least the psychologists continued to do research and at the interface with neuro-science actually developed some real knowledge in relation to perception and even cognition.[4] The development, originating largely in contexts of mental health and social work practice, of a 'community psychology' which often draws on styles of work developed by Jahoda and her colleagues from the

1930s onwards, is an interesting and important development and the extent to which many of its practitioners draw on the insights of Freire is very encouraging.[5] That said, we are now seeing the emergence of an unholy miscegenation of individualistic and asocial economics and individualistic and asocial behavioural psychology in the form of behavioural economics which is set fair to replace current orthodoxies with a more refined but equally useless framework. Having failed with its own naïve psychologism, neo-classical micro-economics is turning to reductionist psychology rather than to the social in order to resolve its fundamental problems of explanation – a case certainly of going from bad to just as bad.

It is very important to recognise that the assertion of market superiority as a resource allocator, the absolute law and the prophets of both neo-liberalism and neo-classical positive economics is not founded on any sort of empirical observation whatsoever. Instead it is a purely deductive consequence of formal modelling, now of ever greater mathematical complicatedness (NOT complexity), on the basis of the establishment of an optimum outcome IF certain severe and inherently unreal conditions are actually in place. All this was more than adequately demolished as any sort of useful description of reality or prescription for social action by Thorstein Veblen (1904) more than a hundred years ago but it remains dominant in the discipline and fundamental to the discipline's role as ideological justifier of the re-commodification of the de-commodified services of welfare states. Only the heretical exponents of political economy in heterodox form challenge this nonsense but until very recently in the UK in particular through the operation of the research assessment exercise (RAE) they have been sidelined in or even excluded from mainstream economics departments. Here we see the dominant tradition in contemporary economics serving absolutely as organic intellectual activity for and on behalf of dominant social interests, particularly corporate interests.

We must distinguish between the work economists do which fits into the framework of mainstream economics as a discipline and work which people who call themselves economists and/or work in economics departments do outside that framework. Much of that work is statistical and can be considered under the general heading of social statistics. The UK has a somewhat unusual separation of social statistics from the social sciences in some universities and in general statisticians as an academic group are more likely to be found in departments of mathematics than in mainstream social science departments. In any event we have a distinctive set of practices and practitioners which together articulate a specifically quantitative social science. We have dealt with both the potential and the limitations of quantitative social science in a general sense in Chapters Two and Seven. Here the intention is to examine the politics of an assertion of the general superiority of quantitative work in relation to applied social science.

Let us reiterate yet again that there is no argument for a dismissal of the general utility of quantitative social science in this text. On the contrary, quantitative work is essential both for an adequate description of the social and trajectories of the social, and for the development of an understanding of social causality. What is at issue here is the kind of scientism which asserts the inherent superiority of any kind of quantitative work but particularly the kind of modelling which underpins especially econometrics but linear variable-based modelling approaches to social causality and prediction in general. Some interesting questions emerge about the politics of this within the academy. Basic description of the social and of social change is a crucial part of applied social science. We have dealt with this in Chapter Three but here we should note the value of such descriptions when generated both as part of official statistics and in the refinement of such statistical descriptions undertaken in the UK particularly by the Institute of Fiscal Studies in relation to taxation, benefits and income distribution. Generally when statisticians (and even economists working as statisticians) are counting and classifying they are doing good and useful work. Why then did for example the UK ESRC and the AcSS Commission attach so much value to competency in complex modelling and mathematical deductive procedures that the second argued for higher rates of grant for PhD students working in that mode, and the first accepted this argument and constantly demands ever greater levels of mathematical sophistication across the social sciences as a whole?

There is a range of answers to that question. One perfectly proper concern derives from the fact that many UK social science undergraduates in disciplines other than economics are to all intents and purposes functionally innumerate. This does not just mean that they are terrified of mathematical calculations, for example those necessary even for the most basic kinds of statistical inference. In fact given the general availability of decent statistical packages students almost never have to perform calculations. They just have to push the right buttons on a Graphical User Interface – say an SPSS window – and then competently interpret output. Rather they are literally terrified of any kind of numeric expression, even of a simple tabular presentation of survey data as percentages. They can cope somewhat better with graphical representation but numbers in the raw intimidate them. The explanation for this is simple. Most UK social science undergraduates do possess an adequate pass in GCSE mathematics, the examination UK secondary school students take at age 16, but most do not continue with mathematics at all after 16 with the exception of those intending to read for degrees in economics. It is not so much that they do not have an advanced grasp of mathematics; they actually forget/abandon skills and competencies they used to possess. It is probably the case that the UK population is less numerate now than it was when the UK was an industrial society and basic mathematical competency was a requisite for many industrial occupations. This is a real problem and must be addressed. The ESRC consultant's report prepared by MacInnes (2009) both provides a good overview of the issue and makes some very useful suggestions for dealing with it. The situation is particularly acute in the UK but Parker et al (2008) show that with the exceptions of Sweden and the Netherlands the degree of quantitative methods training and competency required is much the same in other advanced societies they examined.

So far so good: a concern with improving numeracy among undergraduates and hence providing a basic foundation for postgraduate study and research is entirely proper. The problem arises with an acritical acceptance of the value of complex modelling as not only useful in itself, when, as we have seen in Chapter Seven, it almost always is not useful and generally misrepresents causality in complex social systems, but as actually superior to other modes of social inquiry and explanation. There has been plenty of abuse of the randomised controlled trial in this text but that method does have value in particular, albeit restricted, circumstances. Linear modelling is almost always wrong. The way in which the UK ESRC has thrown money at it, and in particular thrown money at econometric versions of it, just in advance of and through a period during which its almost complete uselessness has played a considerable part in engendering a global economic crisis, belongs in the well-known realm of 'you could not make it up if you tried'.

There is real scope for an actor network theory-based study of the development of the quantitative obsession in UK social science during the 1990s and beyond. That would require a review of the way in which a network of individual key human actors, academic groups expressing particular discourses of practice and understanding, and even non-human actants in the form of new mathematical models and available computing and software resources, came together to shape both intellectual discourse and actual research funding. The suggestion is freely offered to whosoever wishes to take it up. In any event what should be a useful concern with the value of measurement in relation to describing the social and understanding social causality has been taken down a very wrong road indeed. The issue is to get it back on track.

When we turn to sociology, anthropology and geography, the picture is much more complicated than it is for economics and psychology. Here we find a whole range of intellectual complexities in relation to applied social research. Sociologists, anthropologists (especially but not exclusively in development contexts), and geographers all do applied social research. They do it from within discipline-based departments. They do it from within field-based departments in health, urban studies (including housing studies and planning), education, and business schools. Political scientists do it as well, again from within any or all of these kinds of departments. We also have work done, again mainly in development contexts, by specialists in geographically defined area studies. Education and planning departments along with social work departments are primarily engaged in training practitioner professionals but much applied social research is based within them as it also is in terms of the work done by social scientists based in medical schools and even in schools of environmental science or architecture. The fields have become post-disciplinary in that it has long been possible to obtain a PhD in, for example, health studies, education or social work. There has also been an increasing development of professional doctorates in these professional fields. These are intended for practitioners who undertake advanced training and do research while continuing in their professional role.

With the exception of the work of some economists and especially health economists, whose approaches we have considered in Chapter Seven, we can see applied social research as it is done by all the disciplines and fields and wherever it is based in terms of departmental identity as generally post-disciplinary. That is to say, geographers, health studies people, sociologists, educationalists and so on do not do applied social research in any discipline- or field-distinctive fashion. The focus of attention is often different. Urban issues get examined more often by urban studies people or geographers than by say educationalists but even this is not absolute. Applied urban research certainly has been done from education departments or business schools. The key point is that the actual way the research is done bears little relationship to the actual discipline or field label of those doing it. Often of course research teams are composed of people with different disciplinary or field-based training or work record. Often work record, in terms of both topics investigated and mode of investigation, bears little relationship even to the discipline/field in which a PhD was obtained, let alone the content of a first degree programme. Why can we describe this kind of applied work as post-disciplinary? Because the actual nominal classification of those doing it has almost no influence on how it is done. Instead the whole repertoire of social research techniques is drawn on in a sensible 'horses for courses' fashion. Geographers do participatory action research. Sociologists use survey methods. Business school based researchers conduct focus groups. This eclectic catholicism is not confined to methods understood as techniques. A range of methodological programmes inform the way the work is done, more often implicitly but increasingly frequently in explicit terms. Critical realists can be found working in health, education, criminology, urban issues and many more disciplines and fields. A more or less developed phenomenological programme underpins a great deal of qualitative interpretation. Simpler forms of statistical modelling, notably logistic regression, are widely employed in causal work. In practice applied social research is intrinsically post-disciplinary.

There is one great methodological issue to be confronted in relation certainly to the modes of understanding deployed in sociology, anthropology and geography and in a range of substantive fields. This is the pernicious influence of a post-modernist/post-structuralist denial of any possibility of a generalisable account of social reality and social process. Pawson and Tilley called this 'hermeneutics II' (1997), the insistence that all accounts are simply unique interpretations which leads to denial of the possibility of any science. Why the real social sciences should have become, at least in the case of some social 'scientists', so enamoured of an intellectual current which originated in a massive over-reaction to spurious scientism in literary theory is an interesting question. One possible answer is that this current's denial of grand narratives also allows for a renunciation of any commitment to praxis in any form. We find a meta-theory which denies the possibility of any coherent meta-theory of scientific praxis serving as a rationale for sheer cowardice and bone-idleness on the part of intellectuals in post-industrial, post-democratic societies. It is also the case that the structuralism against which post-structuralism rails was constructed in considerable part in the social sciences by Althusser. Althusser's own grasp of the real content of Marxist social theory was weak – Edward Thompson's magisterial demolition of his approach in *The poverty of theory and other essays* (1978) demonstrates that among other things – but he was one in a line of continental European academic 'stars' associated with communist parties, and post-structuralism is also a post-communist intellectual current. Whatever the many defects of formal communist parties, and they were considerable in every respect, the abandonment of a programme of social justice by intellectuals is a bad state of affairs anywhere and anytime but particularly in the current context of social crisis.

In relation to applied social science the pomo line of course does not really inform any actual social research practice. It is a truism to say that postmodernist research is a contradiction in terms. Research which seeks even just to describe can never be postmodernist. The real impact of the pomo current in the disciplines and fields has been to devalue the critical function of any social research, including in particular applied social research. So we have a very odd situation indeed. Scientism in the sense of more or less crude positivist conceptions of research practice comes together with extreme denials of the possibility of science to devalue the critical role of social research as a whole. It all makes the contemporary academy a rather timid and quietist environment. This really will not do!

There is one further aspect of the recent history of the academy in the UK which needs to be considered in relation to applied social research. This is the pernicious influence of the UK's research assessment exercises through which basic resources for academic research are awarded to universities on the basis of an assessment of the research performance of permanently employed academic staff. These began in 1986 and, although somewhat changed in form for the future, are intended to continue despite some reservations expressed in the Roberts Report (2003) to the UK Higher Education Funding Councils. Although the RAE format is perhaps most developed and has had the greatest impact in the UK, similar approaches are taken in many other state-funded university systems. One obvious problem with the RAE has been that it has largely ignored or minimised the actual research done by non-permanent research staff not on teaching academic grades. This has particular significance for applied social research. However, the most important problem for applied social research has been the way in which the assessments have been organised on a discipline/field basis with expert review panels focusing on their own specialisms. Perhaps the most pernicious impact has been in economics where, as Lee (2007) documents, non-mainstream (and therefore possibly useful) approaches have been largely driven out of the main locales for disciplinary research. However, this is an extreme example of an assertion of orthodoxy in the social sciences. The more general problem has been the way in which the RAE process has operated to the disadvantage of all of interdisciplinary work, applied work and work which relates to professional practice. These issues are well reviewed by Barker (2007) but in brutal summary we can say that the RAE process has achieved an outcome which reflects formal rather than substantive rationality. The emphasis on a very limited quantity of 'high quality' research, particularly in the form of journal articles, has devalued not only the production of research-based monographs but that large part of 'applied' output which takes the form of reports. Textbooks are anathema. The engagement aspect of action research has figured not at all in the whole process. The RAE certainly has enhanced the status of a group of elite universities, often at the expense of parts of the academy which emphasise application and practice. This issue has not gone unrecognised and in the Research Excellence Framework (REF) process which will replace the RAE greater emphasis has been placed on an 'impact factor' which characteristically has been defined very much in terms of the UK PLC business model conception of impact. This is being contested but so far not to much effect.

The RAE is a problem in relation to the formal academy. We have already noted that despite the fuzziness of the boundaries around the academy in relation to contract and evaluative research of all kinds, much applied social research is done outside it. Let us turn to one of the most important bases for such research – the world of the 'think tank'.

## Think tanks – post-disciplinary and post-academic

> **Think tank** – A research institute or other organisation providing advice and ideas on national or commercial problems; an interdisciplinary group of specialist consultants. (OED)

The category of 'think tank' constitutes a very fuzzy set. Organisations which have been described as 'think tanks' include for example the Fabian Society founded in 1884 and an affiliate of the UK Labour Party since the party's foundation. Another more recent Left organisation Compass describes itself not as a think tank but as a pressure group.[6] Nonetheless it publishes research reports, albeit ones explicitly intended to influence political process rather than in some neutral fashion inform policy and practice. The explicit commitment of the Fabians and Compass is matched on the Right in the US by the extreme conservative/neo-liberal Heritage Foundation. In the UK the Adam Smith Institute, although lacking the ultra-rightist baggage of the Heritage Foundation, stands explicitly on the Right in political matters. The Institute of Economic Affairs founded in the 1950s played a crucial role in maintaining the ideological assertion of the rationality of market solutions in the third quarter of the 20th century when these were rather out of political fashion. The US Brookings Institution and Political and Economic Planning in the UK (now absorbed into the Policy Studies Institute) while often regarded as centre Left have been much more 'neutral' in terms of their policy analysis and focus of work. In fact their labelling as centre Left seems to reflect nothing more than a view on the extreme Right that any organisation which regards state intervention as any solution to anything is Left.

The AcSS Commission stated that:

> The best think tanks have a sharp focus, high productivity, good connections, considerable influence, relative lack of historical baggage, and speed of action – and a clarity of purpose and recognition that they are not generally involved in fundamental academic research. We entirely accept that some operate at a level of analysis which is wholly inappropriate for research-active universities. But the best of them have some lessons for us. We recommend that deans of social science faculties across Britain should study the nature and successes of think tanks and seek to emulate their desirable features. (2002, p 99)

Certainly there are positive aspects to think tanks. They are inherently interdisciplinary. Even those which advocate the necessity of handing decision making over to markets seldom do so on the basis of impenetrable linear models, however much they may draw on reference to those models to justify the ultimate character of their argument. Generally speaking, think tanks look for what works. Some – the Brookings Institution stands as an exemplar – maintain standards of objectivity and research practice which if anything exceed those characteristic of work done in universities. Actually we have to ask if this is always a good thing. It is a good thing to have bodies like the Brookings Institution or the Policy Studies Institute doing the kind of work they do but one of the advantages of think tanks is that often they work to an explicit ideological agenda. In other words they run under their own political colours. So for example the Adam Smith Institute is explicitly an exponent of privatisation but argues that it is non party political. This is certainly true. It had a continuing influence on New 'Labour' policies for example. However, 'non party political' does not mean 'non political'. Clear political interests are articulated in relation to the privatisation of public health and welfare. Of course the claim is made that this is all in the general public interest and evidence is adduced to demonstrate that this is the case. In effect an ideological expression of interests is transformed into an expression of general public good. Needless to say, the empirical evidence base is slight to non-existent. What we have instead is the usual ideological dross derived from deductive economic theory.

The IPPR is generally described, not least by itself, as a Left leaning body. Interestingly this 'Left leaning' entity has a body of trustees drawn to a considerable extent from business but which includes not one trade union official. It has argued, sometimes on the basis of weak evidence, for developments in health care provision which would facilitate privatisation. While the Adam Smith Institute has been the think tank of Thatcherism, the IPPR has served a similar purpose for New 'Labour'. The similarity of their policy positions illustrates rather well the character of post-democratic politics in the contemporary UK. The only criticisms which can be advanced in relation to the explicitly ideological character of some think tanks relates first to whether their presentation of evidence in support of an argument is selective or just plain wrong, and second to their constant expression of particular elite interests as actually general interests.

So think tanks are contradictory bodies. Their interdisciplinarity is a good thing. Their explicit ideological commitment is honest at least in part. If we understand many of them as actors in a ground of political context then we can accept their operations. That said, there are some real issues in relation to their model of research and intervention. First, they do little original research themselves. Rather they draw on existing research evidence. Such synthesis is perfectly appropriate in itself but it does open up the opportunity for selective presentation and even more for selective interpretation. Second, the targets of think tanks are policy makers generally in central government and the media. In the UK this means that they are overwhelmingly located in London and have a poor direct grasp of conditions and issues, particularly in the English regions. Moreover they have very little in the way of connection with other institutions of civil society. The only real exception to that is that some think tanks have connections to national charitable bodies but almost invariably only with head offices. Some think tanks are charities. Many national charities function to some degree at the boundary between the set of think tanks and the set of pressure groups. Again both operate in a restricted policy and media world – the so-called 'Westminster Village'. This is not absolute. IPPR has a north of England branch and there are at least embryonic think tanks in the capitals of the devolved sub-nations in the UK but metropolitan is the dominant locale and metropolitan elites are the target audience.

The interdisciplinarity which characterises think tank approaches to the application of social research is important in terms of actual research practices but it is not really different from the way in which most applied social researchers work from an academic base. There are academically located institutes which are explicitly founded on an interdisciplinary basis sometimes going beyond the social sciences to incorporate work done in biomedical science or ecology/climate change scientific work. Examples in include the Wolfson Institute at Durham University (with a strong health and bioscience interest) and the Zuckerman Institute for Connective Environmental Research at the University of East Anglia. Many universities have recently established Institutes for Advanced Studies which develop thematically based time-limited interdisciplinary programmes of work. All these are moves in the right direction but disciplinarity still dominates the academic world. However, there is one developing exception – the new practice of translational research.

## Translational research

The idea of translational research has its origins at the interface between biomedical science and clinical practice. In its simplest and crudest form it describes research directed at translating laboratory findings into clinical practice. Woolf (2008) makes the point that there are two phases even to this. First, laboratory work has to inform clinical science in the form of clinical trials. Second, clinical science has to inform actual clinical practice. Plainly transitional research thought of in this way links the deterministic science of the laboratory to the probabilistic science of the randomised controlled trial and leads towards evidence-based clinical practices. However, we can think of the actual practice science as science in the widest sense. While in that model the direction of knowledge is one way – from basic science out to clinical practice – there is an alternative model which recognises a dialogue between practice and research and notes the role of practice in defining the problems which basis science and then clinical science have to address.

The idea of translational research has been extended beyond the specifically clinical, that is beyond the practices of clinical professions, into areas of health service management and 'wicked issue' domains in particular in relation to mental health, health inequalities and problems surrounding ageing. This has opened up the mode to the work of social scientists, and social science has also engaged in translational research in relation to the social aspects of professional practice, particularly in relation to social work and nursing. The English National Institute for Health Research (NIHR) has funded a variety of programmes which can be understood in translational terms. For example, although the expression is not used it fits the NHS 'Service and Delivery Programme' and a range of other initiatives. It is interesting that the Wikipedia entry describing translational research actively associates it with participatory science although the implications of this have not been worked through. The Spring 2010 NIHR call 'Involve' directed at research on public involvement in health care research seems to represent an innovative move in this direction. The Centre for Translational Research in Public Health based on a consortium of universities in the north east of England is developing work in this area. Obviously translational research is not without its contradictions, particularly when it is deployed by big pharma – global pharmaceutical companies – in pushing their products for profit maximisation, but it is an interesting and in many ways positive development.

## Conclusion

Isaiah Berlin is said to have remarked that academic disputes are so vicious because they concern matters which are ultimately trivial. Well, some are about things which matter rather a lot. If we have any ongoing commitment to the role of rationality in the conduct of human affairs and if we think that science, defined in the terms expressed by the Gulbenkian Commission, has a role to play in providing at least part of that rationality, then we should be prepared to be self-critical about how academic work is done. The formal rationality of the organisation of academic work and the privileging of modes of inquiry which have done little but demonstrate a self-referential uselessness over many years are deeply dysfunctional for the application of social science. And to say that is to say very little about the obligations which should emerge in relation to praxis. The harsh reality is that academics have lost most of the status and potential which did reside in their role as 'traditional intellectuals' and have not yet really engaged with how they should function as organic intellectuals in social praxis. It may be fanciful, but perhaps it is not too much so, to assert that the massive expansion of academic positions has absorbed many into roles which distance them from any real engagement with transformatory social practices of any kind. Certainly academic Marxists these days, to say nothing of propagators of pomo, generally are not to be found much engaged in real struggles although there are exceptions which we will come back to in the conclusion to this book. Things should be different and the work we do as applied social researchers matters in making them different.

## Notes
[1] Ormerod has taken a turn to complexity theory to resolve these issues. See for example his *Butterfly economics* (1998). However, in general he works within the framework of restricted complexity.

[2] The maintenance of its separate status is characteristic of a discipline which combines intellectual arrogance with virtually utter uselessness – economics in the contemporary neo-classical mathematically formalistic version which dominates the subject. We are most definitely NOT here referring to political economy in the classical tradition nor to the Keynesian programme in macro-economics.

[3] Outside the domains of practice in education, mental health and occupational psychology where there is a perfectly respectable record of utility in relation to practice.

[4] That said, the current instrument-driven fad for deploying brain scanners in an effort to produce a reductionist neurological explanation for social phenomena is a demonstration of the utter inanity of scientism in practice.

[5] See the website for Community Psychology UK (www.compsy.org.uk/listkb.htm).

[6] The present author has written for Compass.

# TEN

# Concluding

Applied social research is political. In the light of what has gone before in this book that seems a pretty obvious statement but here I want to spell out exactly what it means. To say applied social research is political is to say:

(1) that in complex advanced 'post-democratic' societies, applied social research is part of the whole political process because it:
   (a) is part of the administrative processes of governance as a whole since it provides crucial learning feedback into all governance systems in relation both to:
      (i) accounts of the actual nature and trajectories of all aspects of the social order – the survey function;
      (ii) accounts of the impact of policy and practice interventions – the evaluation function;
   (b) provides descriptions of the outcomes of the actions of governance systems which can be used to legitimate those governance systems in relation to a set of criteria which emphasise managerial competency rather than political ideology – the legitimation function;
   (c) plays a vital role in relation to processes of consultation and participation which are crucial mechanisms for resolving what Bang (2002) has described as the uncoupling problem for relations between political elites and the rest of us – the engagement function;
(2) that it is necessarily engaged with the discourse-based politics of academic and professional life and work in relation to status, resources and overall power in those intersecting systems;
(3) that it has the potential to be part of the basis of an emancipatory politics of social transformation in relation to the central issues which confront us in our lives in a global system in ecological and economic crisis, which dual crisis is reflected in all of the subsystems in which we lead our daily lives – the potential of (and necessity for) praxis.

The task of this conclusion is to see how these things hang together and how the issues raised under numbers (1) and (2) might come together to offer us some possibilities for developing effective praxis in relation to number (3). I am tempted to call (3) the pious exhortatory function since it is raised so often in relation to research practice as a prayer that it might do this without anything very much in the way of practical suggestion as to how it might do it: so a necessary cynicism or let us say pessimism of the intellect is in order. Optimism of the will I hope will follow.

The first thing to recognise is context. Edward Thompson (1981) has reminded us of the reality of those times when 'experience walks in the door without knocking' and the potential which they offer for mobilising people's sense of the problems of their reality in order to make things be different. It is informative to draw on the experience of writing this conclusion in Australia where the position of the Australian economy as a mine for Chinese and other East and South Asian manufacturing industry and power generation means that the economy is still growing. The contrast with the UK where the collapse of the global financial system has imposed an enormous fiscal burden is marked. Australia is still on a rise which reflects its role as a raw materials supplier to the world. However, even here there are serious ecological and social tensions. In countries where the economic crisis is working through rapidly in relation both to employment prospects and massive cuts in the level of public services, the sense of crisis is apparent. Ireland, an extreme case, has already seen cuts in public sector salaries and a slashing of social programmes. We are indeed living in interesting times.

Next, we must note the centrality of applied social research in the whole process of governance in both normal and abnormal times in societies where the abandonment, vastly premature as it has turned out, of ideological/interest-Jbased politics has had profound consequences. If all agents of governance are judged by their technical competence and achievement or otherwise of defined social objectives, then applied social research has twin roles. It is both an enabler of competence and achievement of objectives and an evaluator of both competence and achievement. Enabling is a requisite for performance. Evaluation is central to legitimation of the authority of governing elites and institutions. This means that the doers of applied social research are embedded within governance and central to its activities. In Gramscian terms we can think of them as organic intellectuals but that is perhaps too simplistic a description. Certainly the role of social researcher has intellectual content but really does not have the status which in Gramsci's time was accorded to intellectuals in general. Applied social researchers are, to modify May's (2005) description, both in-house and out-sourced proletarian servants of the evidence-based state. That is to say, the great majority of applied social researchers are employees, albeit relatively well-paid employees. We do not have the direct economic power of the skilled manual working class (and indeed technical workers) of industrial capitalism but we have a central political role.

That role is not merely in the production of knowledge but is also in managing the processes of re-engagement which are crucial to post-democratic governance. Bang explains the necessity for this thus:

> This is an element of what I call culture governance, namely the recognition by the EWP [EU Commission's White Paper on Good Governance, 2001] that involving civil society and citizens in EU's governing processes is becoming a functional steering imperative more than a normative problem of legitimisation. It is not primarily the support of citizens that the EWP is after. It wants their conventional knowledge and participation at close range in their lifeworlds to solve its own steering problems. As most hypermodern administrative systems, [the] EU is beginning to recognise that connecting with laypeople is becoming a precondition of producing more effective and relevant policies. This has been common knowledge in private organizations for a decade, at least. Self-governance and empowerment are here key-notions for connecting management with employees.... the EWP seems to acknowledge that as long as politicians and the media express the sense that politics are exclusively about being able to 'sit at the table' in the city council, national parliament or the EU, the EU citizens and users will continue to experience the 'big' politics as being detached from their immediate everyday problems. (Bang, 2002, pp 4–5)

This of course is about participatory politics. However, there is more to Bang's description than this. He intimately associates cultural governance (CG) with the aims and objectives of New Public Sector Management (NPM). Certainly he recognises, indeed asserts, a radical difference between NPM's insistence on a coupling of elite decision making, which presents a series of choices to individuals who rationally choose among them, and CG's plastic cultural 'diverse modality', which he describes in terms very much like Archer's (1995) discussion of morphogenesis. However, to assert 'Without CG, I shall suggest, it would not be possible for the system to deal with the tension that is built into the NPM-strategy between overriding political leadership, which is to be economically responsible, and a user influence that is supposed to have an optimal range of options from which to choose between freely' (Bang, 2002, p 11) is to suggest a complementarity rather than a contradiction. Bang's argument is more sophisticated as it develops, particularly in relation to his description of the way in which the Danish conception embodied in 'New Perspectives on the Public Sector' rejects the neo-liberal basis of much of NPM. However, he does not develop his discussion in relation to conflict around material product and real resources. This is particularly important in terms of conflict over privatisation of decommodified public services and over confiscatory and exclusionary urban regeneration programmes. In both fields, as is characteristic of post-democratic governance, business/ capital has a loud voice and 'the popular masses' have virtually none.

Bang's academic referents are largely to political science. There is a very similar but interestingly different literature on participation which draws on sociological and related concerns with social movements. The development of participatory budgeting in Porto Alegre (see Sintomer et al, 2005) often provides what we might almost call 'the' example – the defining case of such practices. In Chapter Six we saw how participatory budgeting has become assimilated into Bang's terminology 'cultural governance'. However, in origin the idea was of course much more radical and related to social movements which were emerging from the shadow of authoritarian military dictatorship. Social movements sometimes seem to have had their day, at least in terms of the interests of academia, but we must expect that the crisis will lead to the development of many at all scales. The continuing emergence in England for example of organised resistance to health service reconfigurations is pre-figurative here.

## Applied social science and the politics of the academy

Before developing a discussion of the relationship between applied social research and social resistance (and possibly even social transformation) let us consider the implications of academic politics for any potential radical practice. There are several dimensions to this. First there is the issue of funding. Applied social research seldom raises intellectual property rights issues in relation to commercial value of products.[1] However, grant income delivers a significant income stream to universities and is the funder of employment of the great majority of full-time non-teaching academic social researchers. There is an issue of 'client relations'. Although government and other agencies of governance derive their income from taxes paid by ordinary citizens, in post-democracy they very much run the detail of administrative processes as they choose, subject only to criticism of failures of policy or practice which are taken up by the media as scandals. This means that those who pay for research have contradictory interests in relation to its products. Of course in accordance with principles of rational governance they want accurate description and evaluation. At the same time there is a constant public relations driven pressure to present only good news. What disturbs governance is not wholesale critique in general terms. So long as such critique remains merely academic and confined to the pages of books, learned journals or small-circulation Left magazines it is ignored and may even serve the useful purpose of distracting activity. People who might otherwise do something real in politics instead write articles for *New Left Review*. However, translate a critical frame of reference into detailed critique of real policies and things are very different. The assault on Pollock and her colleagues in response to the criticisms of the Private Finance Initiative (see Pollock et al, 1999, for a summary of these) was severe. More generally evaluations which do not applaud initiatives are not welcome. This is an issue for central and local governance, including health governance, but it is even more of an issue when the governance agency is an arm's-length and usually third sector body depending on maintaining a stream of grant income for its own activities. Bad news is never welcome and too much leads to the drying up of research grant income from sources other than 'science funding' through research councils. Since such science funding is only a small part of the income stream for applied social research, this matters a great deal. Of course this kind of constraint is seldom explicit. It is rather something which develops in day-to-day practice. It is not absolute but it is real.

Who pays the piper is the first issue in relation to the academic politics of applied social research. We also have to address the relationship the applied has to the disciplinary academic empires which dominate universities and 'science' funding bodies. Let me repeat part of the comment of a referee of the proposal for this book[2] who articulated an important part of my argument far better than I had myself: '[Applied social science is] not derivative of conventional social science, stuffed into disciplinary packages, but instead transcends those different "disciplined" ways of doing social research through its engagement with the larger society.' For me this is a clear statement that applied social science is not just different from the 'pure' disciplines. It is far better at dealing with social reality than the pure disciplines and delivers far better science understood, as the Gulbenkian Commission put it, as: 'systematic secular knowledge about reality that is somehow validated empirically' (1996, p 2). Much of disciplinary-based social science bears little if any relationship to social reality. This is particularly the case for the current dominant school in Anglo-American economics. As descriptions of reality and even more as descriptions of the generative causal mechanisms underlying reality, most of this stuff is useless. There was a time when this was said, and said with some force. Richard Titmuss, the doyen of British Social Administration, said it regularly, with particular elegance in *The gift relationship* (1970). Arguments with economics understood in terms of neo-classical micro-economic theory are intensely political. For example the proposals on welfare 'reform' by the former merchant banker Freud (2007), a man whose political career exemplifies post-democratic politics in that he has passed seamlessly from UK New 'Labour' to the Conservatives as an expert on social security policy, are wholly informed by the absurdities of supply side theory.[3] It really is important to take this stuff on its own ground and name it for the dangerous and interest-serving ideological rubbish that it is.

Of course to use the word 'ideological' is to open up a necessary can of worms. If we adopt the position of disinterested science then to describe anything as ideological is to disqualify it as science because it is informed by and expresses interests. Let us call that a thesis. If we consider that ideology is in fact an expression of interests then why should we be concerned with the scientific status of knowledge at all? Let us call that an antithesis. Critical realism offers a synthesis – knowledge is always going to be deployed ideologically but it is made (from something – reality has a role) scientifically. The extraordinary thing is that in social science the more a body of knowledge claims to be completely independent from ideological interest and to have the status of pure science, the less likely it is to provide any sort of empirical description of reality as it is and the more likely it will serve interests, almost always dominant interests. The implication of the realist position is that disputes about the scientific validity of any knowledge claim or body of knowledge-making practices, that is to say disciplines, are profoundly political in character. We have a necessary politics of findings and a politics of methodology.

The real problem with this fight is that most of the time it doesn't happen. From time to time there are skirmishes. The AcSS's (2002) petulance in the face of the Gulbenkian Commission's dismissal of the nomothetic social sciences can be seen as a brief exchange of fire. However, mostly the practitioners of the rubbish deal with criticism by ignoring it. Well, that puts a responsibility on those who feel as I do to take the fight to the enemy. The current crisis provides an excellent opportunity for doing just that. Neo-classical economics is an obvious and easy target but it is not the only one. We also have to contend with sociology considered in two forms. One is as a rather pathetic effort to constitute a quantitative sociological programme based on linear modelling. This tradition has considerable policy influence, largely at its interface with social statistics. It also has an influence on the politics of the UK ESRC in relation to the research training of social science PhD students. At least it generally deals with real data but it does so very badly indeed. The linear modelling quantitative programme has its roots in 'social statistics' considered as a distinctive discipline, and its tentacles extend into political science and many applied fields. Linear modelling and RCTs are both founded on the use of statistical method. The ANOVA and related techniques which are usually used to analyse RCT findings are components of the General Linear Model. Both agree on the value of abstracted quantification and the imposition of linearity on a non-linear world. Let me reiterate that it is not quantification per se that is the issue. Rather it is the form taken by that quantification. There is a necessary fight to be had here.

Positive economics and quantitative sociology/social statistics obviously want to be 'sciences' in the scientistic sense. However, many of those who work in the tradition of the human sciences in sociology, history, anthropology and related fields are also necessary targets on the grounds of 'those who are not with us are against us'. It is really rather sad to see how mainstream interest in most of these disciplines has moved away from work on fundamental issues of social structure towards issues of the construction of personal identities. Let me make it clear. This is not a criticism directed at interest in issues of gender, sexual identity, ethnicity and other dimensions of inequality and differential power. Rather it is the formulation of sociological accounts in terms of individual rather than collective experience which is a problem. Not all of this work by any means follows the postmodernist diversion but much of it does. That turn is the main issue. The denial of science is just as much a problem as the imposition of scientism.

The institutional organisation of 'science' funding for the social sciences causes difficulties for scientific work which is applied in focus but not tied to a specific call by a governance or related body. This is not absolute because for example the UK ESRC does regard education, environmental planning, management and business studies, social policy and social work as 'disciplines' and all are field in nature and have substantial applied components. However, the actual framing of disciplines does privilege to a considerable degree work in a framework which is not post-disciplinary. The specification of an ESRC discipline as 'statistics, methods and computing' demonstrates the privilege attached to quantitative modes of work. In contrast another major UK funder of social research, the National Institute for Health Research, explicitly focuses on applied work which will improve health and social care outcomes. It has for example funded an inter-institutional school for social care research. It is also important to recognise that at the interface of the natural and social sciences, and particularly in relation to ecological issues, there has been funding for projects which have demonstrated the possibility of post-disciplinary work. The approach of integrative methods developed by Lemon and his colleagues (see Lemon, 1999) is an excellent example with considerable methodological implications.

The battles in the academy are complicated and messy. Assaults on scientism are necessary. Its main products – the acritical application of RCTs and linear models and the assertions that form the basis of positive neo-classical economics – have to be confronted in terms of their incommensurability with most (RCTs and linear models) or all (positive neo-classical economics) of reality. Even in relation to simulation, which has some promising characteristics, we have to confront the scientistic desire of those who argue only for restricted complexity and see the simulation rule as something rather like the nomothetic scientific law. These fights are necessary but they are not enough.

## Applied social science and the politics of politics

There are three aspects to the wider political relations of applied social science. We can think of these as its public role, its administrative role, and its role in partisan action. The public role is a developed version of Burawoy's (2004) public sociology. It requires a detailed and critical assessment of public policies and social practices in terms of their implications and outcomes. Much of this work is done particularly in relation to health, education and urban issues. The once thriving critique of tax and benefit regimes is not what it was, at least in the UK. The problem here is not that good multi-, inter- and frequently post-disciplinary work is not done and reported. It is rather what is done with it. Generally speaking this work ends up in the mausoleums of academic journals. Of course it represents a resource. A good deal of this book has been written on the basis of reference to it. But it does not enter into political debate to any very great degree. It was not always thus. For example in relation to social mobility, sociological and related work of the 1950s and 1960s had a considerable influence on policy, providing a justification for the development of comprehensive secondary schools to replace the previous selective system. Likewise work on pensions in the 1960s had a profound influence on Labour government policy in that period. Why have things changed?

The answer lies in the changing relationship between social science and political institutions, particularly political parties of the centre Left. It is important to remember that one of the strands which contributed to the development of social science as a whole and applied social science in particular was a concern with social reform. The London School of Economics and Political Science (LSE) was actually founded by the Fabian Webbs and George Bernard Shaw using a legacy left to the society. The Fabians were interested in good science but they were also proponents of progressive if gradual social change. There are many criticisms which can be directed at the Fabian style of work over the years but there is one outstanding characteristic of the society which marks it out. The Fabians are a society based on a membership and have an explicit political objective. This means that unlike most contemporary think tanks they have not been dependent for funding on the receipt of donations from corporate capital interests or from the super rich. People have donated – the legacy which was used to found the LSE is an example – but the society has continued to exist as a membership organisation within civil society. It is absolutely a place for voices of the Left. The publication of Crouch's seminal piece on post-democracy (2000) illustrates the continuation of this tradition. That is a public social science addressed to the political dimension of civil society itself.

However, the nature of the audience for most Fabian and related publications, including those by think tanks in general, is not what it was. It seems as if most Fabian publications (Crouch's pamphlet being a major exception) and almost all think tank publications are not directed towards a mass audience in civil society but rather towards influential elites in governance and the media. Of course elites were always part of the audience but so was the mass audience because in democratic politics the masses had the capacity to make politics work for them. The popular response to the publication of the Beveridge Report in 1942 and the role that response had in determining the outcome of the 1945 general election is a case in point.

It is not so much that there is no audience for this kind of critical social science, including in particular the products of applied research. It is rather that the audience has lost the institutional framework through which it could translate its informed interest into political outcomes. Again the UK is the extreme case; or rather England is the extreme case since multi-party politics in the devolved nations is much livelier. UK New 'Labour' has systematically dismantled the internal democracy of the party and its membership seems to be in almost terminal decline. Mass parties, particularly mass social democratic parties with strong trade union links, provided a venue for argument and resolution – the resolution being the formal procedural device through which decisions were taken – around issues which could be informed by the public products of social science in all its forms. People read or listened to or watched broadcast documentaries – documentaries being a description of how things are – and that informed their political views and political actions. Of course political activists were always a small minority of the population as a whole but they were embedded in that population and connected it to governance in a way which in the UK at least seems to have gone for good. It should be noted that Left/trade union politics were not the only example of political tendencies which could be informed. In fact all political parties included 'informed activists'. The role of the Workers' Educational Association (WEA) in the formation of the British Conservative Prime Minister Edward Heath (which he always acknowledged) demonstrates that.[4]

If far fewer people are in any way political activists, far more are now social scientists working as social researchers or in administrative and professional roles in which they draw on the findings of applied social science in informing their work. Universities have produced enormous numbers of social science graduates since the mass expansion of higher education which began in the 1980s in most advanced societies. By 2006 in the OECD countries on average 56% of secondary school leavers were entering higher education. It is not so much that most of these will study disciplinary programmes in the social sciences although many will. Rather most studying social sciences will do so as part of a vocationally focused programme in business, nursing, education, social work, and so on. Even medical students have to study some social science these days. Career trajectories may involve a period doing social research which is often the basis for movement through policy advisor roles into higher administrative positions. All this penumbra is in addition to the crucial administrative role applied social research plays in feedback to governance systems.

So we have to think about applied social research as a social practice in and of itself and of applied social research's role in framing professional and administrative practices. Professional practice has contradictory elements. On the one hand there is an emphasis on professionals developing evidence-based practice in which they as competent practitioners review the evidence base constructed by applied social science and apply it in their work. On the other there has been a real de-professionalisation of professional practice, again perhaps most marked in the UK, through the imposition of bureaucratic rules for actions and the recording of actions. This is particularly marked in relation to social work. Le Grand (2003) has argued that the proper treatment of public sector professionals must recognise them as both knights and knaves, as autonomous and competent professionals motivated by a sense of duty and as bone-idle time servers who need to be controlled in all aspects of their work. To say that this is contradictory in theory is obvious. The desire of systems to cover their backs against media scandal has led to a regulation of practice and an insistence on recording actions which in the case of social workers, particularly in child protection, means that their autonomy is minimal. There is a growing recognition that this is profoundly dysfunctional and again England rather than the UK as a whole is a limiting case, so we are likely to see a loosening of such controls in the future. In any event one of the tasks of applied social science is to inform practice and do so in a way which opens up the possibility for radical transformation. Health inequalities are perhaps the most interesting area for developments here. First, in most advanced post-democracies there is a broad agreement in popular political culture that there should be equality of outcome in relation to health. Second, workers in public health, although guided by outcome targets which in any event reflect that political culture, have considerable day-to-day autonomy in their work. Unlike social workers most are free of the tyranny of case management. Since it is evident that inequality in general is the driver of health inequalities, the logic of their actions must always be to attack inequality itself and that leads on to confrontation with the generating mechanisms of inequality. This issue illustrates the complex relationship between reform and transformation. I recently began a presentation to a New Zealand audience by asserting that so far as health inequalities are concerned the problem is capitalism 'innit' but that we ought to engage in practices which challenge neo-liberal market capitalism's overall logic and think about how the accumulation of changes produces a different kind of social order. Applied social research in relation to social practices is a crucial part of this process. To use another Gramscian term, organic intellectuals are engaged in a war of position.

That applies to all domains in which applied social research is practised but it has particular force in relation to research which is part of the participatory process. Bang (2002) indicates very clearly the necessity for post-democratic governance to engage in participatory practices but, as we have seen in Chapter Six, participation is riddled with contradictions. At a large conference which engaged many community activists in Newcastle, UK, I heard members of discussion groups constantly express their disillusionment with participation in governance processes (see Hopwood, 2003). I was struck by the degree to which, far from assimilating them into governance, for many the response was rejection and disillusionment. If 'the community' has no real voice in decision making then, as those people put it, 'we are just there to help them, not to help ourselves'. Applied social researchers, just like community workers (and the roles often are duplicate), find themselves, as the London Edinburgh Weekend Return Group[5] put it, 'in and against the state'.

The literature on community engagement and participation as part of the research process is full of references to Freire and regularly employs the term 'empowerment'. To be blunt this is more often than not rhetorical. If there is no institutional agency to articulate power, then what can the term empowerment actually mean? Mayo (2003) gives us an interesting account of how adult education can offer empowering experiences BUT this was for labour activists in the trade union movement. Mayo is keenly aware of how changes in industrial context have weakened the possibility for this kind of linkage and development. A general problem for those engaged in 'empowerment practices' is that their targets are among the poorest and most dispossessed in society. As Therborn (1986) put it, people on the dole don't make revolutions. In other words empowerment practices are far more likely to be about the social inclusion of marginalised groups than the transformation of marginalising social orders. Generally applied social researchers, because they are engaged with social problems, are less engaged with the 'middle masses' of post-industrial societies although it is precisely from these middle masses that change is most likely to come. There are issues which engage the middle masses. Health is always on their agenda, and educational opportunity and threats to pension systems also matter. However, these are not usually issues which appear collectively in the lifeworld but rather tend to have an individual character. Health service reorganisations which lead to cuts in local services are an important exception here, as are planning proposals with negative environmental or social consequences.

Although in general the middle masses are not perceived as generators of social problems, it would seem necessary in theory at least that they are somehow brought into participatory social mechanisms. It is perhaps indicative that English LSPs, which have very considerable power in relation to joined-up governance, seem almost invariably to draw their community representatives from deprived localities. In other words participation is about engaging those who might help in resolving problems with problem people and problem areas, rather than a means for engaging the citizenry as a whole in political decision making.

Doing something about this is not easy. I am a university professor with 40 years of pensionable service accumulated and not constrained at all these days either by censorship of my work – that has never happened – or the need to get grant income to contribute to school budgets. I make my FEC (Full Economic Cost) largely as a methods technician on other people's projects and by delivering a reasonable amount of teaching. I am not a contract researcher in insecure employment or a local government employed community worker liable to dismissal for challenging my employer's policies.[6] I can shout the odds without much risk, although also, I fear, without much impact. What should be the actual role taken by applied social researchers who are at the sharp end in these sorts of activities? Well, the best answer is a moral imperative: do not use a language of empowerment if there is no empowerment in reality. If empowerment is the objective then recognise that and do something about it. In a time when the notion that a rising tide lifts all boats has demonstrably failed and social and ecological crisis combine to destabilise the lives of people who thought they had it made, then there are real possibilities for doing things differently.

I want to conclude this chapter and this book with an expression of optimism of the will so here goes. Applied social research is a vital process in the maintenance of contemporary social orders. It is a key subsystem of the complex social systems which are the intersection of economy, civil society and state in post-democratic capitalism. Changes in it, in a context when there is a general crisis for social systems which derives from economic and ecological factors, can contribute to changes in the social order as a whole. So it is important to keep chipping away. Any area of social practice in relation to social research matters here. It is important to change the methodological frame of reference of the social sciences as a whole. It is important to use applied social research to demonstrate the current condition and potential trajectories of all levels of the social system in which we live. It is important to try to make participatory processes real and to engage research with genuine empowerment towards social transformation. I worry about the rhetorical nature of those assertions but they have to be asserted, and with that this book ends.

## Notes

[1] The development of GIS is a major exception here.

[2] See the Introduction, p 4, for the fuller quotation.

[3] Accurately characterised by George Bush senior as 'voodoo economics', although when in office he pursued exactly supply side policies.

[4] The WEA of course continues, even if diminished, as a key provider of opportunity for informed dialogical education.

[5] This group emerged from an overlap between CDP workers and members of the Conference of Socialist Economists.

[6] The dismissal of the nurse Karen Reismann for opposing cuts in services in mental health in Manchester is a telling example of what can happen to people who rock the boat.

# Bibliography

Abbott, A. (1988) 'Transcending general linear reality', *Sociological Theory*, vol 6, pp 169–86.

Abbott, A. (1998) 'The causal devolution', *Sociological Methods and Research*, vol 27, no 2, pp 148–81.

AcSS Commission (2002) *Great expectations*, London: Academy of Social Sciences.

Alam, S.H., Meyer, R., Ziervogel, G. and Moss, S. (2007) 'The impact of HIV/AIDS in the context of socioeconomic stressors: an evidence-driven approach', *Journal of Artificial Societies and Social Simulation*, vol 10, no 4, p7.

Alberti, G. (2007) *Emergency access: Clinical case for change*, London: Department of Health.

Allen, C. (2008) *Housing market renewal and social class,* London: Routledge.

Archer, M.S. (1995) *Realist social theory: The morphogenetic approach*, Cambridge: Cambridge University Press.

Arnstein, S.R. (1969) 'A ladder of citizen participation', *Journal of the American Institute of Planners*, vol 35, no 4, pp 216–24.

Audit Commission (2007) *The academies programme*, HC: 254 2006–2007, London: HMSO.

Bahro, R. (1978) *The alternative in Eastern Europe*, London: NLB.

Bains Report (1972) *The local authorities: Management and structure*, London: HMSO.

Balloch, S. and Taylor, M. (2001) *Partnership working: Policy and practice*, Bristol: The Policy Press.

Bang, H. (2002) 'Culture governance: a new mechanism for connecting system and lifeworld', Paper presented at the ECPR joint sessions of workshops, Workshop 6, Turin, Italy, 22–27 March.

Barker, K. (2007) 'The UK Research Assessment Exercise: the evolution of a national research evaluation system', *Research Evaluation*, vol 16, no 1, pp 3–12.

Barnes, D., Wistow, R., Dean, R. and Foster, B. (2006) *National child and adolescent mental health service mapping exercise 2005*, Durham: School of Applied Social Sciences, Durham University.

Barnes, M., Matka, E. and Sullivan, H. (2003) 'Evidence, understanding and complexity: evaluation in non-linear systems', *Evaluation*, vol 9, no 3, pp 265–84.

Bartholomew Working Party on the Measurement of Unemployment in the UK (1995) 'The measurement of unemployment in the UK (with discussion)', *Journal of the Royal Statistical Society Series A*, vol 158, part 3, pp 363–418.

Bateson, N. (1984) *Data construction in social surveys*, London: Allen and Unwin.

Beatty, C., Fothergill, S., Gore, T. and Powell, R. (2007) *The real level of unemployment 2007,* Sheffield: CRESR.

Beveridge, W. (1909) *Unemployment: A problem of industry*, London: Longmans, Green and Co.

Bhaskar, R. (1979) *A realist theory of science*, Brighton: Harvester.

Bierce, A. (1911) *The devil's dictionary* (www.thedevilsdictionary.com).

Blackman, T. (2006) *Placing health*, Bristol: The Policy Press.

Blackman, T., Wistow, J. and Byrne, D.S. (2010, forthcoming) *Variations between Spearhead areas in progress with tackling health inequalities in England*, SDO Project Ref: 08/1716/203.

Blaikie, N. (2007) *Approaches to social enquiry*, Cambridge: Polity.

Blamey, A. and Mackenzie, M. (2007) 'Theories of change and realistic evaluation', *Evaluation* vol 13, no 4, pp 439–55.

Blanden, J., Gregg, P. and Machin, S. (2005) *Intergenerational mobility in Europe and North America*, Bristol: Centre for Economic Performance.

Blowers, A. (2002) 'Political modernization and the environmental question', *Local Government Studies*, vol 28 no 2, pp 69–87.

Borgerson, K. (2009) 'Valuing evidence: bias and the evidence hierarchy of evidence-based medicine', *Perspectives in Biology and Medicine*, vol 52, no 2, pp 218–33.

Bosse, T. and Gerritsen, C. (2010) 'Social simulation and analysis of the dynamics of criminal hot spots', *Journal of Artificial Societies and Social Simulation*, vol 13, no 2, pp 5 (http://jasss.soc.surrey.ac.uk/13/2/5.html).

Boyle, R. (2006) *Mending hearts and brains: Clinical case for change*, London: Department of Health.

Bradley, W.J. and Schaefer, K.C. (1998) *The uses and misuses of data and models*, London: Sage.

Brady, D. (2004) 'Why *public* sociology may fail', *Social Forces*, vol 82, no 4, pp 1629–38.

British Academy (2008) *Punching our weight: The humanities and social sciences in public policy making*, London: British Academy.

Burawoy, M. (2004) 'Public sociologies: contradictions, dilemmas and possibilities', *Social Forces*, vol 82, no 4, pp 1603–18.

Burns, D. (2006) 'Evaluation in complex governance arenas: the potential of large system action research', in B. Williams and I. Imam (eds), *Using systems concepts in evaluation*, Fairhaven, MA: American Evaluation Association.

Burns, D. (2007) *Systematic action research*, Bristol: The Policy Press.

Byrne, D.S. (1998) *Complexity theory and the social sciences*, London: Routledge.

Byrne, D.S. (2000) 'Newcastle's going for growth: governance and planning in a postindustrial metropolis', *Northern Economic Review*, vol 30, pp 3–16.

Byrne, D.S. (2002) *Interpreting quantitative data*, London: Sage.

Byrne, D.S. (2005a) 'Complexity, configuration and cases', *Theory, Culture and Society*, vol 22, no 5, pp 95–111.

Byrne, D.S. (2005b) 'Theory, role of', *Encyclopedia of social measurement*, Los Angeles: Elsevier Inc, pp 785–9.

Byrne, D.S. (2009a) 'Complex realist and configurational approaches to cases: a radical synthesis', in D.S. Byrne and C. Ragin (eds) *Sage handbook of case based methods*, London: Sage, pp 101–12.

Byrne, D.S. (2009b) 'Using Cluster Analysis, Qualitative Comparative Analysis, and NVIVO in relation to the establishment of causal configurations with pre-existing large N data sets: machining hermeneutics', in D.S. Byrne and C. Ragin (eds) *Sage handbook of case based methods*, London: Sage, pp 260–8.

Byrne, D.S. (2010) 'Idleness' in G. Calder, J. Gass and K. Merrill-Glover (eds) *The British welfare state at 60*, Cardiff: University of Wales Press.

Byrne, D.S. and Doyle, A. (2005) 'The visual and the verbal – the interaction of images and discussion in exploring cultural change', in C. Knowles and P. Sweetman (eds) *Using visual methods*, London: Routledge.

Byrne, D.S. and Ruane, S. (2007) 'The case for hospital reconfiguration – not proven: A response to the IPPRs *The Future Hospital*', www. nhscampaign.org.uk/uploads///documents/Reconfiguration%20 Not%20Proven.pdf

Byrne, D.S., Williamson, W. and Fletcher, B. (1975) *The poverty of education*, London: Martin Robertson.

Byrne, D.S., Olsen, W. and Duggan, S. (2009) 'Causality and interpretation in Qualitative policy-related research', in D.S. Byrne and C. Ragin (eds) *Sage handbook of case based methods*, London: Sage, pp 511-21.

Cabinet Office Strategy Unit (2008) *Getting on: Getting ahead*, London: HMSO.

Callaghan, G.D. (2008) 'Evaluation and negotiated order', *Evaluation*, vol 14, no 4, pp 399–411.

Cameron, S. (2003) 'Gentrification, housing redifferentiation and urban regeneration: 'Going for Growth' in Newcastle upon Tyne', *Urban Studies*, vol 40, no 12, pp 2367–82.

Campbell, D.T. (2003) 'Foreword', to R.K.Yin *Case study research: design and methods*, London: Sage, pp ix–xiii.

Carlisle, E. (1972) 'The conceptual structure of social indicators' in A. Shonfield and S. Shaw (eds) *Social indicators and social policy*, London: Heinemann, pp 23–32.

Carpenter, J. (2006) 'Addressing Europe's urban challenges: lessons from the EU URBAN Community Initiative', *Urban Studies*, vol 43, no 12, pp 2145–62.

Carr, W. (2006) 'Philosophy, methodology and action research', *Journal of Philosophy of Education*, vol 40, no 4, pp 421–35.

Carter, R. and New, C. (2004) *Making realism work*, London: Sage .

Carvel, J. (2006) 'Plan for wave of closures of NHS services', *Guardian*, 13 September.

Checkland, P. and Holwell, S. (1998) 'Action research: its nature and validity', *Systematic Practice and Action Research*, vol 11, no 1, pp 9–21.

Checkland, P.B. (2000) 'Soft systems methodology: a thirty year retrospective', *Systems Research and Behavioral Science*, vol 17, pp 11–58.

Cicourel, A.V. (1964) *Method and measurement in sociology*, New York: Free Press.

Cilliers, P. (1998) *Complexity and postmodernism*, London: Routledge.

Cilliers, P. (2001) 'Boundaries, hierarchies and networks in complex systems', *International Journal of Innovation Management*, vol 5, no 2, pp 135–47.

Commission on Public Private Partnerships (2001) *Building Better Partnerships*, London: IPPR.

Crotty, M. (1998) *The foundations of social research*, London: Sage.

Crouch, C. (2000) *Coping with post-democracy*, London: Fabian Society.

Crutchfield, J.P. (1992) 'Knowledge and meaning: chaos and complexity', in L. Lam and V. Naroditsky (eds) *Modelling complex phenomena*, New York: Springer-Verlag.

Danermark, B., Ekstrom, M., Jacobsen, L. and Karlsson, J.C. (2002) *Explaining society*, London: Routledge.

DCSF (Department for Children, Schools and Families) (2010) *DCSF News*, 13 January (www.dcsf.gov.uk/pns/DisplayPN.cgi?pn_id=2010_0014).

Dennis, N. (1972) *Public participation and planners' blight*, London: Faber.

Department for Communities and Local Government (2007) *The English indices of deprivation*, London: Department for Communities and Local Government.

Donaldson, S.I. (2009) 'In search of the blueprint for an evidence based society', in S.I. Donaldson, C.A. Christie and M.M. Mark (eds) *What counts as credible evidence in applied research and evaluation practice?* London: Sage, pp 2–18.

Dorling, D. (2008) 'Do three points make a trend?, asks Danny Dorling', 4 November (www.compassonline.org.uk/news/item.asp?n=3340).

Drogoul, A. and Ferber, J. (1994) 'Multi-agent simulation as a tool for studying emergent processes in societies', in N. Gilbert and J. Doran (eds) *Simulating societies,* London: UCL Press, pp 127–42.

Duncan, C., Jones, K. and Moon, G. (1996) 'Health-related behaviour in context: a multilevel modelling approach', *Social Science and Medicine*, vol 42, no 6, pp 817–30.

Dyer, W. (2006) 'The psychiatric and criminal careers of mentally disordered offenders referred to a custody diversion team in the United Kingdom', *International Journal of Forensic Mental Health*, vol 5, no 1, pp 15–27.

Elster, J. (1989) *Vitenskap og politikk (Science and Politics)*.

Energy Intelligence and Marketing Research (2003) *Building the environmental partnership*, www.newcastle.gov.uk/condiary.nsf/all/2B B85F70DE6754898025712B0042FF9C/$FILE/Building%20the%20 Environment%20Partnership.pdf

Eve, R., Horsfall, S. and Lee, M. (eds) (1997) *Chaos, complexity and sociology,* Thousand Oaks, CA: Sage.

Everitt, B.S. and Dunn, G. (1983) *Advanced methods of data exploration*, London: Heinmann.

Farrall, N. (2006) *Health futures: Final report on the consultation outcome 2006–7*, Salford: University of Salford.

Farrington-Douglas, J. and Brooks, R. (2007) *The future hospital: The progressive case for change.* London: Institute for Public Policy Research.

Flyvbjerg, B. (2001) *Making social science matter*, Cambridge: Cambridge University Press.

Freeman, H.E. and Sherwood, C.C. (1970) *Dilemmas of social reform*, Englewood Cliffs, NJ: Prentice-Hall.

Freire, P. (1972) *Cultural action for freedom*, Harmondsworth: Penguin.

Freud, D. (2007) *Reducing dependency, increasing opportunity: Options for the future of welfare to work*, London: Department for Work and Pensions.

Gadamer, H.G. (2004) *Truth and method*, London: Continuum.

Garson, G.D. (1998) *Neural networks*, London: Sage.

Geddes, M. (2000) 'Tackling social exclusion in the European Union? The limits to the new orthodoxy of local partnership', *International Journal of Urban and Regional Research*, vol 24, no 4, pp 782–99.

George, A.L. and Bennett, A. (2005) *Case studies and theory development in the social sciences*, Cambridge, MA: MIT Press.

Gilbert, N. (1995) 'Emergence in social simulation', in N. Gilbert and R. Conte (eds) *Artificial societies*, London: UCL Press, pp 144–56.

Gilbert, N. and Conte, R. (eds) (1995) *Artificial societies,* London: UCL Press.

Gilbert, N. and Doran, J. (eds) (1994) *Simulating societies,* London: UCL Press.

Gilbert, N. and Troitzsch, K.G. (1999) *Simulation for the social scientist,* Buckingham: Open University Press.

Goldenberg, M.J. (2009) 'Iconoclast or creed: objectivism, pragmatism and the hierarchy of evidence', *Perspectives in Biology and Medicine*, vol 52, no 2, pp 168–87.

Goldstein, H. (1995) *Multilevel statistical models*. London: Edward Arnold.

Goodhart, D. (2008) 'More mobile than we think', *Prospect*, vol 153, 20 December, www.prospectmagazine.co.uk/2008/12/moremobilethanwethink/

Gorard, S. (2008) 'Research impact is not always a good thing: a re-consideration of rates of "social mobility" in Britain', *British Journal of Sociology of Education,* vol 29, no 3, pp 317–24.

Gouldner, A.W. (1971) *The coming crisis of Western sociology*, London: Heinemann.

Greenberg, D. and Poole, L. (2007) 'Designing a social experiment for the UK; how it was done and some lessons learned', *Evidence & Policy*, vol 3, no 1, pp 5–29.

Greene, J.C. (2009) 'Evidence as proof and evidence as inkling', in S.I. Donaldson, C.A. Christie and M.M. Mark (eds) *What counts as credible evidence in applied research and evaluation practice?*, London: Sage, pp 153-67.

Greenhalgh, T. and Russell, J. (2009) 'Evidence based policy making: a critique', *Perspectives in Biology and Medicine*, vol 52, no 2, pp 304–18.

Greenwood, D.J. and Levin, M.L. (2007) *Introduction to action research: Social research for social change*, London: Sage.

Gulbenkian Commission (Wallerstein, I., Chairman) (1996) *Open the social sciences*, Stanford: Stanford University Press.

Gutiérrez Romero, R. and Noble, M. (2008) 'Evaluating England's "New Deal for Communities" programme using the difference-in-difference method', *Journal of Economic Geography*, July, pp 1–20.

Hammersley, M. (1999) 'Sociology, what's it for? A critique of Gouldner', *Sociological Research Online*, vol 4, no 3 (www.socresonline.org.uk/4/3/hammersley.html).

Hamnett, C. (2003) *Unequal city: London in the global arena*, London: Routledge.

Hargadon, J. and Plsek, P. (2004) *Complexity and health workforce issues*, Working paper, Boston, MA: Joint Learning Initiative.

Harrison, S. (1998) 'The politics of evidence based medicine in the United Kingdom', *Policy & Politics*, vol 26, no 1, pp 15–31.

Hawe, P., Shiell, A. and Riley, T. (2004) 'Complex interventions: how "out of control" can a randomised controlled trial be?', *British Medical Journal*, vol 328, no 7455, pp 1561–3.

Hawkes, G., Houghton, J. and Rowe, G. (2009) 'Risk and worry in everyday life: comparing diaries and interviews as tools in risk perception research', *Health, Risk and Society*, vol 11, no 3, pp 209–30.

Hayles, K. (1999) *How we became post-human*, Chicago, IL: University of Chicago Press.

Head, B.W. (2008) 'Three lenses of evidence based policy', *Australian Journal of Public Administration*, vol 67, no 1, pp 1–11.

Healey, P. (2006) 'Consensus-building across difficult divisions: new approaches to collaborative strategy making', *Planning Practice and Research*, vol 11, no 2, pp 207–17.

Hedstrom, P. (2005) *Dissecting the social*, Cambridge: Cambridge University Press.

Higgs, P., Rees-Jones, I. and Scambler, G. (2004) 'Class as a variable, class as a generative mechanism: the importance of critical realism for the sociology of health inequalities', in R. Carter and C. New (eds) *Making realism work*, London: Sage, pp 91–110.

Holland, J.H. (1998) *Emergence*, Reading, MA: Addison-Wesley.

Hopwood, B. (2003) *Report of the 'Whose City?' conference*, 24–25 January, Newcastle: Sustainable Cities Research Institute.

House of Commons Select Committee on Health (2009) *Health inequalities*, HC 286-1, London: HMSO.

Hubble, N. (2006) *Mass observation and everyday life*, Basingstoke: Palgrave Macmillan.

Irvine, J., Miles, I. and Evans, J. (eds) (1979) *Demystifying social statistics*, London: Pluto.

Johnson, P. (2004) 'Making social science useful', *British Journal of Sociology*, vol 55, no 1, pp 23–30.

Kritzer, H.M. (1996) 'The data puzzle: the nature of interpretation in quantitative research', *American Journal of Political Science*, vol 40, no 1, pp 1–32.

Krueger, R.A. and Casey, M.A. (2008) *Focus groups: A practical guide for applied research*, London: Sage.

Krzanowski, W. (1998) *An introduction to statistical modelling*, London: Edward Arnold.

Law, J. (2004) *After method: Mess in social science research*, London: Routledge.

Lawless, P. (2006) 'Area-based urban interventions: rationale and outcomes: the new deal for communities programme in England', *Urban Studies*, vol 43, no 11, pp 1191–2011.

Lawless, P., Foden, M., Wilson, I. and Beatty, C. (2010) 'Understanding area based regeneration: the New Deal for Communities Programme in England', *Urban Studies*, vol 47, no 2, pp 257–75.

Le Grand, J. (2003) *Motivation, agency and public policy: Of knights and knaves, pawns and queens*, Oxford: Oxford University Press.

Lee, S.L. (2007) 'The Research Assessment Exercise, the state and the dominance of mainstream economics in British universities', *Cambridge Journal of Economics*, vol 31, no 2, pp 309–25.

Leisering, L. and Walker, R. (1998) *The dynamics of modern society*, Bristol: The Policy Press.

Lemon, M. (ed) (1999) *Exploring environmental change using an integrative method*, Amsterdam: Gordon and Breach.

Levitas, R. (1996) 'The legacy of Rayner', in R. Levitas and W. Guy (eds) *Interpreting official statistics*, London: Routledge and Kegan Paul, pp 7–25.

Levitas, R. and Guy, W. (1996) *Interpreting official statistics*, London: Routledge and Kegan Paul.

Liebrand, W.B.G., Nowak, A. and Hegselmann, R. (eds) (1998) *Computer modeling of social processes*, London: Sage.

London Edinburgh Weekend Return Group (1980) *In and against the state*, London: Pluto Press.

Machin, S. and Wilson, J. (2009) *Academy schools and pupil performance*, Paper CEPCP280, London: LSE Centre for Economic Performance.

MacInnes, J. (2009) *Final report of the strategic advisor on quantitative methods*, Swindon: ESRC.

Macmillan, L. (2009) *Social mobility and the professions*, Bristol: Centre for Market and Public Organization.

Marris, R. and Rein, M. (1967) *Dilemmas of social reform,* London: Routledge.

Marsden, D. and Oakley, P. (1991) 'Future issues and perspectives in the evaluation of social development', *Community Development Journal*, vol 26, pp 315-28.

Mason, P. and Barnes, M. (2007) 'Constructing theories of change', *Evaluation*, vol 13, no 2, pp 151–70.

Matheson, A., Dew, K. and Cumming, J. (2009) 'Complexity, evaluation and effectiveness of community-based interventions to reduce health inequalities', *Health Promotion Journal of Australia,* vol 20, pp 221–6.

May, C. (2005) 'Methodological pluralism, British Sociology, and the evidence based state', *Sociology*, vol 39, no 3, pp 526–7.

Mayo, P. (2003) 'In and against the state: Gramscii, war of position and adult education', *Journal for Critical Education Policy Studies*, vol 3, no 2 (www.jceps.com/index.php?pageID=article&articleID=49).

Milligan, C., Bingley, A. and Gatrell, T. (2005) 'Digging deep: using diary techniques to explore the place of health and well-being amongst older people', *Social Science and Medicine*, vol 61, pp 1882–92.

Moore, P. (1991) 'Report of the Royal Statistical Society's Working Party on Official Statistics, "Official statistics: Counting with confidence"', *Journal of the Royal Statistical Society Series A*, vol 154, pp 23–44.

Morin, E. (2006) *Restricted complexity, general complexity* (http://cogprints.org/5217/1/Morin.pdf).

Morris, S., Greenberg, D., Riccio, J., Mittra, B., Green, H., Lissenburgh, S. and Blundell, R. (2004) *Designing a demonstration project: An employment retention and advancement demonstration for Great Britain*, London: Government Chief Social Researcher's Office.

Murtagh, B. and McKay, S. (2003) 'Evaluating the social effects of the EU URBAN Community Initiative Programme', *European Planning Studies*, vol 11, no 2, pp 193–211.

Newman, J.F. (2001) *Modernising governance: New Labour, policy and society*, London: Sage.

Newman, J. (2005) *Remaking governance: Peoples, politics and the public sphere*, Bristol: The Policy Press.

Newman, J., Barnes, M. and Sullivan, H. (2004) 'Public participation and collective governance', *Journal of Social Policy*, vol 2, no 33, pp 203–23.

Nutley, S.M., Walter, I. and Davies, H.T.O. (2007) *Using evidence*, Bristol: The Policy Press.

Oakley, A. (2000) *Experiments in knowing*, Cambridge: Polity.

Office of the Deputy Prime Minister (2001) *A new commitment to neighbourhood renewal: National strategy action plan*, London: Cabinet Office.

O'Hagan, A. and Luce, B.R. (2003) *A primer on Baysian statistics in health economics and outcomes research*, Sheffield: Bayesian Initiative in Health Economics & Outcomes Research and Centre for Bayesian Statistics in Health Economics.

Ormerod, P. (1998) *Butterfly economics*, London: Faber and Faber.

Ormerod, P. (1994) *The death of economics*, London: Faber and Faber.

Ostrom, T. (1988) 'Computer simulation: the third symbol system', *Journal of Experimental Psychology*, vol 24, pp 381–92.

Oswaldo, A., Abland, J., Manuel, M. and Manuel, J. (2007) 'Characterising emergence of landowners in a forest reserve', *Journal of Artificial Societies and Social Simulation*, vol 10, no 36 (http://jasss.soc.surrey.ac.uk/10/3/6.html).

Parker, J., Dobson, A., Scott, S., Wyman, M. and SjostedtLanden, A. (2008) *International bench-marking review of best practice in the provision of undergraduate teaching in quantitative methods in the social sciences*, Swindon: ESRC.

Parry, J. and Judge, K. (2005) 'Tackling the wider determinants of health disparities in England: a model for evaluating the new deal for communities regeneration initiative', *American Journal of Public Health*, vol 95, no 4, pp 626–8.

Pawson, R. (2006) *Evidence-based policy: A realist perspective*, London: Sage.

Pawson, R. and Tilley, N. (1997) *Realistic evaluation*, London: Sage.

Payne, G. (1981) *Sociology and social research*, London: Routledge and Kegan Paul.

Petticrew, M., Tugwell, P., Welch, V., Ueffing, E., Kristjansson, E., Armstrong, R., Doyle, J. and Waters, E. (2009) 'Better evidence about tackling wicked issues in health inequities', *Journal of Public Health*, vol 31, no 3, pp 453–56.

Player, S. and Leys, C. (2008) *Confuse and conceal: The NHS and independent sector treatment centres*, Monmouth: Merlin Press.

Plowden Report (1967) *Children and their primary schools*, London: HMSO.

Plummer, K. (1983) *Documents of life*, London: Allen and Unwin.

Polanyi, K. (2001, orig.1945) *The great transformation: The political and economic origins of our time*, Boston, MA: Beacon Press.

Pollock, A. (2005) *NHS plc: The privatisation of our health care*, London: Verso.

Pollock, A.M., Dunnigan, M.G., Gaffney, D., Price, D. and Shaoul, J. (1999) 'Planning the new NHS: downsizing for the 21st century', *British Medical Journal*, vol 3, no 19, pp 179–84.

Pollock A.M., Shaoul J., Rowland D. and Player S. (2001) 'Public services and the private sector: a response to the IPPR Commission', *Catalyst*, January.

Posnett, J. (1999) 'The hospital of the future: is bigger better? Concentration in the provision of secondary care', *British Medical Journal*, vol 319, pp 1063–5.

Price WaterhouseCooper (2008) *Academies programme 5th annual report*, London: Department for Children, Families and Schools.

Ragin, C. (1992) 'Casing and the process of social inquiry' in C. Ragin and H. Becker (eds) *What is a case?*, Cambridge: Cambridge University Press.

Ragin, C.C. (1994) *Constructing social research*, Thousand Oaks, CA: Pine Forge Press.

Ragin, C.C. (1987) *The comparative method: Moving beyond qualitative and quantitative strategies*, Berkeley, CA: University of California Press.

Ragin, C. (2000) *Fuzzy set social science*, Chicago: University of Chicago Press.

Ragin, C. and Rihoux, B. (2004) 'Qualitative comparative analysis (QCA): state of the art and prospects', *Qualitative Methods. Newsletter of the American Political Science Association Organized Section on Qualitative Methods*, vol 2, no 2, pp 3–13.

Reed, M. and Harvey, D.L. (1992) 'The new science and the old: complexity and realism in the social sciences', *Journal for the Theory of Social Behaviour*, vol 22, pp 356–79.

Reed, M. and Harvey, D.L. (1996) 'Social science as the study of complex systems', in L.D. Kiel and E. Elliott (eds) *Chaos theory in the social sciences*, Ann Arbor, MI: University of Michigan Press, pp 295–324.

Rittel, H.W. and Webber, M.M. (1973) 'Dilemmas in a general theory of planning', *Policy Sciences*, vol 4, pp 155–69.

Rivlin, A. (1971) *Systematic thinking for social action*, Washington, DC: The Brookings Institution.

Rothschild Report (1972) *A framework for government research and development* (Cmnd 5046), London: HMSO.

Ruane, S. (2005) 'The future for health care: the prescriptions of UK think-tanks', in M. Powell, L. Bauld and K. Clarke (eds) *Social policy review 17*, Bristol: The Policy Press.

Ruane, S. (2007) *Report Commissioned by Rochdale Borough Council re: The Health Futures and Making it Better proposals for health services in Rochdale* (www.nhscampaign.org.uk/uploads///documents/Reconfiguration%20Not%20Proven.pdf).

Sanderson, I., (2000) 'Evaluation in complex policy systems', *Evaluation*, vol 6, no 4, pp 433–54.

Savage, M. and Burrows, R. (2007) 'The coming crisis of empirical sociology', *Sociology*, vol 41, pp 885–99.

Sayer, A. (2000) *Realism and social science*, London: Sage.

Sintomer,Y., Herzberg, C. and Rocke, A. (2005) 'From Porto Alegre to Europe: potentials and limitations of participatory budgeting' (www. dpwg-lgd.org/cms/upload/pdf/participatory_budgeting.pdf).

Skeffington Report (1969) *Report of the Committee on Public Participation in Planning: People and Planning*, London: HMSO.

Sohng, S.L. (1995) 'Participatory research and community organizing', Working paper presented at The New Social Movement and Community Organizing Conference, University of Washington, Seattle, WA, 1–3 November 1995 (www.interweb-tech.com/nsmnet/docs/sohng.htm).

Stafford, M., Nazroo, J., Popay, J. and Whitehead, M. (2008) 'Tacking inequalities in health: evaluating the New Deal for communities initiative', *Journal of Epidemiology and Community Health*, vol 62, pp 298–304.

Tappenden, P., Chilcott, J.B., Egginton, S., Oakley, J. and McCabe, C. (2004) 'Methods for expected value of information analysis in complex health economic models. Developments on the health economics of beta interferon and glatiramer acetate in the management of multiple sclerosis', *Health Technology Assessment*, no 8, p 27.

Taylor, D. and Balloch, S. (2005) *The politics of evaluation*, Bristol: The Policy Press.

Teisman, G., Van Buuren, A. and Gerrits, L. (2009) *Managing complex governance systems*, New York: Routledge.

Therborn, G. (1986) *Why some peoples are more unemployed than others*, London: Verso.

Thompson, E.P. (1978) *The poverty of theory and other essays*, London: Merlin.

Thompson, E.P. (1981) 'The politics of theory', in R. Samuel (ed) *Peoples' history and socialist theory*, London: Routledge and Kegan Paul, pp 396–408.

Timmins, T. (2008) 'Can do better in the social mobility class', *Financial Times*, 4 November.

Titmuss, R. (1970) *The gift relationship*, London: Allen and Unwin.

Troitzsch, K.G. (1998) 'Multilevel process modeling in the social sciences', in W.B.G. Liebrand, A. Nowak and R. Hegselmann (eds) Computer modeling of social processes, London: Sage, pp 20–36.

Tukey, J.W. (1977) *Exploratory data analysis*, Reading, MA: Addison-Wesley.

UNDP (United Nations Development Programme) (2009) *Annual Report*, New York: UNDP.

Unger, R.M. (1998) *Democracy realized*, London: Verso.

Uprichard, E. and Byrne, D.S. (2006) 'Representing complex places: a narrative approach', *Environment and Planning A*, vol 384, pp 665–76.

Veblen, T. (1904) *The theory of business enterprise*, New York, Charles Scribner's Sons.

Von Hayek, F. (1974) 'The pretence of knowledge', Nobel Prize Lecture in A. Lindbeck (ed), *From Nobel Lectures, Economics 1969–1980*, Singapore: World Scientific Publishing Co.

Walker, R., Hoggart, L. and Hamilton, G. (2006) *Making random assignment happen: Evidence from the UK Employment Retention and Advancement (ERA) demonstration*, Research Report No 330, London: Department for Work and Pensions.

Wall, M., Hayes, R., Moore, D., Petticrew, M., Clow, A., Schmidt, E., Draper, A., Lock, K., Lynch, R. and Renton, M. (2009) 'Evaluation of community level interventions to address social and structural determinants of health: a cluster randomised controlled trial', *BMC Public Health,* vol 9, p 207.

Walton, M., Signal, L. and Thomson, G. (2009) 'Household economic resources as a determinant of childhood nutrition: policy responses for New Zealand', *Social Policy Journal of New Zealand*, vol 36, pp 194–207.

Westergaard, J. (1978) 'Social policy and class inequality: some notes on welfare state limits', *Socialist Register*, vol 15, pp 71–99.

Westergaard, J. (2003) 'Interview with John Westergaard', *Network*, vol 85, pp 1–2.

WHO/Europe HEN (Health Evidence Network) (2003) 'Are bigger hospitals better?', HEN summary of a network member's report, (www.euro.who.int/en/what-we-do/data-and-evidence/health-evidence-network-hen/publications/hen-summaries-of-network-members-reports).

Williams, R. (1979) *Politics and letters*, London: Verso.

Williams, R. (1980) 'Base and superstructure in Marxist cultural theory', in *Problems in materialism and culture*, London: Verso.

Woolf, S.H. (2008) 'The meaning of translational research and why it matters', *Journal of the American Medical Association*, vol 299, no 2, pp 211–13.

Wright, J., Parry, J.M., Mathers, J.M., Jones, S. and Orford, J. (2006) 'Assessing the participatory potential of Britain's New Deal for Communities', *Policy Studies*, vol 27, no 4, pp 347–61.

Wright, J.S.F., Parry, J. and Mathers, J. (2007) 'What to do about political context? Evidence synthesis, the New Deal for Communities and the possibilities for evidence-based policy', *Evidence & Policy: A Journal of Research, Debate and Practice,* vol 3, no 3, pp 253–69.

Znaniecki, F. (1934) *The method of sociology*, New York: Farrar and Rinehart.

# Index

Home Office and CDPs 163-4, 166
hospital size: evidence and policy 105-9,
    116, 129
House of Commons Select Committee
    on Health 50, 53-5, 116
housing
    action research and CDPs 165-6
    Pathfinder projects 67, 93
Human Development Index (UNDP)
    67, 94
hydrography and complex systems 61
hypothetico-deductive method 63,
    158-9

**I**

impact models 48
Incapacity Benefit and unemployment
    figures 64, 110, 111
Independent Sector Treatment Centres
    (ISTCs) 116-17
Index of Multiple Deprivation 67-8
inequality
    policy and social mobility 102, 103
    and urban interventions 171
    *see also* deprivation; health inequalities
information
    access to public sector data 67, 75-6
    and capitalism 70, 109-10
    *see also* evidence; knowledge; statistical
    data
Institute of Economic Affairs 188-9
Institute of Fiscal Studies 183
Institute for Public Policy Research
    (IPPR) 105-6, 107, 190
Institutes for Advanced Studies 191
institutional audits and urban initiatives
    90, 91
institutional memory 75-6
institutions: data on 66-7, 75-6
interdisciplinary work
    and applied social science 175-6, 191,
    199-200
    meaning of term 16, 178
    of think tanks 188, 189, 190, 191
inter-generational social mobility 101-3
International Micro-Simulation
    Association 147-8
interpretative approaches 9, 24
    and evaluation of urban initiatives
    90-1
    measurement as interpretation 32-3
    and qualitative methods 71, 72
interventions
    evaluating worth 79-97
    evidence and evaluation 48-52
    evidence and 'wicked issues' 52-9, 191

privileging of RCTs 49-50
    *see also* NHS reconfiguration; urban
    interventions

**J**

Jahoda, M. 181-2
Joseph, Sir Keith 181
Judge, K. 87, 95

**K**

Keep our NHS Public (KONP)
    campaign 107-8
'knowing capitalism' 70
knowledge
    and action research 155, 156, 159, 163
    and actor-network theory 24-5
    corporate interests and production of
    knowledge 16
    and evidence-based policy 4-5
    'knowing capitalism' 70
    multiple evidence bases 51
    and praxis 34, 35
    role of research and policy 41-2
    and science 1, 2-3
    synthesisation 10
    *see also* epistemology; evidence;
    information
Kritzer, H.M. 32
Krzanowski, W. 140-1

**L**

Labour Force Survey 110
Labour Government
    and Community Development
    Projects research 167-8
    *see also* New Labour
Law, J. 25-6, 56
Lawless, P. 91, 93
Le Grand, J. 205
leadership and local government 124
league tables *see* rankings
Lee, S.L. 187
legitimating role of applied social
    research 5-6, 35, 99-119, 195
    and official statistics 5, 12-13, 64, 100,
    109-12
    policy-based evidence 105-9
    and social mobility 100, 101-4
    and think tanks 189-90
Leisering, L. 101
Lemon, M. 202
Levin, M.L. 155-6, 159-60
liberation theology 28, 134
linear modelling techniques 183
    limitations 15, 47, 95, 142-3, 146, 153,
    176, 184, 189, 201, 202
    *see also* regression modelling

and qualitative methods 9, 29-33, 128, 201
social surveys and data collection 11, 62-3
and variables 64-5, 141-2
*see also* linear modelling techniques; randomised control trials (RCTs); statistical data

# R

radical social work 158
Radical Statistics (Radstats) movement 117-18
Ragin, C. 23, 65, 141, 142-3
randomised control trials (RCTs)
and action research methodology 158
effect of demi-regs 55-6
evaluation and ERA Demonstration 84, 85-6
and hierarchy of evidence 44-51
and hypothetico-deductive method 63
New Zealand health assessments 96
and quantitative research 29-30, 63, 184, 201, 202
retention rate problems 86
'Well London' project and evaluation 94-5, 96
rankings: data on public institutions 66-7
rapid reviews and evaluation 81
realism
and evaluation 81, 82
and evidence 43
and methodological foundations 8-9, 20-1, 186
*see also* complex realism; critical realism; scientific realism; social realism
redistributive welfare and health inequalities 170-1
Reed, M. 20-1
reflexivity of applied social science 20
reform 56-7, 203
regression modelling 33, 47, 140, 142-3, 153
logistic regression technique 87, 142, 143, 186
and New Deal for Communities evaluation 92, 95
Rein, M. 57-9, 89, 163
relativism 9, 43
research
and action 57-9
requirements of government 44, 51, 179-80
and scientific method 1

*see also* academy; acting and action research; evidence; qualitative research methods; quantitative research methods
research assessment exercises (RAFs) 182, 187-8
Research Excellence Framework (REF) 188
resource allocation
Baysian techniques and health 'economics' 143-4
and evaluation 79, 92
failure of economics as applied social science 182
funding and politics of the academy 198-202
and NHS reconfiguration 129-30
participatory budgeting 133-5, 198
*see also* Private Finance Initiative (PFI) funding
restricted complexity 21, 26-7, 154, 202
and agent-based modelling 150, 151-2, 153
Rihoux, B. 142-3
Rittel, H.W. 52
Roberts Report 187
Rochdale: NHS reconfiguration consultation 126-8, 129
Rockefeller Foundation 85
Romero *see* Gutierez Romero, R.
Rorty, Richard 159, 160
Rothschild Report 181
Royal Statistical Society 62-3, 110, 111
Ruane, S. 107-8, 129-30
Russell, J. 47

# S

Salford University Market Intelligence Unit: Healthy Futures report 126-7, 129
Sanderson, I. 81
Savage, M. 70
Schaefer, K.C. 139
Scholar, Sir Michael 111
schools
academies and legitimating evidence 101, 112-15, 116
data and rankings 67, 77*n*
obesity initiative in New Zealand 96
'science': meaning(s) of term 1-3
scientific method 1, 2, 3, 159
and evidence 42-3
scientific realism 43, 157, 162
scientific research based knowledge 51
'scientism' 2, 3, 183, 186, 187, 201, 202
Select Committee on Health 50, 53-5
Sen, Amartya 67
Sherwood, C.C. 48-9, 95, 156